CW00547141

PUBLICATIONS
OF THE
ARMY RECORDS SOCIETY
VOL. 16

SIR HUGH ROSE
AND THE
CENTRAL INDIA CAMPAIGN
1858

The Army Records Society was founded in 1984 in order to publish original records describing the development, organisation, administration and activities of the British Army from early times.

Any person wishing to become a member of the Society is requested to apply to the Hon. Secretary, c/o the National Army Museum, Royal Hospital Road, London, SW3 4HT. The annual subscription entitles the member to receive a copy of each volume issued by the Society in that year, and to purchase back volumes at reduced prices. Current subscription details, whether for individuals living within the British Isles, for individuals living overseas, or for institutions, will be furnished on request.

The Council of the Army Records Society wish it to be clearly understood that they are not answerable for opinions or observations that may appear in the Society's publications. For these the responsibility rests entirely with the Editors of the several works.

Sir Hugh Rose.

SIR HUGH ROSE
AND THE
CENTRAL INDIA CAMPAIGN
1858

Edited by
BRIAN ROBSON

Published by
SUTTON PUBLISHING LIMITED
for the
ARMY RECORDS SOCIETY
2000

First published in the United Kingdom in 2000 by
Sutton Publishing Limited · Phoenix Mill · Thrupp · Stroud
Gloucestershire · GL5 2BU

Copyright © The Army Records Society, 2000

All rights reserved. No part of this publication may be reproduced, stored in a retrieval system, or transmitted, in any form, or by any means, electronic, mechanical, photocopying, recording or otherwise, without the prior permission of the publisher and copyright holders.

British Library Cataloguing in Publication Data
A catalogue record for this book is available from the British Library

ISBN 0-7509-2541-8

Typeset in Ehrhardt.
Typesetting and origination by
Sutton Publishing Limited.
Printed in Great Britain by
Bookcraft, Midsomer Norton, Somerset.

ARMY RECORDS SOCIETY
COUNCIL FOR 1999–2000

PRESIDENT
Field Marshal the Lord Carver GCB CBE DSO MC DLitt

VICE-PRESIDENT
Field Marshal Sir John Chapple GCB CBE MA FZS FRGS
The Rt Hon Sir Frank Cooper PC GCB CMG
Professor Sir Michael Howard CBE MC DLitt FBA FR Hist S

COUNCILLORS
Professor John Gooch BA PhD FR Hist S (Chairman)
Professor Jeremy Black MA PhD FR Hist S
Professor Brian Bond MA FR Hist S
John Bourne BA PhD FR Hist S
Lieutenant-Colonel Simon Doughty MA
General Sir Anthony Farrar-Hockley GBE KCB DSO MC BLitt
Professor David French BA PhD FR Hist S
Alan Guy MA DPhil FR Hist S
Major-General Alistair Irwin CBE MA
Major-General John Kiszely MC
Brigadier Allan Mallinson BA
The Rt Rev Michael Mann, KCVO
William Philpott BA DPhil
Colonel John Power FCIS
Brian Robson CB MA FR Hist S
Peter Simkins MA
Keith Simpson BA MP

HONORARY SECRETARY
Professor Ian Beckett BA PhD FR Hist S

HONORARY TREASURER
Mrs Marian Mollett BA ACA

Contents

Preface   xi

Introduction   xiii

Abbreviations   xxii

Glossary   xxiii

I   Bombay to Jhansi, June 1857 to March 1858   1

II   Jhansi to Kalpi, March to May 1858   115

III   Kalpi to Gwalior, May to June 1858   192

Notes   290

Biographical Notes   308

Bibliography   311

Index   315

Maps

1.   Operations in Malwa   xxvi

2.   Sehore to Jhansi   5

3.   Jhansi   116

4.   The Betwa, 1 April 1858   149

5.   Jhansi to Gwalior   163

6.   Kalpi   196

7.   Gwalior   233

Sir Hugh Rose, *c.* June 1858, by an unknown artist (possibly Captain Wood, the AAG), on the last page of the Field Force Order Book. Reproduced by permission of the Trustees of the British Library.

Preface

'Sir Hugh Rose himself seems to be beyond dispute the ablest man who appeared in that field.'

Sir John Fortescue

Many years ago I read Fortescue's assessment and it lodged in my memory. When the Publications Committee of the Society expressed a wish to publish a volume on 'the Mutiny', Rose seemed an obvious subject and I was honoured to be asked to proceed accordingly.

The written material available on the insurrection of 1857 as a whole is very large. The shocking nature of the event and the exotic setting encouraged a flood of memoirs and narratives; the bibliography in P.J.O. Taylor's *What Really Happened During The Mutiny* (New Delhi, 1997) runs to some 900 items, excluding contemporary newspapers and journals. If one adds the mass of paper produced by the bureaucracies in India and London, then the material can properly be described as immense. But the content is skewed. The great mass of material relates to events in Northern India – Delhi, Rohilkhand, Oudh (Awadh), Bihar and the Punjab – the foci of the insurrection in its mutiny phase. Material on events in the Central India campaign is very much more limited, and even to military historians Rose and the campaign there are largely unknown. But, as this volume seeks to show, it was not a backwater and the events there in 1858 were not only directly linked to the outcome in the north but were of comparable importance.

In selecting material for publication, the primary aim has been to provide a connected, chronological account of the operations of Sir Hugh Rose's Central India Field Force between December 1857 and June 1858. These chronological limits have been slightly transgressed in order to provide a more comprehensible context. A secondary objective has been to provide, via the various Introductions, a compact free-standing outline of the campaign for the general reader who may not wish to wade through all the documents. Fortescue's account of Rose's campaign (in Volume 13 of his *History of the British Army* (London 1899–1930)) is sadly marked with uncharacteristic errors. The only published history of the campaign as a whole is the official history published in 1908, primarily for the purposes of a staff ride conducted by the then General Officer Commanding Bombay; it is a competent factual history, with useful plans of the various actions and valuable factual annexes but it eschews comment or analysis. T. Lowe, *Central India during the Rebellion of 1857 and 1858* (1860) is perhaps more of a personal account than a true history. A full-scale modern account is needed; a biography of Rose himself even more so.

In preparing the present volume I am indebted to many people and institutions. I am grateful to the Council of the National Army Museum for permission to publish material in its possession, and to the Director and his staff for their unfailing help and courtesy. I am similarly grateful to the Trustees of the National Library and Museums of Scotland, the Trustees of the British Library, and the Regimental Headquarters of the Worcestershire and Sherwood Foresters Regiment. Mr A.I. Annand very graciously gave me permission to quote from John Henry Sylvester's diary and Major David Downe generously lent me his excellent transcription of John North Crealock's diary. Material in the Crown copyright is published by permission of Her Majesty's Stationery Office.

On a more personal level I am grateful for advice and assistance to Stephen Wood, Tony Bennell, Professor Ian Beckett, Pat Shipp, Dr Iain Brown, Peter Taylor and Dr Kirti Narain, with whom I had the pleasure of visiting some of the sites in India in 1997 and to Mrs Annie Jackson for her impeccable and helpful copy-editing.

The Society for South Asian Studies and the General Palit Trust awarded me grants to travel in India; in the event, I did not need to make use of these grants but I wish to record my appreciation of their generous treatment.

This volume is dedicated to my wife, whose love and support I can now never repay.

Brian Robson
Hove
January 1999

Introduction

The campaign in Central India in 1858 has been overshadowed by the more dramatic events in Northern India, in Delhi, Cawnpore (Kanpur) and Lucknow (Lakhnao). But in strategic importance and brilliance of execution, as well as in the light that it sheds on the Mutiny as a whole, it stands on its own. Its commander was one of the most remarkable generals in British military history but remains an enigma.

Historians recognised long ago that the term 'Indian Mutiny' was inadequate to describe the events of 1857–9. That it was in the first instance a military mutiny is beyond dispute; by its close, all 10 regular cavalry regiments of the East India Company's Bengal Army, 17 out of 18 irregular cavalry regiments, 59 out of 74 infantry regiments, a third of the artillery and nearly all the 12 companies of Sappers and Miners had either mutinied or been disarmed or disbanded. There had been significant outbreaks in the Bombay Army and signs of unease in the Madras Army. That the mutineers – Hindu, Sikh and Muslim alike – turned instinctively to the deposed Mughal emperor, living in Delhi as a British pensioner, as their leader gave the insurrection an immediate political dimension.[1]

From the beginning, moreover, the mutineers were joined by important elements of the civilian population – the minor feudal nobility, major and minor landholders, tenant farmers and peasants. The sepoys threw up no leaders of consequence;[2] virtually without exception, the important leaders came from the minor nobility and squirearchy. Some nationalist historians have, therefore, sought to portray the events as a 'War of Independence'.[3] That was clearly not so. There is no persuasive evidence of any widespread conspiracy or coordination.[4] The majority of the troops used against the insurrection were Indian, and the European troops would have been helpless without the support of huge numbers of Indians. The support, tacit and active, of the major Indian rulers such as the Maharaja of Gwalior and the Nizam of Hyderabad was critical to the ultimate British success. Yet there is a sense in which the nationalist historians are right, because the thread which connected all the elements in the insurrection was the rejection of British rule. To contemporary

Europeans, the events were so unexpected, so widespread and so shattering to their beliefs that a rational explanation became a necessity. Until the 'Mutiny' could be explained, future British policy in India could have no clear direction. To attempt here even a bare explanation of those events is a task of foolhardy proportions. Yet it must be made in order fully to understand the documents in this volume.[5]

In very broad terms, it may be said that at the root of the uprising lay the reaction of a deeply traditional, conservative society to a radical programme of social and politico-economic change imposed by alien rulers. To the early Victorians, change was the driving force of society – by a singular coincidence, Darwin's theory of evolution, with its emphasis on natural selection and competition as the basis of evolution (and, by implication, progress) was published while the embers of the insurrection still smouldered. To Indians, however, there was no natural link between change and progress; the hard-edged Utilitarian theories of Malthus and Ricardo, eagerly and confidently applied by influential administrators such as Thomason, were alien and incomprehensible. What to British administrators seemed an enlightened programme of social and economic reform was seen by Indians as an attack on their religion and culture. As Dr Sen has put it

> The English Government had imperceptibly effected a social revolution . . . The Mutiny leaders would have done away with the new reforms, with the new order, and gone back to the good old days . . . In short, they wanted a counter-revolution.[6]

Two developments particularly affected attitudes in Central India. The first was Dalhousie's doctrine of 'lapse', under which the territory of a ruler who died without a natural male heir fell to the British Government.[7] The policy fell with peculiar force on the Maratha states. In the five years before 1857, three Maratha states of particular significance fell into British hands. The Bhonsla Rajas of Nagpur and Berar were one of the four greatest Maratha families. Sattara was the home of Shivaji, the Maratha national hero, and Jhansi was a Maratha state of long standing and importance. The most important event ultimately was the refusal to allow an adopted son of Baji Rao II to succeed him as Peishwa (or hereditary Chief Minister) of the Maratha Confederacy. Dhundu Pant (or the Nana Sahib, as he became known), his nephew (the Rao Sahib), the Rani of Jhansi and the Nana Sahib's ADC, Tantia Topi, would be among the most prominent and determined leaders of the uprising. Moreover, when states were annexed, widespread unemployment tended to follow; in Oudh (Awadh), it has been estimated, some 45,000 soldiers were left without employment when that state was annexed in 1856.[8] Dalhousie's policy of abolishing many of the traditional forms of landholding in order to simplify and standardise the tax system caused hardship and grievance. The best known example is the dispossession of the *taluqdars* of Oudh and the North West Provinces[9] but much the same policy was applied by the Bombay Government through the Imam Commission of 1852.[10] Although these could be applied only to those areas under direct British rule, no one could be sure when a territory might not fall to the British. It might be said therefore that the uprising was about the mismanagement of change.

Traditionally, the outbreak of the insurrection has been located at Meerut (Mirath) on the evening of 10 May 1857. But the beginning can be traced back some months earlier, to unrest in the 19th and 34th Bengal Native Infantry, at Berhampore and Barrackpore.[11] Indiscipline had long been endemic in the Bengal Army; John Jacob went so far as to say, in 1851, that mutiny was the normal state of that army. It was almost inevitable in an army dominated by caste, where rank did not equate with caste:

> I cannot conceive of the possibility of maintaining discipline in an army where a non-commissioned officer will, when he meets off-duty a Brahmin sepoy, kneel down and put his forehead to the ground. I have seen this done. The sepoy thus treated is the master of the officer.[12]

The insurrection quickly spread into Central India. Within three weeks of the outbreak at Meerut, regiments had mutinied at Jhansi, Nowgong (Naogaon), Saugor (Sagar), Nimach, Jubbalpore (Jabalpur) and as far south as Hyderabad;[13] by August 1857 only one regular regiment in Central India remained basically loyal and only one major post, Mhow (Mau), remained in British hands. The great trunk road from Bombay to Agra and Delhi and, ultimately, Calcutta, was cut off and all of India south of the Jumna (Yamuna) was open to rebel penetration.

It was not until November 1857, with Delhi and Cawnpore recaptured and the garrison of Lucknow out of danger, that serious attention and resources could be devoted to the recovery of Central India. While it remained in a state of insurrection, the operations in Oudh and Rohilkhand, under the Commander-in-Chief, Sir Colin Campbell, remained exposed to attack from the rear, across the Jumna. Equally, rebel forces could find sanctuary south of the Jumna. In October 1857, Sir Robert Hamilton, Agent to the Governor-General in Central India, arrived in Calcutta from a curtailed leave in England, to be consulted by Lord Canning and Campbell. The plan which emerged [197] provided for two columns, from Mhow/Sehore and Jubbalpore, to move north eastward in parallel towards the Jumna. The objective of the first column, composed of Bombay Army troops, was the rebel stronghold at Kalpi, on the Jumna, 45 miles south of Cawnpore. The second column, of Madras troops commanded by Major-General Whitlock, was to occupy Banda, 40 miles east of Kalpi.

Canning's first choice to command the Mhow column was John Jacob but he was detained in Persia in the aftermath of the Anglo-Persian war and command devolved unexpectedly on Sir Hugh Rose, who had arrived in September 1857 to command the Poona (Pune) Division of the Bombay Army.

The two columns were intended to co-operate but Whitlock's force was slow in assembling and in the upshot there was effectively no co-operation.[14] It may almost be said that the two forces met only in the Admiralty Court in 1866 in the famous dispute over the Banda and Kirwi prize money.[15]

In 1858 Central India comprised the territory between the Nerbudda (Narbada), Jumna and Chambal rivers. The western end was known as Malwa and blended imperceptibly into southern Rajputana (Rajasthan); the eastern end was Bundelkhand. The western half of the area is hilly and heavily forested; the eastern half merges into the alluvial plain of the Jumna and Ganges. Most of Central India was ruled indirectly, through the chiefs of the large number of Indian feudal states; the districts of Hamirpur, Banda, Jalaun, Jhansi and Lalitpur, comprising the major part of Bundelkhand, were administered directly by the British Commissioner for the Saugor and Nerbudda Territories, at Jubbalpore. The rulers of the smaller states had obligations of military service to their feudal overlords such as the Maharaja of Gwalior (Sindhia) and all maintained armed retainers. The major rulers – Sindhia, Holkar (Indore) and the Begum of Bhopal – remained loyal; the majority of the smaller ones rebelled. The population was mainly divided between Marathas and Bundela Rajputs,[16] with large pockets of Muslims and earlier Dravidian races such as the Gonds and Bhils.

Properly to understand the insurrection one needs to analyse in detail the varied motives of those concerned.[17] In broad terms, the mutineers of the regular Bengal regiments and of the Contingents shared the grievances of their colleagues in the north; they were the most formidable element because of their equipment (including artillery), discipline and training, and because their fate if captured was instant execution. For the same reasons, the Arab, Pathan and Baluch mercenaries – known as *vilayatis* – would fight hard. Many of the minor rulers and landowners were actuated primarily by motives of self-interest – to pay off old scores, to throw off feudal obligations, to carve out new territories or to regain what had been lost earlier. Of all classes, it was perhaps the squirearchy – the *thakurs* – who proved the most determined opponents:

> In all the major battles that Hugh Rose had to fight in the plains of southern Bundelcund, it was fundamentally the resistance of the thakurs which he had to overcome.[18]

In 1857 Rose was a man of 56, past the age at which modern major-generals retire. He came from a line of politicians and diplomats but was commissioned into the 92nd Highlanders in 1821, transferring almost immediately into the 19th Foot. In 1839 he became a lieutenant-colonel by purchase but there was no regimental vacancy and he went on half pay. A few months later he was appointed to the liaison team attached to the Turkish Army in Syria in the operations against Mehemet Ali.[19] He remained as Consul-General until 1848 when he joined the Diplomatic Service as Secretary to the Embassy at Constantinople. He played a key role in the events leading up to the Crimean War in 1854 and was appointed liaison officer at French Headquarters in the Crimea, earning a reputation for coolness and courage under fire. On the outbreak of the Mutiny he volunteered for service and was appointed to the Poona Division. He had seen a good deal of war as an observer but had never commanded troops in action. In giving him the Poona command, it seems unlikely that any one envisaged a command in the field. There was much criticism of his appointment,[20] and a good deal of cynicism in India as to his capacity as a commander.[21] His force, originally called the Nerbudda Field Force but later christened the Central India Field Force, consisted of two self-contained brigades, containing both European and Indian troops of all arms. The 1st Brigade, under Brigadier C.S. Stuart, Bombay Army, had been in the field since June 1857, originally as part of a force despatched from Bombay to relieve Mhow, and then as the Malwa Field Force; the 2nd Brigade, under the confusingly-named Brigadier

Charles Steuart, HM 14th Light Dragoons, began to form at Sehore in November 1857. Hamilton accompanied the Force as Political Officer.

It had been intended that Rose should move directly on Jhansi as soon as Whitlock was ready to advance from Jubbalpore. But Whitlock was late and Rose, with one brigade, was diverted to Saugor, where the European garrison had been under siege since June 1857,[22] while his other brigade moved directly on Jhansi.

Rose's advance began inauspiciously with a furious quarrel with Hamilton over the punishment of the Begum of Bhopal's mutinous troops. He ran into further controversy at Sehore over the punishment of mutineers from the Bhopal Contingent. His campaign got under way in the middle of January, almost at the depth of the cold weather season; from then on the troops would be steadily marching into the hot weather. He had his first major success at the end of January when he captured the formidable fortress of Rahatgarh, relieving Saugor on 3 February 1858. After a delay to repair his siege artillery and amass supplies, he moved on to capture Jhansi on 4 April, fighting off a relieving army under Tantia Topi. He fought another major action at Kunch and captured Kalpi on 23 May 1858. The campaign was apparently at an end and he handed over his command to Robert Napier and prepared to resume his command at Poona. On 4 June he received news that the defeated rebels from Kalpi had seized Gwalior, with its wealth of money, ammunition, stores, and men, thus reviving the threat to India south of the Jumna. He immediately reassumed command, marched on Gwalior, defeated the rebels and brought the campaign to a final close.

It had been conducted in very harsh physical conditions; at times the troops had been short of food, water, ammunition and clothing, especially boots, and the murderous heat towards the end had killed almost more men than the rebels [145, 179]; Rose collapsed at least five times with heatstroke [135, 136]. On the British side it had been conducted without mercy; Rose, with his exacting concepts of duty and discipline, spared few mutineers or rebels who fell into his hands.[23]

The success of his campaign did not mean that rebellion had been eliminated in Central India, as has often been assumed. The paucity of troops to garrison the reconquered territory allowed insurrection to flare up after Rose had passed, and localities temporarily cleared of rebels were often reoccupied within weeks; the fortress of Chanderi, captured by Stuart on 17 March, was back in rebel hands by the end of the month, fortunately for only a brief period. Indeed, there were probably as many troops engaged in operations in Central India in 1859 as at the height of

Rose's campaign. What his campaign had done was to destroy the organised rebel armies and to occupy their bases, thus eliminating any real threat to India south of the Nerbudda. What remained was essentially guerilla war.

Refusing with some hauteur the offer of a divisional command at Gwalior, Rose resumed his command at Poona where he continued to exercise some responsibility for operations against rebels in the Bombay Presidency. In March 1860 he became Commander-in-Chief Bombay Army, holding the post for only three months before succeeding Colin Campbell as Commander-in-Chief in India on 4 June 1860. He inherited the problems arising from the transfer of the East India Company's armies to the Crown and, in particular, of the mutiny of the Bengal European regiments.[24] The remainder of his tenure was devoid of major problems. On leaving India in 1865 he became Commander-in-Chief in Ireland, retiring in 1870. He was raised to the peerage as Baron Strathnairn and promoted to field marshal. He volunteered to take over command in Zululand after the defeat at Isandlwhana but his offer was tactfully refused on account of his age and seniority. He died in Paris in 1885.

Relations with other commanders

Relations between Campbell and Rose were cool despite, or perhaps because of, previous acquaintanceship in the Crimea. Campbell was clearly jealous of Rose's success and he was aided in this by his Chief of Staff, Mansfield, but Rose's imperious manner and his easy access to Canning no doubt played a part. While he cannot have been the easiest of subordinates he nevertheless remained loyal to Campbell.

With his subordinate commanders, he seems to have got on best with Orr, the commander of the Hyderabad Contingent force, and Robertson, commanding the 25th Bombay Native Infantry. He worked generally amicably with Stuart but his other brigade commander, Steuart, forfeited his confidence at Kunch and Rose took steps to ensure that he never had another active command [191]. Steuart's successor, Robert Campbell, remained a cypher. Napier arrived with an established reputation and the aura of a coming man, and Rose treated him accordingly.

Rose remains an enigma. He had all the qualities of a great commander – quickness of perception, boldness, decisiveness, physical courage, determination and thoroughness, and luck, the quality which Napoleon prized above all others in a general. He was not a popular commander and criticisms of him persisted among his officers. His reputation rests on one short campaign against an indifferent foe; what he was really capable of is part of the enigma. He never married and appears to have had no close friends; while he was capable of generosity, arrogance, vanity and selfishness were important features of his character.[25]

Communications

The electric telegraph played a major part in operations and it is surprising that the rebels did not make a more concerted effort to destroy it [25]. In January 1858 the line from Bombay ended at Mhow and then Indore; telegrams from there to Bombay took an hour or so. Beyond Indore, draft telegrams had to be sent thence by messenger and telegrams to Bombay might then take a matter of days. As he advanced, Rose was able to restore the line behind him. At Kalpi, telegrams could go via Cawnpore; at Gwalior he could use the telegraph at Agra. Beyond Indore, the normal mail system – the dak – had largely disintegrated but there seems to have been little difficulty in individual messengers getting through albeit sometimes by long detours [124].

Linked with the problem of communications was that of intelligence. Rose had no intelligence department and he depended primarily on Hamilton and his political assistants. They depended upon extensive use of Indian spies who seem to have been able to move freely, even within the rebel camps, and upon information from loyal officials and rulers; no doubt the rebels had an equally efficient spying system. On the whole, Rose seems to have had fairly good information on the movements of his opponents, the conspicuous exception being the move on Gwalior by the rebels in June 1858. What Rose generally lacked was detailed information about the places that he had to attack and he devoted much time and effort to personal reconnaissance [70, 99, 102, 130].

Sources

The bulk of Rose's papers (42 volumes) are in the British Library but contain relatively little on his campaign. His despatches are conveniently collected in Forrest (Volume IV) but I have gone back to the original copies which, however, differ only in minor details. Elphinstone's papers and a volume of memoranda and letters of Mansfield are in the India Office Collections, as are Sylvester's diary and narrative[26] and a number of other letters and diaries. The Collections also contain Rose's Field

Force Order Book. A particularly valuable source, the papers of J.G. Lightfoot, used by the Marquess of Anglesey and Christopher Hibbert, cannot now be traced.

There was much correspondence among the rebel leaders and some of this is reproduced in S.A. Rizvi and M.L. Bhargava (eds.), *Freedom Struggle in Uttar Pradesh*, 6 vols. (Lucknow, 1957–61). We know very little about the internal economy and command structure of the rebel forces but Sir John Kaye's papers in the British Library contain a translation of a document listed as Tantia Topi's order book but more accurately described as the order book of the Kalpi garrison. It gives a highly revealing picture of the command structure, and particularly of the relative positions of the Nana Sahib, the Rao Sahib and Tantia Topi, and shows how closely the rebels attempted to follow administrative and disciplinary procedures inherited from the British. It throws little light, unfortunately, on the rebels' logistic arrangements, which remain a virgin field for study, as indeed do the British.

Editorial method

Documents are reproduced as far as possible exactly. The Indian clerks employed in copying telegrams and outgoing letters were not always familiar with the subtleties of English spelling and syntax, and errors are common and occasionally impenetrable; nevertheless no attempt has been made to amend spelling or punctuation. Minor excisions are marked by ellipses, major ones by asterisks. Missing or indecipherable words are shown in square brackets. Opening and closing salutations are omitted, and dates and addresses at the beginning of documents are given in a simplified, standardised form.

Abbreviations

Add MSS	Additional Manuscripts, British Library
BL	British Library
Forrest	G.W. Forrest (ed.), *Selections from the Letters, Despatches and other State Papers preserved in the Military Department of the Government of India, 1857–1858*, 4 vols., (Calcutta, 1893–1912)
FPP	Foreign Department Political Proceedings
FPC	Foreign Department Political Consultations
FSC	Foreign Department Secret Consultations
FSP	Foreign Department Secret Proceedings
FSUP	S.A. Rizvi and M.L. Bhargava (eds.), *Freedom Struggle in Uttar Pradesh*, 6 vols. (Lucknow, 1957–61)
MDP	Military Department Proceedings
NAM	National Army Museum, London
NLS	National Library of Scotland
OIOC	Oriental and India Office Collections, British Library
SUSM	Scottish United Services Museum (now the National War Museum of Scotland)

Glossary

Amil, *Amildar*	a revenue-collecting official for a particular area
atta	coarse ground wheat with husks included
batta	monetary allowance granted for active or foreign service
bhang	cannabis, the drug made from Indian hemp (*cannabis indica*)
bhisti	a water carrier
Brahmin	a member of the highest Hindu caste, often but not exclusively priests or soldiers
caste	the Hindu class system. The principal castes are the Brahmins (qv), the Kshatriyas (warriors), Vaishyas (traders), and Sudras (artisans and agriculturalists). The so-called Untouchables were outside the caste system. Each caste is broken down into sub-castes
crore	100 lacs or 10,000,000
dak (*dawk*)	the mail or letter post
dhooli	a covered stretcher or litter, carried by bearers
Durbar (*Darbar*)	a ruler's Council; (by transference) a levee or audience
Firingi (*firinghee*)	a derogatory term for a European
garhi (*ghurree*)	a small fort cf. -garh
gharry	a horse-drawn cart or carriage
havildar	an Indian NCO equivalent to a sergeant
Hindustan	an old name for India south of the Himalayas but often used in the 19th century to refer to the area north of the Narbada river
Holi	the Hindu spring festival, characterised by coloured powders or liquids being thrown at passers-by
Jagirdar	the holder of a *jagir* (grant of land)
Jat	an Aryan people, located mainly in North-West India and the Punjab, mainly farmers, and Hindu or Sikh by religion

jemadar	an Indian officer roughly equivalent to a warrant officer or company sergeant-major
Kotwali	a police station
lac (*lakh*)	100,000 (written 1,00,000)
Maratha	member of a war-like Hindu race from Central India; at their zenith in the late 18th century, famous as cavalry
naik	an Indian NCO equivalent to a corporal
nullah	a ravine or ditch, normally dry
pagri	a loose cloth wound round a helmet to give added protection against the sun
palki	a covered, man-carried litter or stretcher
paltan	a regiment
Pathan	generic term applied to the Muslim tribes of Afghanistan and the North-West Frontier
Peishwa (*Peshwa*)	originally the hereditary chief minister of the Maratha confederacy but later in effect the head of the confederacy. The last Peishwa, Baji Rao II, was stripped of his powers by the British in 1817 on the conclusion of the Third Maratha War and exiled to Bithur, near Cawnpore
Raj	the common term for the British empire in India, literally meaning rule or sovereignty
Raja (or *Rao*)	from the Sanskrit, meaning 'king' and applied to a ruler; often given as a title of honour; Rani is the female form. Maharaja is a superior version
Rajput	an imprecise term denoting a class of warriors or aristocracy, often identified with the Hindu Kshatriya caste but perhaps more accurately denoting a social class
risaldar	the equivalent in the cavalry of a *subadar* in the infantry, commanding a troop
ryot (*raiyat*)	a cultivator or small farmer
Sahib	term of deference usually applied to Europeans but often applied as an honorific to Indians, e.g. the Nana Sahib and the Rao Sahib
sepoy (*sipahi*)	strictly speaking an Indian infantry soldier but often applied loosely to all Indian soldiers, cf. Kaye's *History of the Sepoy War*
serai	a resting place for travellers

sowar (*sawar*)	literally a horseman, but usually meaning a cavalry trooper
subadar	(1) an Indian officer of status roughly between a warrant and a Queen's commissioned officer, commanding an infantry company (2) a local commandant or chief officer of a town or district
suttee (*sati*)	the practice of widows and concubines immolating themselves on their husband's funeral pyre. Also applied to the widow or concubine
taluqdar (*talukdar*)	the holder of a *taluq* or permanent tenancy of a piece of land or the revenue attached to it in Oudh and the North-West Provinces
tank	an artificial pond or lake, a reservoir
thakur	a term of respect applied usually to a type of feudal landlord or petty chieftain, cf. 'squire'
thanadar	the officer in charge of a police station (or *thana*)
tulwar (*talwar*)	a curved Indian sword
Walayati (*vilayati*)	a mercenary soldier of Pathan, Afghan, Baluchi or Arab descent, common in Central India in 1858
zamindar	a landholder, originally in Bengal but later used elsewhere

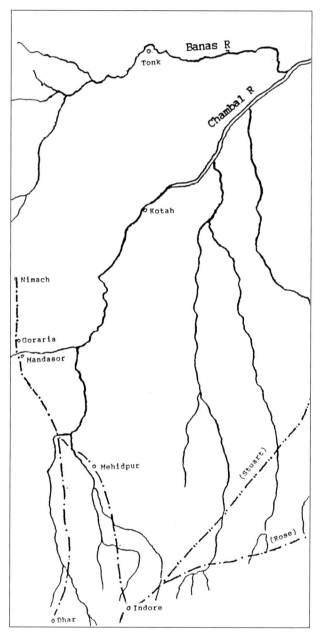

Operations in Malwa

I

Bombay to Jhansi, June 1857 to March 1858

The first stirring of a campaign in Central India was the despatch in June 1857 by Lord Elphinstone, the Governor of Bombay, of a column under Major-General Woodburn.[1] After suppressing a mutiny of the 1st Cavalry of the Hyderabad Contingent at Aurangabad [1], it moved on to Mhow and Indore, where the acting Agent to the Governor-General in Central India (Colonel H.M. Durand) had been expelled and the Residency sacked by mutineers from the Bhopal Contingent and Bhopal state forces in July 1857.[2] Woodburn retired sick and the column was taken over by Brigadier C.S. Stuart, reaching Mhow on 2 August.

When the monsoon ended, Stuart and Durand conducted a short campaign in Malwa,[3] where three strands of insurrection had become intertwined, in a microcosm of the rebellion as a whole. At Nimach (Neemuch) the 72nd Bengal Native Infantry, a wing of the 1st Bengal Light Cavalry and the 7th Infantry of the Gwalior Contingent, had mutinied in June 1857; at the end of August the Shahzada Firuz Shah, a nephew of the Emperor, raised the flag of revolt at Mandasor, defeated a small Bombay force outside Nimach and besieged the remaining British garrison in Mandisore; finally, a dynastic struggle in the small state of Dhar led to British authority being thrown off.

Dhar was besieged and taken by Stuart on 31 October 1857 [3], and the rebels under Firuz Shah were defeated at Goraria on 23 November [9], allowing Nimach to be relieved. With Malwa temporarily quiet, the column returned to Indore on 15 December where it became, in due course, the 1st Brigade of Rose's force. Meanwhile, troops to form a second brigade[4] were collecting at

Sehore, where the British had been expelled earlier, and where mutinous troops of the Bhopal Contingent had collected [17].

Rose was appointed to command the Nerbudda (later the Central India) Field Force at the end of November 1857 [10] and reached Mhow with Hamilton, who relieved Durand, early in December 1857. Their first task was to punish the rebels who had attacked the Residency at Indore. Despite apparent amity earlier [10,34], it led to an immediate breach, Rose believing that Hamilton was obstructing efforts to punish the mutinous troops of the Begum of Bhopal. There may well have been some truth in that, in view of Hamilton's earlier association with Bhopal [38] but Rose was clearly at fault in questioning Hamilton's motives [33]. Elphinstone attempted to smooth matters over but Rose took the matter to Canning who, clearly exasperated, appears to have contemplated Rose's supersession [60]. At the beginning of January, Rose was persuaded to move towards the relief of Saugor but he ran into fresh controversy at Sehore over the punishment of mutineers of the Bhopal Contingent [40, 42, 94] which was to dog him until 1859 [193]. Hamilton disapproved of Rose's harshness and although they subsequently achieved a reasonable working relationship, members of Hamilton's staff lost no opportunity to snipe at Rose.

The relief of Saugor had been allotted to Whitlock but he was behind schedule. Rose was in some doubt as to the real urgency [37] particularly since it meant dividing the operations of his two brigades but he eventually moved from Sehore with his 2nd Brigade on 15 January 1858, leaving the 1st Brigade under Stuart to move via the Grand Trunk Road to Guna and thence to Jhansi [43, 54].

Rose had been criticised for his relative inexperience[5] but he had seen a good deal of war. Conversely, many of his troops had seen no active service; the 86th Foot had seen no service since 1819 and the 3rd Bombay Europeans, raised in 1853, had seen no service of any kind. The 25th Bombay Native Infantry had been in Malwa but the 24th had not seen service since 1839. Rose's Field Force Order Book suggests that his troops had a good deal to learn [53, 72, 73, 75, 78, 85, 98]. The total strength of the Force was about 5,700, of whom about 3,000 were in the 2nd Brigade with Rose.

Rose encountered his first serious opposition at Rahatgarh, 24 miles from Saugor, where the very formidable fortress had been held since the previous August by Fazl Mahomed Khan, a rebellious *jagirdar* of the ruler of Bhopal.[6] It was typical of many fortresses in Central India, perched high on a rocky outcrop rising almost sheer from the surrounding country and enclosed in thick jungle, with the Bina river protecting the west face. Some 4½ miles in circumference, the fortress was garrisoned by about 600 mercenaries[7] in the pay of the local ruler, the Bundela Raja of Banpur, Mardan Singh,[8] who was nearby with a large army. Rose arrived on 24 January, hacked his way through jungle, established his siege battery on the east side and opened fire on the 26th, and by the 28th had made a practicable breach. The bulk of the garrison escaped that night but Fazl Khan was captured next day and hanged over the main gateway the same evening. A relieving army under Mardan Singh, which arrived a mile or so from the fort on the 28th, was defeated, and the remnants followed up and defeated again at Barodia, 12 miles north of Rahatgarh, on 31 January. Rose was blamed by some officers for the escape of the garrison[9] but the size of his force, the extent of the fortress, and the jungly nature of the surrounding country prevented him establishing a tight cordon [64]. More importantly, Rose had shown boldness, decisiveness and a steady nerve; the speed of his operations and the punishment which followed made an immediate impact on the rebels.

He entered Saugor on 3 February and five days later moved out to attack the fortress of Garakhota, 28 miles east of Saugor, held by troops of the Raja of Shahgarh[10] (but including sepoys of the 52nd Bengal Native Infantry). It was a repetition of Rahatghar. The fortress was immensely strong, protected on three sides by rivers, but the garrison, warned by the fate of Rahatghar, escaped before Rose could open fire [69]. After destroying the fort [71], the force was back in Saugor on 15 February. Rose remained in Saugor, accumulating supplies and transport, repairing the carriages of his siege artillery and, in accordance with his instructions, waiting for Whitlock to start from Jubbalpore.[11] The latter finally started on 17 February and, ten days later, Rose left

Saugor for Jhansi. Thirty miles north of Saugor the route crossed a line of hills, penetrated by three passes. The main pass (the Narut) was held in force by the Rajas of Banpur and Shahghar, assisted by mutineers from the 31st and 42nd Bengal Native Infantry from Saugor.[12] Rose feinted against this and attacked the middle of the three, the Madanpur pass, forcing it for the loss of 12 men wounded [79, 81, 82, 83]. There was now no major obstacle between him and Jhansi, which he reached on 20 March; the 1st Brigade arrived two days later, having besieged and taken the powerful fortress of Chanderi, 55 miles south-west of Jhansi, on 17 March [92, 96].

Jhansi was an immensely powerful fortress, defended by some 11,000 men, including 1,500 sepoys. Unsurprisingly, Canning and Campbell were apprehensive of a reverse and Rose had authority to by-pass it if he found it too strong [67, 68]. Indeed, on the evening his troops reached Jhansi, he and Hamilton received orders from Canning and Campbell to divert eastwards to relieve the loyal Raja of Chirkari, under attack from an army under Tantia Topi [80, 87]. By Hamilton's account, Rose was opposed to this diversion but felt unable to disobey and Hamilton took it upon himself to direct Rose to continue against Jhansi. His reasons were deployed in a long letter for Canning [95] and his action was approved. His reasoning was eminently sound and it seems a classic case of dangerous long-range meddling.

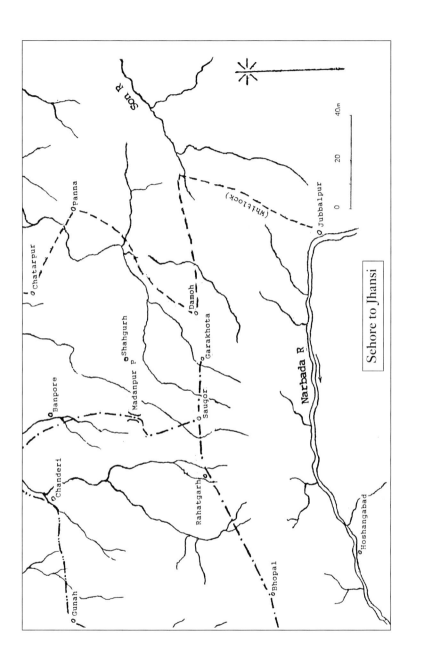

Sehore to Jhansi

Captain Edward Lowry[1] to his wife

Aurangabad

[Holograph]   24 June 1857

. . . I will now tell you what has taken place since I last wrote when I told you we were sharp off to this place. Our last march was 37 miles in 24 hours and out of 48 hours I got but 3 of sleep, not because I had no opportunity but you know over excitement makes me restless. Well! last night we marched at 5 o'clock and after having gone about 14 miles we halted and were ordered to lie down for two hours and to take it out in sleep on cold mother earth. At 3 o'clock a.m. we were ordered to march into Aurangabad where we arrived at 10 A.M. We marched straight to the lines of the mutineers, the artillery guns were pointed towards their lines at a distance of 50 yds, the 25th regiment in quarter distance column on their right and the Cavalry on left and right rear of the guns, after this a parley took place and the result was about 150 mutineers stood to us and came over to our side, the remainder yelling like devils ran to their horses in the lines; when we received the order to load and form square for cavalry; the guns then opened on them with grape and canister, they all bolted right and left when the 14th Dragoons went after them and brought in several prisoners, killing only 5 men. 60 prisoners taken, many of them are going to hang.[2] About half an hour ago one man was hanged close to my tent. The mutineers are being cut up in every direction, so do not be alarmed dearest. I was president of a Court Martial yesterday and the man who I tried is to be shot this evening, he is a Havildar in the Nizam Artillery. I felt much distressed when signing the proceedings which were his death warrant, he was a fine, handsome youth, it seems to me cruel work, dear Rose, to hang and shoot the men by wholesale, it is not like killing a man in a fight, for tho' the scoundrels deserve it and have brought all this on themselves, one cannot help feeling for them, they have no fear of death, the man hanged just now, when at the foot of the gallows, asked for water to wash his feet and hands as he was going straight to Paradise.[3] Poor creature, he was hanged for trying to murder his Commanding Officer – 5 more men are to be hanged this afternoon.

The courts sit every day, one is called 'Follett's Court'[4] and the other 'Lowry's' so you see I have plenty to do . . .

NAM 6711–24

2
Colonel H.M. Durand to Elphinstone

Dhar

[Manuscript telegram] 23 October 1857

Brigadier Stewarts[5] column attacked the Dhar and Anjheera insurgents this morning and drove them from their positions which were supported by the fire of the Dhar fort. Three guns were taken from the Enemy by a charge of H.M[s] 14th Dragoons under Captain Gall[6] and 1st Nizams Cavalry under Captain Macdonald.[7] Our loss small chiefly in 3rd Nizams Cavalry which did good service under Captain Orr.[8] Small loss attributable to Brigadier Stewart and Major Kean making good use of Woolcombe[9] and Hungerfords[10] guns, practice by both excellent.

OIOC MSS Eur F87, Box 9D, Letter Book 3

3
J.H. Sylvester – diary

[Holograph]

[25 October 1857] . . . ye Brig[r11] who issued no order of any kind the village was not properly occupied even though he was advised to do so. The consequence was the men off duty & even some native soldiers but chiefly the 86th and Artillery were frightfully drunk having seized the native liquor shops. They then commenced looting & killing every thing black, old men, young women and children!! This of course was to be deplored but I had anticipated this. They shouted Cawnpore, Delhi and down they went. [Indecipherable] says he saw a room full of dead women with children sucking at their breasts. Other women brought out dead, children supplicating for mercy. Officers rushed down, the Provost Marshal & some Dragoons & they soon put a stop to it and destroyed all the liquor.

OIOC MSS Eur C241, p. 31

4
Captain H.O. Mayne[12] to Quartermaster-General Bombay
Dhar
[Manuscript telegram]   2 November 1857

Mhow – Monday 10.9 A.M. The Breach in the Dhar fort having been reported practicable last night the assault was ordered for this morning but about 10 P.M. last night the 3rd Cavalry[13] outpost to the N.W. were heard to be engaged – the force turned out and the 3rd Cavy. started immediately in that direction. The Dragoons followed speedily – the Infantry moved down quickly to the head of the Pettah[14] and at 11 P.M. rushed up the breach and found the fort evacuated.[15] The fort was held during the night inside by the 25th and outside by 1st Cavalry detachment. The unconfirmed report is that 500 rebels with about 30 wounded and their baggage on Camels and Tattoos[16] have escaped. The Cavalry returned before 3 A.M. without finding the fugitive Enemy except ten men. Further particulars will be reported. Our shells have greatly damaged the fort buildings except the Treasury and Ordnance. The place is completely empty.

OIOC MSS Eur F87, Box 9D, Letter Book 3

5
Sylvester – diary

[17 November 1857] A Drum Head Court Martial sat immediately on the 78 prisoners taken by Major Orr's people.[17] They were sentenced to be shot. We paraded that evening at 5 p.m. 74 prisoners had their hands tied behind them, their eyes bandaged were shot by one detachmen[t] 86th. Most fell dead instantly, some having their brains shot out, others shot through the heart, the blood came pumping out & some shot in ye abdomen showed signs of agony afterwards & so received an extra bullet. I walked past them lying in a bloody line. We dined in the open air . . .

OIOC MSS Eur C241, p. 41

6
Colonel Le Mesurier to Colonel Melvill[18]

Asirgarh

[Holograph]   13 November 1857

A detach[t] of the Hyderabad Contingent under Cap[t] Hare[19] en route to Mhow arrived here yesterday – strength

80 sabres
4–6 Pounders
250 Bayonets
3 Officers.

Several Mules preceding them passed on without halting, destined, I suppose, for Mhow.

I have every thing nearly ready for the reception of the Company of Europeans to be here stationed. The Native Hospital has been adapted for the purpose, and a more splendid place there could not be. I have all their Stables & Barracks & Cots for the Sick ready. The Sleeping Cots, for the number required, will not be ready for a few weeks, as the Wood is to be brought from a great distance. I received the order here on the 12th Ul[t] to prepare, and within the Month every thing has been arranged, under the steady exertion of my Staff Officers, with a daily superintendence on my part. I have done every thing to make the Men very comfortable. Major Landon & L[t] Louis[20] are to be the officers with the company; but Col. Liddell[21] tells me that Landon knows nothing, and never did know any thing, of Soldiers. This is extremely unsatisfactory. I shall therefore apply for the services of Cap[t] Sandwith[22] to be sent here on his arrival from England. He was in the 2nd Europeans under my Command – a very intelligent officer & well acquainted with all the details of Regimental Work – indeed an invaluable officer. Whatever he does he does well.

1¼ Lac of rupees arrived here yesterday from [indecipherable] for the use of Steuart's force. The Aurangabad force arrived this morning and halts here tomorrow.

I have no *proper* Commissariat Agent here. I wrote long ago to Davidson,[23] and he promised to write to Major Ramsay[24] at Poona to send me an efficient man to Assurghur, which is indespensible. The present is inefficient. God knows what Major Ramsay has done. Had he sent a man he would have apprised of it e'er this. He was never a quick moving man.

The force, that is the infantry portion of it, arrived at 7 this morning. I have just received a note from Major Landon – 1 P.M. telling me the Europeans had not, when he wrote, ½ to 11 A.M., breakfasted. How badly off the 3rd Europeans appear to be for Regimental Captains. Stockley the 2nd Major,[25] now at Mhow, would be of great assistance to Liddell if he were to join.

NAM 6408–16–12

7
Le Mesurier to Melvill

Asirgarh

[Holograph]   15 November 1857

Steuarts' force left this morning en route to Mhow. He received an Express post before he left for Mhow, on which he made a requisition for the Services of the Company of Europeans, which he had been ordered to detach for garrison duty here, to go on with him. I immediately complied with his request, & hope it will be approved by the Chief. I had every thing ready to receive the Company, & most comfortable they would have been. For some months, I & my Staff have been at work to prepare for them. Landon has been directed by Steuart to join the Depot of his Reg^t at Nuggur.[26] His C.O. reported that he could get Landon to do nothing. Landon is the senior Captain in the Reg^t – a high position with his Reg^t in the field – Liddell only above him, who, if he fell sick, Landon was next & unfit. Instead of being sent to Nuggur it is more than probable that he will be attached to a Reg^t where so many better men have been *recently* sent.

These are curious times, Melvill. Everything will, e'er one year passes, give way to 'The Imperial Army of India'. How slow the Troops that left England in July for Bombay are in arriving. You will have two or three of them arriving by the day you receive this. I am surprised that your Health has not given way from the tremendous work you have to get through daily, and no Central India to set you up as formerly. I am going to apply for leave to visit the Presidency on Privilege Leave from the 2nd January – to take Medical advice – *for no other object*. I shall get back again as quick as I can.

I am afraid Durand is not doing as well as was expected of him. It will require a larger force than we have at Mhow to settle Central India. Before January next the British Troops will be marching in every direction. How little we appear to know of the real state of things with Outram at Lucknow.[27] I hope all is going right with him.

NAM 6408–16–12

8
Le Mesurier to Melvill

Asirgarh

[Holograph]   23 November 1857

4 P.M.

> 80 Bearers
> 60 Horsemen
> 1 Elephant
> 1 Howdah
> 1 Palanquin

arrived this morning from Indore for Sir Robert Hamilton.[28] It looks as if he intends coming by Assurgurh.

On the 16th Inst. it appears that 18 Cartloads of Treasure, escorted by 400 Peons[29] from Bombay en route to Indore have been plundered by the Bheels at Cundwah.[30] The Peons joined the Bheels & have shared the Booty which was under their protection. These Bheels are giving much trouble on that line of road.

Steuart's Force left Cundwah, 24 miles from this, on the 21st towards Hooshingabad.[31] The force that is to leave Nuggur on the 6th [of] next month to join them is a very respectable addition: but they will be a long time reaching them, they cannot well be here before the end of next month, & by the end of January before they join the Column.

NAM 6408–16–12

9
Stuart to Adjutant-General Bombay

Mandasor

[Printed copy]   27 November 1857

I have the honour to forward . . . full particulars of the successful operations . . . against the rebel enemy in the vicinity of Mundesore.

(2) On the morning of the 21st November the Force, accompanied by the Field Force, Hyderabad Contingent . . . under command of Major Orr, arrived within three miles and a half of

Mundesore about 9 A.M., and as I had no good information as to the roads or the country in the immediate vicinity of the town, neither as to the fords of the river Sowna, which it was necessary to cross before reaching the town, I determined upon camping until a good reconnaissance had been effected. The Rebel enemy at Mundesore, hearing of our approach, had posted pickets entirely covering the country over which we were advancing, and, observing our pickets thrown out, they mustered in some force outside the walls of the town and appeared inclined to attack. I, however, contented myself with reinforcing the pickets, and leaving the whole charge of the front to Major Robertson, 25th Regiment Native Infantry,[32] the Field Officer of the Day, returned to camp. About 3 o'clock P.M. I received intimation from him that the enemy were advancing in force, and threatening both our flanks and centre at the same time. I accordingly moved out to meet them; they advanced steadily, with banners flying, and appeared in great numbers. On approaching our right front, however, they were most gallantly charged by Lieutenant Dew, Her Majesty's 14th Light Dragoons,[33] who, with some of his men, occupied that ground as a picket. Major Orr, Commanding 3rd Regiment Cavalry Hyderabad Contingent, supported Lieutenant Dew and the Enemy were driven back with great loss, and before our guns, which had quickly moved up, could open upon them, the attack on our centre was repulsed by a few rounds of our Artillery, whilst that on the left was successfully met by the Field Force under Major Orr. The enemy having thus been driven back at all points, were pursued for some distance, in fact until they nearly reached the walls of the town, and nothing further occurred that day.

(3) Having received intelligence from the Governor General's Agent that the portion of the Rebel army before Neemuch, amounting to about 5,000, would probably raise the siege of that place and endeavour to effect a junction with their Head-Quarters at Mundesore, I determined to frustrate this by intercepting them. Accordingly, early on the morning of the 22nd Instant, I moved forward my force in order of battle, our advance was unopposed, and on my left flank reaching the village of Kulgipore, I made a flank movement to the left, as previously determined on, leaving

the advance guard to cover it, and to reinforce the rear guard as we crossed the Bakri ford of the river Sowna, about 1,400 yards to the south-west of the town of Mundesore. Thus secured, the movement was safely effected, opposed only by a slight and ineffective fire from a gun on one of the south-west bastions of the town. I then encamped facing the west of the town, my flanks well protected by the two branches of the river and my line running at right angles to the right of Sir Thomas Hislop's camp in 1817. Just previous to the camp being marked out, it was reported that Cavalry were seen on the left, and Major Orr, taking the 1st Cavalry Hyderabad Contingent, under Captain Abbott, and 4th Cavalry Hyderabad Contingent, under Captain Murray,[34] saw about 300 Horse, supposed to be under Heera Singh, endeavouring to draw them off in a north-westerly direction, but keeping at too great a distance to allow of being attacked. Reinforcements of Cavalry were sent for, and whilst the Left Wing, Her Majesty's 14th Light Dragoons under Captain Gall, and 3rd Cavalry Hyderabad Contingent under Lieutenant Clerk,[35] were moving up, intelligence was brought to Major Orr that Heera Singh's baggage had just left the village of Goraria, on the Neemuch road, the object of Heera Singh's party, to draw our Cavalry away from his baggage, thus being apparent. Her Majesty's 14th Light Dragoons, the 1st Cavalry Hyderabad Contingent and the 4th Cavalry Hyderabad Contingent galloped off in pursuit, the 3rd Cavalry Hyderabad Contingent remaining as reserve. They caught up the Enemy about two miles south of Peeplia and, after cutting up about half of them, halted at a nullah, a mile to the south of the village. On perceiving it strongly held by the Enemy's Infantry, who showed many standards, they then returned to camp.

(4) Feeling assured that the Infantry seen in Peeplia formed the advance guard of the Enemy, I moved at 8 o'clock A.M. on the 23rd Instant by my left, and crossed the northern branch of the river Sowna. I then halted my column, and collected all my baggage on the reverse flank, then moving on to my proposed camp on the Neemuch and Mundesore road, ready to oppose the enemy either from one or the other direction. On coming on to the ground, the enemy appeared in great force to the north; so, ordering my

baggage to be collected on a strong mound, I strongly reinforced my rear-guard and proceeded to meet them. After a short advance, I formed line to my front, facing northward and found the Enemy occupying a very strong position, with their right in and beyond the village of Goraria, their right centre covered by a date nullah and lines of date trees, their battery of six guns on a rising ground, with a large mud hut protecting their gunners, and their left stretched along the ridge running east from the village. My line advanced covered by skirmishers; the Enemy's Infantry, with banners flying (many of them green), moved down to meet us through the intermediate fields of high jowarry[36] and their guns opened fire. I immediately halted my line and replied to the fire with Captains Hungerford's and Woolcombe's batteries, at a range of about 900 yards. After a few rounds, I again advanced the line, and permitted Captain Hungerford to move his half battery to a position on our right front, from which he could enfilade the Enemy. After an advance of about 300 yards, our line was again halted and firing resumed, that from both batteries being very effective. A most gallant charge was then made on the Enemy's guns by the escort of Her Majesty's 14th Light Dragoons, attached to Captain Hungerford, under Lieutenant Martin,[37] who found, however, that the positon was still very strongly held by the Enemy's Infantry, and was compelled to retire, he himself being very severely wounded. Captain Hungerford's half battery was again advanced to within 100 yards, and after a round or two of grape, the guns were once again charged and captured, the enemy flying in great numbers into the village to their right. The 3rd Regiment of Cavalry Hyderabad Contingent, under Major S. Orr, was just at this moment rapidly advanced to our right front, and having been wheeled to the left, it swept down upon them in their retreat and killed great numbers. Our line then changed front about the eighth of a circle, right thrown forward, and moved steadily on the village, which evidently held great numbers of the Enemy. Their skirmishers disputed our advance but were soon driven back. Having halted within about 300 yards of the village, our Artillery opened upon it with shot and shell, after which I directed the Infantry to advance and carry it.

The men of the 86th and 25th regiments dashed forward in the most gallant manner, and, having entered the village, commenced to drive all before them. They soon met, however, with very warm opposition, the Enemy having taken possession in great force of many houses, from which a most harassing fire was kept upon our men. Under these circumstances, and, as, moreover, I could get no satisfactory accounts of what was passing in my rear which I knew from the firing I heard, as also from the pressing applications I received for reinforcements, had been warmly engaged, I recalled the Infantry and posted strong pickets all round the village, and moved the remainder of the men a short distance off to where the baggage had been passed up from the rear. I then learnt that, during the afternoon, when we were hotly engaged in the front, a strong body of the Enemy from Mundesore attacked our rear, and endeavoured to carry off the siege train, baggage etc. They were, however, most gallantly repulsed on every occasion.

(5) On the 24th Instant I arranged with Captain Hungerford Commandant of Artillery, that the village of Goraria in which the rebels had taken refuge, should be well shelled and again assaulted by the Infantry. Accordingly, I moved up to it about noon, and found that the Enemy were as I had left them the preceding evening, excepting that a few had attempted to escape, nearly all of whom were killed. After a heavy fire of three hours duration, the detachment of Her Majesty's 86th Regiment under command of Major Keane,[38] and the 25th Regiment Native Infantry, under Major Robertson, again stormed the village and carried it, killing great numbers of the Enemy; they themselves also suffering severely. At sunset I withdrew the Troops, intending to move against the Fort of Mundesore the next day. Early, however, on the morning of the 25th Instant, intelligence reached me that the Enemy had, during the night, completely evacuated Mundesore, and were scattered in flight throughout the country, in various directions, having lost, it is computed, about 1,500 of their number during our operations against them. I accordingly removed my

Camp to Mundesore, and am now engaged in dismantling the Fort, destroying the Guns etc., before leaving the neighbourhood.

❋ ❋ ❋

Forrest, IV, Appendix E, pp. lvii–xxi

10

Rose to Elphinstone

Poonah

[Holograph]   28 November 1857

I cannot *say* how much obliged I am to you for sending me to Central India. I hope Sir Robert will come soon. We came from Marseilles to Suez & I believe we both liked each other, at least I know I did him; he seemed to me to be thoroughly practical and sensible, with a singularly good knowledge of the scene of his labours. I am sure that we shall work perfectly well together. Almost the last thing he said to me on board was that he hoped I might accompany him to Indore.

I am just going to inspect the Troop of the 14th, at Kirkee which is to join Brigadier Steuart; they will be 90 sabres strong.

The 3rd39 I am to see in a day or two; they are described as remarkably fine men; not so tall as broad and muscular. The country people say 'England has now sent some of her peasants'.

OIOC MSS Eur F87, Box 6A, No. 4

11

Officer Commanding Mhow to Rose

Mhow

[Manuscript telegram]   30 November 1857

The seige [sic] train consists of five 18 Pounder guns, four 12 Pounder guns, one 10 and one 8 [inch] howitzers,40 one 10 inch, one 8 inch and two five and half [inch] mortars, of the above two 18 pounder guns, the 8 inch howitzer and the 8 and five and half mortars are with the field force. The force at Mhow consists of Bengal Artillery, 1 Subaltern, 44 Non Commissioned and gunners, 3 nine pounder guns with horses but no drivers, HMs 86th, 1 Ensign and 49 Non Commissioned and Privates, natives 25th Bombay N.I. 2 Subalterns, 3 Native Officers, 111 Non Commissioned and Privates, Hyderabad Contingent Artillery, 3 Native Officers, 73 Non Commissioned and privates with 6 six pounder guns, Cavalry 3 native Officers 135 Non Commissioned and Privates, Infantry 3 European Officers, 4 Native Commissioned Officers, 12 native officers and four hundred and thirty nine Non Commissioned Officers and privates, Bombay Sappers and Miners two European Officers, 4 Sergeants, one native officer, 36 Non Commissioned and privates, Bhopal Contingent Artillery 1 native officer, 9 Non Commissioned and privates, two nine pounder guns, Cavalry two native officers, 57 Non Commissioned and sowars. Malwa Bheel Corps 1 Lieut (which commanding station), 4 native officers, 131 Non Commissioned and Privates . . .

OIOC MSS Eur F87, Box 9D, Letter Book 3

12
Rose notebook

[Holograph]   [c.1 December 1857][41]

Malwa & Deccan F.F.
Malwa F.F. at Neemuch

	E.	N
Left Wing 14th Lt Drs	213.	
4th Comp.2nd Batt Arty		
	99.	77
No 4 Light Field Batt		
Sappers & Miners (Bomb)	4.	30
Ditto (Madras)	4.	117
Detach HM 86th	244.	
25th Regt N.InfY		920
	564	1144

564
1144
————
1708
————

Deccan Field Force[42]

	E.	N
Right Half 1st Troop H.A.[43]	70.	12
Detach[t] Sappers and M[s]	2.	34
D[o] H.M. 14th L[t] Drag[s]	180.	
3rd European Reg[t]	449.	
24th N. Inf[y]		891

Under orders to join from Nuggur 7th December

	E	N
Detach[t] 1st Troop H.A.	23	6
2nd Comp. Reserve Ar[t]. ⎫		
⎬	105	74
N[o] 18 Light Field Batt ⎭		
Detach[t] HM. 14th D[t] Dr[s]	159	
3 Light Cavalry –		240
Detach[t] 3rd Europ. Reg[t]	255	
Total	1243	1257

1807
2401
————
4208
————

Grand Total	1807	2401[44]

To join from Bombay on arrival there
H[d] 2nd Wing H.M 86th Reg[t]
One Reg[t] Europ. Inf[y][45]

SUSM M1994.100.2

19

13
Rose to Somerset

Indore

[Manuscript telegram]   6 December 1857

I arrived with Sir R.H. at Indore yesterday even[g]. Holkar disarmed his Cav[y] with his Police before the arrival of the Malwa Brigade wh[ch] arrived at 10 o'clock a.m. He disarmed his Infantry during the day without British assistance. All is quiet here; and the culprits will speedily be brought to justice.

Many of the Troops require shoes. Could Your Excellency supply these from Bombay or elsewhere.[46]

When may I expect the Royal Artillery and Engineers?

BL Add MSS 42811 ff. 41a–b

14
Rose to Elphinstone

Nassick[47]

[Holograph]   9 December 1857

I received last night a telegraphic message from the Officer Com[g] at Mhow that the whole of the Siege Train is mounted on the Fort of Mhow with the exception of the part of it which is with the Bheelsa Field Force[48] – consequently the Deccan Brigade, now at Sehore, will be without Siege Train, unless supplied with it from Bombay, or Ahmed Nugger, as it would not be prudent to dismantle the Fort of Mhow of its guns, particularly in the absence of the Nerbudda Field Force. I have telegraphed this to the Chief.[49]

The Bullock Train is excellent; if prolonged to Mhow it will bring all that part of the country conspicuously close to Bombay our great, or general Base of Supply for Troops and their Materiel. At all the halting places, there are Commissariat Supplies etc. for the Troops. I have seen them here myself – Tea, Biscuit, Medical Comforts. Major Kane[50] is just the man for the direction of the Train. I think that I could give it a simple, military organisation like the English, French and Austrian Military Transport. When not employed in the Transport of Troops, and Military Stores (which would often be the case) it might be kept in being, and pay for itself by conveying Treasure,[51] valuable merchandise, and hereafter, when the speed of the Train improves, it might convey the Post. The Road is very good except the first part . . .

I shall halt the Malwa Field Force at Indore, so that Sir Robert may begin his operations at once, and the Reinforcements can continue their march to reinforce the Deccan Brigade without a check.

OIOC MSS F87m Box 6A, No.4.

15
Rose to Steuart[52]

Mallegaum[53]

[Holograph copy]   11 December 1857

N° 1 of 1857

With reference to your Conf[ll] letter, N° 57 of 1857, to the Q[r] M[r] Gen of the Army, I beg leave to request you to send me a detail of the Medical Transport which you require for y[r] Brigade.

I request you also to let me know

1st The amount of rounds of ammunition wh[ch] your Brig. has for each man, & for each piece of Artillery.

2. The mode of transporting the Reserve Ammn. of your Force; whether the mode works well, and if it does not work well, I should be glad to receive your suggestions for improving it.

3. Whether your Force has sufficient Dhoolies,[54] and Tents and other arrangements for Flying Ambulances.

4. The fullest information you can collect as to the State of the Country, particularly Saugor, and the movement of the Rebels. It will be advisable to obtain all the information you can on these points, by addressing letters to the Officer Comm[dg] at Saugor.

BL Add MSS 42811 ff. 2b–3

16
Durand to Governor-General (Lord Canning)

Mhow

[Manuscript telegram]   16 December 1857

The regular Cavalry and Infantry of Holkar were quietly disarmed
yesterday the presence of the Mhow Column enabling the Durbar
to execute my requisition. The punishment of the guilty remains
to be carried into effect but the Durbar have repeatedly promised
that the disarming once effected justice would have its course.
I handed over charge to Sir Robert Hamilton this morning, the
16th, at Indore.

OIOC MSS Eur F87, Box 9D, Letter Book 3

17
Hamilton to Captain H.O. Mayne

Indore

[Holograph copy]   22 December 1857

Information has reached me that several men of the disarmed
Bhopal Contingent are collected at Sehore, in respect of whom it
is necessary that the orders of the Government, No. 733, copy of
which is annexed for your information, be fully carried out whilst
Brigadier Stewart[55] and his force are encamped at Sehore.

2. Major Genl Sir H. Rose concurs with me in considering that
the best mode of giving effect to the desire of Government will be
by your proceeding without delay to Sehore taking with you all the
remnants of the disarmed Contingent now at Indore for it is only
by the faithful amongst them that evidence could be produced to
convict the culpable.

3. As Brigadier C. Stewart will halt at Sehore for the next
15 days, in this interval the whole enquiry may be concluded. Any
men who may not be tainted can enter the service of the Regent of
Bhopal should she desire to entertain them; those whose fidelity to
the British Government is beyond question may be retained on
their former rate of pay, until the further orders of Government,

but the Bhopal Contingent as a body can no longer be recognised nor any permitted to wear the uniform.

4. With regard to the Bhopal guns now at Indore it is not intended that they should leave this, they will continue here with the Golundaze[56] under charge to Lieutenant Martin, with the men of the extinct Gwalior Contingent.

5. No orders having been received from Government in respect of the United Malwa Contingent, the men of that force must remain under the command of Major Timins.[57]

6. I request you will inform Lieutenant Martin that he is to command my personal Escort which will be formed of the men and guns you may leave behind, and such others as may hereafter be added. The Escort will move to ground which Lieutenant Shakespear[58] will point out to Lieutenant Martin.

BL Add MSS 42807

18
Hamilton to Elphinstone

Indore

[Manuscript telegram]   23 December 1857

All going on satisfactorily here. Holkar has blown away another ringleader from a gun this evening. Trials going on and punishment being inflicted on guilty. The wire within a mile and half of Indore and the Office is opened there, we are short of wire. Colonel Stockley with a force is going to Sindwa today and will keep open the communication. Mr Beauvais accompanies him to put on the mail carts and horses and also to see the Bullocks are placed and properly protected.[59]

OIOC MSS Eur F87, Box 9D, Letter Book 4

19
Hamilton to Elphinstone

Indore

[Manuscript telegram]   23 December 1857

The Aunjeera Raja,[60] his minister and 3 officials tried by us this morning and sentenced to be hung (sentence suspended as to Raja) – three executed, one commuted to transportation for life. Eight mutineers blown from guns this evening, one hung. Let me know any news from Cawnpore.[61] All quiet here.

OIOC MSS Eur F87, Box 9D, Letter Book 4

20
Rose to Elphinstone

Indore

[Manuscript telegram]   24 December 1857

The Political Agent at Hoasungabad writes on the 16th Instant from a place ten miles north of the Nerbudda to Captain Richards that, on the 14th inst., a detachment consisting of 3 nine pounders, two hundred sepoys,[62] thirty Europeans and 40 sowars were sent to Bhopal six miles from Saugor against rebels – that the detachment was surprised, lost 12 men killed and wounded, left their dead and wounded on the ground and retired in confusion. The writer adds on a slip of paper marked private that the 31 NI are not to be trusted. Sir Robert Hamilton and myself are of opinion that this news is serious and consequently I have determined to have my first Brigade at Indore to preserve order during the executions. I am expediting the repairs of the seige train of the 2nd Brigade and shall proceed with it, two troops 14th Light Dragoons, a detachment of the Hyderabad Contingent and Colonel Turnbulls[63] reinforcements to Saugor as soon as possible. Three more mutineers were executed by the troops at Indore. All is quiet here.

OIOC MSS Eur F87, Box 9D, Letter Book 4

21
Le Mesurier to Melvill

Asirgarh

[Holograph]   27 December 1857

Forbes Detachment[64] arrived this morning at ½ past 7. I heard from Turnbull's Camp last night at Dhorgaun on the 25th four marches from this, a Letter had been received that morning from Sir Hugh Rose directing him to branch off to Sihore. He will do so when he gets within 9 miles short of Mhow, & then strike off to the right into the Saugor Road. Sir Hugh writes to his A.D.C. to join him with his kit at Mhow; and that 2 days after his arrival, he, Sir Hugh, shall start and overtake the Column in 5 marches. Wood, Ashburner and Jones[65] go on with Turnbull. I hear that Turnbull has no route of his march after he strikes into the Saugor Road. He will find no difficulty – Sihore is about half way between Mhow and Saugor. Turnbull was to be at Bumai on the right bank of the Nerbudda this morning (27th Dec[r]) where he halts.

5 men have been hung at Mhow, and some are being tried at Indore – chief hands in the late disturbances.

Col. Durand, Cap[t] Cobbe[66] & Mrs Knapp the Residency Doctor's Lady will be here tomorrow, en route to Bombay. Durand's fun in hanging a lot of fellows at Indore was spoilt by the arrival of Sir Rob[t], who is supposed to be less viciously disposed. Neither of these two great Men met. Durand handed over charge officially and came away at once to Mhow. All this Gordon Cumming writes me.[67]

The expedition against the Bheels is to begin soon. Stockley is to have charge of the Advance on his side. Bheels against Bheels is of little use. Until the Jungle is dry enough to burn nothing can be done against them. Morefull writes me that they are getting very troublesome. The Troops of the 14th Dragoons have now arrived under Prettijohn. He has 100 Store Carts with him; what Stores they are I know not. Forbes halts tomorrow. I shall leave this about the 1st next month and reach Malligaun on the 3rd.

NAM 6508–16–12

22
Rose to Somerset

Indore

[Manuscript telegram]   29 December 1857

The Durbar of Indore have not evinced either good faith or promptitude in punishing those who were concerned in the massacre and plunder of thirty eight British subjects and attack of the Residency in July last.

. . . Decided measures have ameliorated this state of things and two demands which I induced Sir Robert Hamilton to make have been granted. He told me that he should use force if they were not granted. I ordered the 1ˢᵗ Brigade from Mhow, where it had gone to refit for the Field, to Indore, for the purpose of enforcing these demands.

The reinforcements under Lt Colonel Turnbull arrive at Mhow on the 30ᵗʰ Instant, as he is obliged to take them there to sharpen their swords. I intend to march with them to Saugor.

In order to carry out all the instructions of the Governor General & Lord Elphinstone I have in unison with Sir Robert Hamilton ordered Major Orr to go from Mundisore via Augher with his Force to Shajeehanpoor on the Indore & Agra road to open that road as far as Biowra[68] and protect the reconstruction of the Electric Telegraph along it. A party of Cavalry marches from here to do the same from here to Shahjeehanpoor.

Did your Excellency receive my Telegram about Saugor.

BL Add MSS 42811 ff. 15b–16b

23
Rose to Elphinstone

Indore

[Telegram]   29 December 1857
Telegram No.48

I regret to say that the Durbar of Indore[69] notwithstanding my earnest and repeated representations has not given any satisfaction for the rebels against the Government, the massacre of the British subjects, the attack on the Residency, the plunder of British property, and the mutiny of Holkar's troops which took place at Indore in July last. With the exception of blowing one man away from a gun today a continuation of the same earnest representations was the cause of seventeen men being executed, not one officer was amongst them. The men themselves cried out before their execution, why are we executed and not one officer who made us do what we did. The Durbar has acted equally ill in the matter of the Amildar of Mahidpoor.[70] This man organised the rebellion and mutiny in that town. The Durbar in order to shield this man tried him on a minor charge and got him out of the way. Sir Robert Hamilton has addressed the following demands to the Durbar and tells me that if they do not grant them, he will have recourse to force. I require a list of every officer of the Maharajah's and [? Busrung] Paltans to be sent to me immediately by the bearer. The Amildar of Mahidpoor must be sent forthwith to me. I have read this Telegram to Sir Robert and he said yes. The Inhabitants of Indore are completely armed. They ought to be disarmed. I could do it.

OIOC MSS Eur F87, Box 6G, Packet 20

24
Elphinstone to Hamilton

Bombay

[Telegram]   29 December 1857

Sir Hugh Rose's telegram of the 29th tallies strongly with disclosures made by the adopted son of the ex-Raja of Sattara – & by three or four of his advisers who have been examined separately. They all declare that they were told to expect assistance from Indore – that Holkar deceived them etc. A letter has been found written in [indecipherable] from Shenamund Shastri Punditjee from Indore to Doorga Singh Seenaputtee at Sattara dated 25th Nov' year not given – saying that Holkar & Sindia are coming to Satara in six weeks with an army – & that Holkar has himself told this to the writer – answer to be sent to the house of Bhagwandass Choonilal at Oujein. Holkar alone is to be written to and none of his Sirdars. You will know whether Shenamund Shastri is likely to be employed in such a correspondence by Holkar and whether the house of Bhagwandass Choonilal is likely to have been made use of. This letter and former intercepted ones, together with his present vacillating conduct, lead me to suspect that he has been playing a double game, affecting to favour both sides. Neither Sir Hugh Rose nor his force should on any account leave Indore till the matter is settled and all demands complied with. You will be the best judge as to the advisability of disarming the town.

OIOC MSS Eur F87, Box 6G, Packet 20

25
Ootum Ram[71] to Hamilton

Bajrungarh[72]

[Holograph copy translation]   30 December 1857

I have according to orders enquired about the Telegraph wires and the poles. In the village of Dheerpore in the Rajhogurh Haka the wire is kept in a room by the Rajhogurh people and a portion of the wire is also kept in a Rajghur village near Barasat. Enquiry is also been made about the wire in the Bujrungurh Haka but I don't think these enquiries can proceed satisfactorily for in the Rajhogurh country the anarchy and plunder is such that no person or functionary or a common traveller can pass without 2 or 300 armed men and even such parties are sometimes plundered. How is it then possible that a Dak can be re-established or an Enquiry made in such a state, which I have already reported to you.

The plunder was less when I had just arrived, but after the defeat of the rebels at Mundisore they fled towards Bujrungarh. Some were disarmed by the Sur Soobah of that place and sent to Gwalior, about 500 Vullayatees and the horse and foot came to Rajhogurh and kept at Ramnuggur. About 2,000 other vagabonds were let loose to plunder in the hills. These villains plunder all travellers, even a Fakeer, within a range of 12 Coss;[73] and their example is beginning to be imitated by others between Koolarie and [?Mummia],[74] the country about which places is regularly raised. The Vullayatees show an implacable enmity towards the British servants and kill any one who can be caught, though I am, as yet, quite safe, thank God.

I have ordered Muthrapershad, the Goonah writer,[75] to enquire about the wire and the poles in the Sepree district but with his small escort of 3 or 4 men he was obliged to retire, and an escort of 100 men also, the Thakadars can't give, of course.

If I had your support in men and money at the first outset, with about 100 or 200 of the former I would have dispersed the rebels but they have now accumulated to 2 or 3,000 in number and if not sharply looked after, may make another Mundisore affair of it and probably give great trouble to the rulers.

Their object is plunder and devastation, and they are about to commit the mischief and ruin of the country; Scindia's troops with Sir Soobah are not enough to stay the storm; and I hope you will refer the matter to Sir Robert Hamilton. Letters from H.H. Scindia and the Pol. Agent were received by the Maharajah Rajah, calling upon him to make proper arrangements for the protection of the post but he falsely answered that nothing was wrong in his Hoka.

BL Add MSS 42812 ff. 10–12

26
Hamilton to Elphinstone

Indore
[Manuscript telegram]   1 January 1858
Secret

There is no reason to detain the force. It should go to Saugor as quickly as possible. There is a perfect panic in Indore. We have had executions and the very faithful sepoys of Holkar had quitted service. The disarmed went off and though the town was surrounded by two A.M. today *not* many were taken. I went through the lines they were empty. You will hear by post.

OIOC MSS Eur F87, Box 6G, Packet 20

27
Nana's ADC to Bundelcund chiefs

Kalpi

[Printed copy]   2 January 1858
Translation

My master Sreemunt Maharajah Peshwa Bahadur[76] at the sacrifice of every ease and comfort as well as of his wealth, property etc. has for the purpose of defending the religion both of the Hindoos and Mahomedans prepared himself to slaughter the followers of Christ as they are the enemies of the faith of the Mussulmans and Hindoos. The said Maharajah has, by waging a war with the Christians, put several of them to the sword and has resolved not to refrain himself from killing them as long as he breathes his living air, and to annihilate at once the people of this race now in India. The object which the Maharajah has in view to expel all the Christians from Hindoostan is not to take possession of all the territories and property of the Rajahs and Chiefs of India, or to assume the supreme command of the country, but on the other hand, it is his sole desire that after a victory shall have been obtained over the enemy, all the Chiefs may in peace enjoy the possession of the territories which they at present hold as well as those which they formerly possessed, and pass their days in the enjoyment of ease and happiness. Those provinces which are now exclusively in the British possession, shall, after a due consultation, be distributed to such Chiefs as will by exhibiting cordial spirit offer their services in slaughtering the followers of Christ. If all the Chiefs for the purpose of defending their religion and faith, join together and be of one mind, and render as much assistance as they respectively can, it will not be difficult to annihilate through the divine favor, all the remaining Christians. Under the orders of the aforesaid Sreemunt Peshwa Bahadur, I beg to inform you all that in a recent war at Cawnpore, our force has for some reasons retreated, and that troops are now being assembled at Calpee for the purpose of opposing the enemies at Cawnpore.[77] It will be a friendly act on your part if you now render assistance by sending troops and guns without loss of time. My employer warmly hopes that all the Chiefs of Bundelcund will be of one mind to assist him in the undertaking as formerly the Peshwa of Poona, when he was in power, rendered assistance to the Chiefs of this country and paid every regard to their honor and dignity. Under these circumstances it is hoped that you should as soon as possible despatch to Calpee in charge of a trustworthy person such number of men and guns as you may be able to furnish. An early reply to this is solicited, inasmuch as the above Maharajah is daily expected at Calpee. You shall also inform me whatever you think advisable.

FPC, 31 December 1858, No.2132; FSUP, III, pp. 211–12

28
Babu Ramcomal Roy[78] to Hamilton

Mandisore

[Holograph copy translation]   3 January 1858

From the day of taking Mandisore to the present all is going on well with the Post Office here and every one does his duty.

I also beg leave to state that the first disturbances in Mandisore had arisen on the part of the Mewattees and the Vullayatees, which had destroyed the Postal arrangements. These fellows who are caught and brought in are generally released and allowed to live in the town and the suburbs and their pursuers are lenient to them. The lower classes, washers, smiths, butchers, bearers etc. are punished more than the armed men. Innocent people, traders, poor and widows, who had run, fearing the approach of British troops, are subjected to the confiscation of their property which remains in the town, and there is also religious bigotry. If this way becomes the foundation of another jihad[79] where is the wonder?

The old Tussaldar and Kotwal, whose folly and prejudice formerly led to such disturbances ought to be changed by the new Soobah.[80] You should recommend it together with the apprehension of the villains, otherwise a derangement is possible which might cause interruption of the Daks.

If the civil authorities want the Mewattees to settle for the sake of cultivation they could give them places in the hundreds of desert[ed] villages in this district which will be a blessing to the peaceful and respectable inhabitants of the town and remove their apprehension.

BL Add MSS 42812 ff. 12–13

29
Rose to Elphinstone

[Manuscript telegram]   3 January 1858
Secret

I have received your letter of the 30th Dec[r]. Sir R. Hamilton never showed me your telegram to him of the 31st Dec[r].[81] Immediately on receiving your letter of the 30th of Dec[r] I asked Sir Robert Hamilton why he had not shown such an important communication to me, in reply he made an unworthy excuse. Sir Robert Hamilton's conduct in not obtaining prompt and sufficient retribution has caused me most serious anxiety. My baggage marched this morning and 'en route' for Saugor. Sir Robert Hamilton's conduct about your telegram has increased my mistrust of him so much that I have suspended my departure till I receive your orders. Our prestige is restored but the Durbar has not given a satisfaction to Sir Robert Hamilton which is either just, sufficient or honourable to the British Government. The Durbar is either powerless, or has allowed the leading and great majority of offenders against British rights to run away.

OIOC MSS Eur F87, Box 6G, Packet 20

30
Elphinstone to Hamilton

                                                                  Bombay
[Manuscript telegram]   4 January 1858

Unless you have obtained complete satisfaction I doubt the policy of sending away the means of obtaining it. If the Durbar is unable or unwilling to afford it, I would exact it by force, treating the Durbar with consideration if its backwardness arises from weakness and with severity if it arises from unwillingness. General Whitlock's column marched from Hyderabad on the 15th inst. and should reach Saugor early in February. Sir Hugh Rose's column would not arrive there more than a week or at most a fortnight before him.[82] If Saugor is not in immediate danger it would be as well to adhere to your original plan of re-opening the communication with Agra thus cutting off the Kotah and Rajpootana rebels from Bundelcund & Oude, and placing Sir H. Rose *en rapport* with the C. in Chief who is now advancing with his force in two parallel columns upon Mynpoorie.

OIOC MSS Eur F87 Box 9B, Letter Book 8

31
Erskine[83] to Steuart

Jubbulpore

[Holograph copy]   4 January 1858

I have been informed that you are marching with Sir H. Rose's Force via Sehore to Saugor. I hope this is the case, for altho' perhaps not in immediate danger the Saugor garrison would hardly hold the Fort long if attacked by a large body of mutineers, with Artillery, and the city would assuredly be plundered.

The Rajah of Banpore (in Chundera)[84] was by the last account at Jhansi, and the Ranee of that place and he were not only recruiting their armies of Bundeelahs but have got a good many of the Gwalior and other mutineers to join them. Some had been sent to the Rajah's entrenched camp at Nurreewalee[85] near Saugor and if he succeeds in collecting a large body of mutineers he intended to come down and attack Saugor. If he does so, the 52nd Mutineers who are still close to Rehly and Gurrakotta (in Saugor) would probably join him and the Shahgurh Rajah (who is the chief Rebel of Bundelkund and whose troops took possession of our old forts at Gurrakotta, Benaika and Nursingpore,[86] and still holds them) would very likely do the same.

A portion of Gen. Rose's force would soon settle the Saugor district, cut up the 52nd and take the forts I have mentioned, as well as Ratgurh, near which he would pass on his way to Saugor. I shall feel greatly obliged by your letting me know your plans as early as possible. We are still awaiting reinforcements here slowly coming from Secunderabad and Bangalore, and cannot I fear advance in any force or do much till the end of January or early in February but we are not idle and every week attack the Rebels. We have cleared them away entirely from the south of the Nerbudda and had we only one more Native Infantry and a few more Europeans and a few large guns we might go and take Bejiragurh and Myheer instead of allowing the Rewah troops to attempt doing this for us, and then advance to Dummuh and Saugor. I suppose you will take the whole of the Shahgurh country and confiscate it.

The Gov. Gen. authorised me to offer a reward of 10,000 Rs for the apprehension of the Rajah of Shahgurh. I also offered 8,000 for the apprehension of the Banpore Rajah. The latter and the Ranee of Jhansi should be hanged when caught but as the Shahgurh man did no harm to his European prisoners and eventually released them, I would not hang him, though I would confine him for life and confiscate his country.

If you intend going to Chundera and Jhansi, I would much like to join you at Saugor, and accompany you to the north, but I fear I must remain with Gen. Whitlock when he arrives, however if you go up in advance of me, I could send D^y Commiss. for Chundera and Jhansi to join you at Saugor via Mersinghore provided you can leave troops at Chundera & Jhansi till we can relieve them.

BL Add MSS 42612 ff. 8–10

32
Canning to Elphinstone

Calcutta

[Manuscript telegram]   4 January 1858

I have received the message of Sir Hugh Rose on the 29th December. With respect to disarming Indore two precautions must be observed, the force employed must be sufficient to prevent any possibility of failure, and provision must be made for protecting the town by police or otherwise after the arms shall have been taken away. Subject to these conditions Sir Robert Hamilton and Sir Hugh Rose may take such measures for disarming Indore as they think best. This authority is given at once because much time will be lost. Sir Robert Hamilton's plan is awaited and Sir Hugh Rose's force should be set free to move onward with the least possible delay. Holkar's consent should be obtained to place his guns in such keeping as Sir Robert Hamilton may consider trustworthy.

OIOC MSS Eur F87, Box 9D, Letter Book 4

33
Rose to Elphinstone

Indore

[Holograph copy] 4 January 1858

I cannot say how sincerely I regret the fall of Sir Robert Hamilton, which I regret to say, is inevitable. You know better than any one what a high opinion I had of him, and how much I was taken with his cleverness, his decision, and knowledge of the country. We were together in your hospitable house, we travelled for eight days in a Bullock gharee together and came from Marseilles together as far as Suez. In all these journeyings there was nothing but the most complete union of opinion and it was only at Indore that the divergence of opinion commenced, becoming each day greater and greater. Sir Robert Hamilton appeared to be spellbound by all belonging, however remotely, to Holkar. The only persons at Indore with respect to whom he showed energy were the imprisoned officials of the Rajah of Amjeera.

✳   ✳   ✳

But Sir Robert Hamilton, I venture to think, should be removed *at once*. If you want an honest and clear-headed Agent in the meantime, there is Major Robertson, altho' I should be most sorry to lose such an excellent leader of his gallant Regt the 25th. I get on famously with the native troops. I got for the Hyderabad Contingent the same allowances as the Native Regular Troops, which has made them very happy. It was their right.

❋ ❋ ❋

The defeat of the rebels at Mandasore and other places and my humble little operation of surrounding the City restored our prestige. A picket of the Hyderabad Cavalry intercepted two letters from Indore which show that the Indorean heroes of July last are quite 'poules mouillées'.[87]

OIOC MSS Eur F87, Box 6G, Packet 20

34
Elphinstone to Rose

Matheran
[Holograph copy]   4 January 1858

I am sorry to perceive that a want of confidence and mutual cordiality exists between you and Sir R. Hamilton. I can perfectly understand that there should be a difference of opinion between you on the subject of Holkar's conduct. To me, as well as to you, it appears open to much suspicion. At the same time, it is perhaps capable of being explained satisfactorily and I must admit that Sir R. Hamilton is in a much better position to judge of it than I am – probably the explanation which Sir R. Hamilton would give of Holkar's apparent backwardness in punishing his troops and not surrendering the Amuldar of Mehidpore is the same which you yourself have suggested viz. his want of power. He is more or less dependent on those who surround him – and it is quite possible that with all the good will in the world he may not be able to give us the satisfaction which we are entitled to ask.

I certainly thought that Sir R. Hamilton would have shewn you my secret telegram of the 29th Dec[r] but his not doing so was occasioned probably by his unwillingness to prejudice you against

Holkar – and not by any wish to withhold information which he considered important. He may have good reasons for discrediting the disclosure and the other suspicious circumstances alluded to in that telegram. I have not heard from him on the subject but it occurs to me that this is not improbable and that it would explain his keeping back what he considered an unfounded rumour. I do not say that he ought to have done so – it is sufficient that his silence may thus be accounted for without imputing any improper motive for it.

I have told Sir R. Hamilton that I doubt the policy of letting your column leave Indore until he has received the most ample satisfaction that can now be given for the events of July but it rests with him and not with me to determine what amount of satisfaction should be accepted. I have suggested to him that as General Whitlock will probably reach Saugor with his column in February, if that place is not immediately threatened, it w^d be as well to adhere to your original plan of opening the direct communication with Agra[88] at the same time cutting off the Kotah & Rajpootana rebels from Bundelcund and Oudh. This might be done by taking Jhansi or even by holding Sipri. One great advantage from taking this line is that you would place yourself in communication with the Commander in Chief who is now advancing from Cawnpore up the Doab – his force is in two parallel columns one on the right bank of the Ganges the other on the left bank of the Jumna. Sir Colin Campbell hopes by this means to clear the Doab of mutineers & rebels. The two columns are ordered I understand to unite at Mynpoorie.

But upon that point (of your movements) Sir R. Hamilton and yourself are much better judges than I can be. If the difference of a week or perhaps a fortnight in the relief of Saugor is of importance that place must of course be first attended to. If it can wait for Genl. Whitlock's advance the other movement appears to me the most desirable. At the same time I believe that there are mutineers at Bhopal to be punished but probably Col. Stewart who is now at Sehore will be strong enough for this.

I have no time for more but I think I have not omitted anything of importance.

Pray let me impress upon you how desirable it is that you and Sir R. Hamilton should be on good terms. Remember that in all small societies there are two parties and do not listen with too much facility to those who w^d willingly *blow the coals* between you.

OIOC MSS Eur F87, Box 9B, Letter Book 8

35
Hamilton to Elphinstone

Indore

[Holograph copy]   5 January 1858

. . . Matters are really going on quite well, but it requires the utmost strength of patience & temper to keep things together. The feeling among the troops & officers is beyond anything violent, to use the words of Major Robertson. They are disorganised. The wildest rumours are spread in camp to the infinite annoyance of the Europeans so that they have little rest. I have done all I can to meet Sir H. Rose's wishes. I do not at all interfere with his military arrangements & I really do wish that he would be equally considerate & not interfere with political matters. The inconvenience is very prejudicial to the public service & very embarrassing. Holkar is true himself & there are none about him that are good, there are some whose names have been taken & whose conduct requires enquiry but not the enquiry of a Courtmartial. The case of the Colonel [indecipherable] is one; Captain Hutchinson[89] is making an enquiry. I have heard what he has to say, he was the head of the infantry portion of Holkar's army & styled Colonel, his subordinates mutinied, it was clear that he had no control over them for long before he had been virtually superseded, an enquiry into corruption having been commenced months before I left India & daily reported by the Government newswriter. Now with this case Sir H. Rose I cannot think has any business to interfere, the enquiry & its results will be submitted to the Governor General, the Colonel is a cousin of the Maharajah's & no partiality to him exists, he is sure to appear whenever required. That I have told Sir H. Rose & I told him at first every thing but when I found my words were Taken up & liable to have a wrong construction I became reserved, for to argue on this point was useless & only would lead to differences which I have happily avoided up to this, but in truth Sir Hugh is too eager to listen & take up every rumour & act on it as true rather too hastily. If you could give him a hint, we might do business much faster. The interviews between Holkar & Sattara were well known *here* at the time. I declined to see the Ex-Rajah, but Holkar did & it was all reported at the time & the Gov^t newswriter had all the details, my records are gone. Sindia & Holkar will never agree, they had a disagreement when Sindia was at Oujein & have never met. Sindia has explained his affairs to Major Macpherson[90] & I send you a copy of a Telegram. Holkar only needs time to re-establish his Government, he has now our support. Police included, there are not 3,000 armed retainers at Indore, no regular paltans or sowars, in short *no* force sufficient to protect the town from rebels. He will do his utmost but bullying him will not assist him. It is the policy of the Nanna & Marhatta party to do all that can be done to run down & excite distrust against those chiefs who are known or supposed to be friendly to us & it would be a victory to them & the cause of great embarrassment to us if anything like a collision with Holkar took place. The population is between 70 & 75,000, the police now is weak, the Maharajah has ordered no one shall carry arms without a licence, this is a first step towards disarming, but we have not disarmed Mhow cantonment & Bazaar in wh. are some 20,000 inhabitants as bad as any. I have issued this licencing order in the Residency Bazaar. We could not organise a Police as required by the Governor General as a condition. I think Walker is doing right. Therefore, on this point, I see no cause to interfere. I dare say the Division here is strong enough, but I would not incur the risk. We might not be opposed, but if we were, it would be in streets and alleys. As to their artillery, I hope before post times, to tell you what has been done, they are all in an enclosed place, & under trusty men. Some are only for this eye, but more hereafter, but I am now going to speak to Holkar, & perhaps had better despatch this first.

Sir H. Rose has sent me no distribution of the force or told me what he is going to do. I think he would like to abandon the

Residency, but this will never do. Our Opium merchants[91] are here & not at Mhow & to leave Indore would have a most prejudicial effect. I know the want of Europeans is great, but if you were to send a Dragoon Regiment to Mhow, & a troop to Indore their horses might be collected & sent to them here & their presence be of the greatest importance. I must have Captain Hutchinson at Indore & he ought to have an escort. In Calcutta so important was Indore considered that holding it & abandoning Mhow would have been approved. That cannot be now, but the Fort at Mhow is reported today to be in charge of the Nizam's Contingent, no Europeans in it, some 7 to 11 lacs of rupees & all our stores & magazines. It would be better to march Colonel Stewart there at once, at least a portion of his force, but I, you will see by Sir H. Rose's letter, cannot issue any instructions to him as he is to act under orders from you or the C. in C. at Bombay.

OIOC MSS F87, Box 6G, Packet 20

36
Elphinstone to Rose

[Holograph copy]

Bombay
6 January 1858

I have just received the enclosed from Sir Robert Hamilton – as he says that Holkar has done all that he requires there could be no use in your remaining at Indore and Sir Robert is anxious that Saugor should be first relieved. I have of course nothing more to say. There can be no doubt that Saugor is now in a position of some danger for its safety depends upon the fidelity of a regiment of Bengal sepoys! I hope that you will arrive in time to prevent any disaster and that you will then be able to turn your face towards Tehree and Jhansi, leaving Jubbalpore and eastern Bundelkund to the Madras column and General Whitlock. By turning to the North you would have a better chance of intercepting the Kotah rebels – and you would place yourself in communication with the C. in Chief.

OIOC MSS Eur F87, Box 9B, Letter Book 8

37
Rose to Steuart

Camp Ashtar
[Holograph copy]   8 January 1858
Private

I hope to have the pleasure of seeing you on the morning of the
10th. The Siege Train, of two 18 [pdrs], one 8 inch Howitzer, one 8
inch Mortar and two 5½ inch Mortars, 80 men of the 14th L[t]
Dragoons, 2 Cos of the 3rd Europeans, about 400 of all arms of the
Hyderabad Contingent, one Company of Madras Sappers and
Miners, 50 men of Captain Woolcombe's Battery to work the siege
train, and about 40 Bombay Sappers and Miners, will arrive about
5 days after me at Sehore.

My movements from Sehore must depend on what I hear from
yourself and the other Quarters about Saugor; I am quite puzzled
by the conflicting accounts which I hear about Saugor; that is to
say Brigadier Sage[92] is the only person who represents it in a
flourishing state. All other accounts make out that Saugor is in an
unfavourable state; that the 31st are shaky; that there is smallpox in
the Fort; and that the rebels are increasing all round it. I look to
you for a real account. Major Erskine has so often cried 'Wolf' that
I confess I am not much influenced by his opinion but those of a
Captain Western[93] which are very favourable, appear to me more
worthy of credit.

BL Add MSS 42812 ff. 7–8

38
Elphinstone to Rose

Bombay
[Manuscript copy]   10 January 1858

✳ ✳ ✳

It is for the Gov[r] General to decide the case between you and Sir
R. Hamilton and it is not for me to anticipate his decision, but

I cannot help as a friend expressing my regret that you should have forwarded what appears to me a very hasty judgement on his conduct. I should have expected a leaning on the part of Sir R. Hamilton towards Holkar. He was his guardian and may be said to have brought him up. He has lived at Indore among his people for many years, and he would naturally be unwilling to believe anything against them. Again it must be admitted that Holkar's conduct at the time of the mutiny was such as to disarm suspicion. Captain Hungerford who at first believed him to be treacherous, has now become convinced that he was acting in good faith. He did all he could to assist the little garrison at Mhow. He opened the communication with Dhodia & Bombay. He acted in short exactly like a man who was anxious to justify himself and to prove that he had nothing to do with the mutineers – and however open to suspicion his recent conduct may have been, & whatever the grounds for distrusting him may exist, I think he is entitled to the benefit of these facts.

I have nothing to do with your movements now – you and Sir R. Hamilton must decide upon them. My advice will be as soon as Saugor is safe, to place yourself in communication with the Commander in Chief,[94] and to endeavour to cut off the retreat of any body of rebels who may be driven southward by him – & to endeavour to intercept any who may be endeavouring to come across from Kotah to Beundelkhand & Oude. Jhansi appears to me to be an important position & if you can establish yourself there, you would be able to accomplish all the objects I have alluded to.

OIOC MSS Eur F87, Box 9B, Letter Book 8

39
Elphinstone to Hamilton

Bombay

[Manuscript copy]   10 January 1858

I received yesterday your letter of the 5th, and two letters, one official & one private, from Sir Hugh Rose. I was very sorry to find from these letters that there was very little chance of your acting together with cordiality, and as it was necessary to forward Sir Hugh Rose's official letter to the Gov[t] of India, I at the same time sent both his and your private letters to the Governor General which will enable him to form a better opinion of the state of affairs between you than if he only saw the official correspondence.

I am extremely sorry that those differences should have proceeded to such a length. I feared from an expression in one of Sir Hugh Rose's telegrams that there was something wrong, but I wrote to him strongly advising him to defer to your opinion. He could not have received my letter when he wrote the two letters which I have forwarded to the Gov[r] General.

With regard to the movement of the columns & reinforcements I think that as you have decided that Saugor is the first object, the plan which you propose of turning from that place to the north punishing the Banpore man[95] and advancing as far as Jhansi – while a smaller force from Mhow moves along the Agra road to Goonah & Sipri, is the best that can be adopted, but Sir Hugh Rose and you are in a much better position for judging than I am.

The Nana was still in Oude about the middle of December, when Brigadier Grant's column[96] moved to the bank opposite to and within five miles of Futtehpore Chowrassie where he was staying, he retreated northwards i.e. further into Oude, and was believed to have gone to a place of Hindoo pilgrimage abt 30 miles from Futtehpore Chowrassie. Captain Bruce[97] who gave this information adds 'He at present fears to cross through the Doab[98] towards Indore'.

OIOC MSS Eur F87, Box 9B, Letter Book 8

40
Lieutenant Bonus[99] to his parents

Sehore

[Typewritten copy]   10 January 1858

Sir Hugh Rose and his Staff arrived this morning with some reinforcements viz one gun Horse Artillery, 3 guns Field Artillery, a squadron of the 14th Dragoons, and two companies 3rd European regiment. We have now a compact little force viz 4 guns Horse Artillery, 3 guns Field Artillery, two squadrons 14th Dragoons, about 700 men of the 3rd Europeans, nearly all of the 24th NI, and our few Sappers; we are quite strong enough to dispose of 10,000 rebels. I am told that Sir Hugh Rose is very bitter against the native, not so Sir Robert Hamilton who also came in today, he accompanies the force in a civil capacity. It is whispered that the two are not very good friends; I daresay there is some truth in this, the Soldier and the Civilian who is to keep the former in check seldom hit it off. Sir R.H. is a very great man in these parts, he is Agent to the Governor General for Central India, and a King in Malwa.

On the 4th we had a Parade to see two men hung: the business was quietly and quickly done. The troops were formed up into three sides of a square, there was a large tree in the centre, ropes were fastened to a couple of boughs, the prisoners, each in a cart, were brought under the tree, the ropes adjusted and the carts were driven away. Death came quickly. A grave was dug beneath the tree and the bodies were buried before the parade was dismissed. The whole affair lasted only half an hour. Their crime was murder; they killed a native collector, and one of them proclaimed himself Nawab of some place . . . when I returned I was surprised to find an order that all Officers commanding regiments and detachments were to go to the Brigadier at 5 o'clock . . .

It turned out to be a consultation as to the disarming of the Bhopal Contingent. These troops mutinied some little time ago, with the exception of a few men, they overran the country round about. Then for some reason which is not at all clear, they began to return in driblets. Now they are nearly all back, about 600

Infantry, 100 Cavalry and 4 guns. The meeting at the Brigadier's was to make a plan for disarming the whole lot. After some discussion it was agreed that Captain Mayne (who came here with a troop of Sikh Horse to enquire into the circumstances attending the late mutiny) should order a parade the next morning, and that he should march the whole contingent past our camp into the open plain under the pretence of a grand parade. In order to avert any suspicion or distrust, all our men were to be about their tents as usual. But Commanding Officers were to take measures to have all their men in camp between 7 and 8 a.m. There was, of course, some danger of the Contingent refusing to pass in front of our camp but by keeping the matter perfectly secret, we hoped to avoid trouble . . . Well, the next morning the Contingent about 7.30 a.m. marched past our camp much to the astonishment of all those not in the secret. As soon as the Contingent was out of sight beyond a slight rise all was bustle with us in camp and in a quarter of an hour our whole force was between the Contingent and the village [diagram inserted] the Infantry loaded with ball. The mutineers were no doubt greatly upset by our appearance. The troops were soon in position when the rebel Infantry were ordered to pile arms; this they did at once, but the Cavalry at first refused to drop their swords. Instantly our Guns, loaded with grape and [?canister] faced them and there was no more trouble. All uniform was stripped off and 116 were made prisoners; these were known as the worst of the lot.

After the disarming, the Lines were searched and all arms and ammunition taken away. Part of ladies dresses were found and some trinkets telling of robbery if not worse.

OIOC IOR neg. 4395

45

41
Memorandum by Major Charters Macpherson

Agra

[Typed copy] 12 January 1858

✻ ✻ ✻

I do not know what people will say to my views and Dinkur Row's[100] that the *primary* cause of the revolt was – the deep dissatisfaction of the Army with our rule – our Government; and our manners, shared with the whole population of Hindustan. I can get at nothing but this I grieve to say for a primary cause. The Army was fully predisposed by this cause to revolt. It made the Cartridge grievance a pretext to rise; and the foremost malcontents, Princes etc. seized the opportunity to stimulate and head the Rebellion. The Soldiery had a true religious panic from a true grievance, but had they not been ripe for revolt, they had not revolted about the Cartridge but had sought and found satisfactory explanations and assurances. But they *would* have no explanation and made the Cartridge the pretext for revolt. The Mahomedans who struck for both Religious and Secular Supremacy desired both our overthrow and our extinction. The Hindus, who happily did not make a Religious context of it desired the overthrow of our [? rule] but protected life. Had the Hindus made a matter of religion of it no one had remained to report . . .

Had Scindia gone not a Prince would have stood a day. I got him to act in antagonism to the revolt until the Contingent[101] mutinied – and then to keep the Contingent quiescent until we were quite ready to crush them – although they chased Wyndham ignominiously. The Army revolted in the face of matchless class advantages[102] because we do not even attempt to carry the mind of the people with us – no Civilian under 15 years standing that I see ever conceived such a thing as to do so.

✻ ✻ ✻

OIOC MSS Eur D 706/2, f. 6

42
Bonus to his parents

Sehore

[Typewritten copy]   13 January 1858

What painful duties we have yet to do in India, what scenes of bloodshed yet to witness. But I do trust that never again shall I have to take part in such a terrible business as that of last night. The Brigade was suddenly called out at 5 p.m. for the execution of 149 men who had been found guilty of mutiny by a Drum-head Court Martial in the morning.[103] Before we reached the place of execution it was quite dark. The prisoners blindfolded were made to kneel in a long line; then the firing party of European Infantry was marched up behind them, man to man, so that the muzzles of the rifles almost touched the heads of the prisoners. The next instant 146 were dead or dying, three escaped in the darkness though they were blindfolded, and their hands tied behind them. At the moment I was sick and faint, but I suppose that will not occur again. Later, while we were at dinner we heard shots and of course ran out to see what was the cause of the firing. It turned out that the remainder of the prisoners about 267 in number had made an attempt to escape, 45 got clean away I believe, 13 were shot down, the rest were secured . . .

OIOC IOR neg. 4395

43
Rose to Elphinstone

Sehore

[Manuscript telegram]   14 January 1858

As soon as the Seige Train arrives at Mhow my 1st Brigade will march with half of it and the company of Royal Engineers and Artillery to Goonas to cooperate with me in attacking Jhansee. I shall be at Saugor on or about the 28th instant and shall march as soon as possible against Jhansi from Saugor. It is of great importance that the 1st Brigade should take with it as many of the

86th regiment as possible because the 21st Native Infantry[104] will be obliged to leave 200 men on account of their having the Scurvy at Mhow. Consequently if the reinforcements for the 86th regiment do not arrive before the 1st Brigade leaves Mhow it will not have sufficient infantry to guard its seige train and Artillery. I earnestly beg that the reinforcements for the 86th regiment may be sent up by Bullock train from Bombay to Mhow. 149 men of the Bhopal Contingent were tried and shot yesterday. The communications of Saugor are cut off by the rebels except by a circuitous road. Brigadier Sage says that he cannot send me any supplies. I am obliged to take them with me. Pray send me the Depots of my regiments to Mhow soon.

OIOC MSS Eur F87, Box 9D, Letter Box 4

44
Kalpi garrison orders

Kalpi

[Holograph copy] 17 January 1858
(translation) [1 Jamadusani 1274]
Parole Choorkhee

Orders by Tantia Sahib. All Commanders, Sepoys and Sowars are hereby informed that from this date whoever applies for his discharge will forfeit any pay that may be due to him, and will be punished by order of the Court. The Brigadiers of Divisions should be very attentive to his duty and not neglect it, and no Sepoy should be allowed to go in the city during the night, no noise should be made in the Fort or outside, and no fire should be lighted, and every day at 3 P.M. Choona Sing and the Brigade Major should inspect the picquets and place them in proper positions. And there should be a Muster daily at 10 A.M. and 4 P.M., and every Brigadier should make a report at 10 A.M. Every Brigadier should warn the men under his Command not to cut down trees belonging to ryots.[105] Many complaints have been made, in future if any one does so He will be punished.

OIOC Home Miscellany 727 f. 23

45
Rose to Sage

Balampur

[Holograph copy]   18 January 1858

. . . I am marching as fast as I can with my Force to Saugor, not halting anywhere except at Bhilsa,[106] one day, to allow the Siege Train to come up; but should the rebels disappointed at Saugor being safe, press you pray let me know, and I will make forced marches to relieve you, as no consideration weighs *so strongly* with me as the thought of 170 of my countrymen of all ages and sexes, being in danger from vile rebels.

I am much obliged to you for your useful suggestions about Ratghur; I shall do my best to catch its garrison; I gladly accept the amiable offer of the points of your Indian experience. I am much stronger in Artillery and Cavalry than in Infantry. I must therefore act accordingly, guard the Artillery with Infantry, pound our adversaries with Artillery, and pursue them with Cavalry and 4 Horse Artillery guns which I have . . .

BL Add MSS 42812 ff. 19–20

46
Kalpi garrison orders

Kalpi

[Holography copy]   19 January 1858
(Translation)   [3 Jamadusani 1274]
Parole Sreenuguree

From this date Gungahdeen Sepoy of the 3rd Reg[t] has obtained leave to write papers etc. and will be present at the Brigade Office. All Havildar Majors should attend the Brigade Office for orders daily and Kote Havildars not to go out except when [indecipherable] are sent and from tomorrow morning gun should be fired daily with country powder. A Brigade Court will be assembled at 2 o'clock at the Quarters of Brigadier Sheopershad of

Artillery, for appointing Officers in the 5th and 6th Reg^{ts} and 1 Sepoy to be present from every Reg^t & Artillery. No grasscutters or strangers should be admitted in the fort. Every Commandant of Regiment & Artillery should state the number of orders received through the Regimental Moonshee which will be compared with the Brigade order book.

Tomorrow Brigade Court will be assembled in the fort to enquire into the case of the man who was shot by a sepoy.

OIOC Home Miscellany 727 f. 24

47
Private Wood[107] to his mother

Indore

[Holograph]   19 January 1858

. . . since our arrival at Indore I think we have paid off the Mutineers to their hearts content for our force have blown away from Guns the number of 41 and hung about 150 and we have about 300 prisoners transported to be sent to Bombay and Shipped for Aden to work in the mines we are expecting an escort to take them down to Bombay daily. We also sent a portion of Infantry and Cavalry into Mhow on the 13 Inst. and disarmed the whole of the Native Inhabitants of the Bazaar and collected about 3 or 4 Cart loads of arms of various descriptions in the place and the force returned here the following day. Our force is dwindling down to a very small one for we have sent 1 Troop of ours away and 2 regiments of Irregular Cavalry, 50 European Artillery and a great number of other native troops to join our 2nd Brigade at Sehoor where our Colonel Stewart is in Command with 5 Troops of the 14th he has got a very fine Brigade of Europeans with him, and I hear that they have disarmed a Cavalry reg^t and shot 150 of the rascals and as many more remaining to be dealt with and as soon as they have settled with them they go on to Bopall and from thence to Saugor. They have got a fine seige train with them so that I expect they have got some Forts to go against for the rascals like to get behind stone walls where they can fight like cowards through loop holes they are afraid to come on the plains for it. I believe the columns about Cawnpore and Lucknow are paying them off nicely and surely they cannot be many more to settle with. It is my opinion we are getting them together as much as possible in Oude so that we will make that place our last grand attack and at the fall of that place I think that I can safely say that the war in India will be all over, but there will still be the Hill Tribes to annoy us for some time.[108] The sooner it is over the better say I so that I can once more return to Old England and they will soon have to recall some of the troops from here and the 14th are the first Cavalry regiment from home so that I think there is some little chance.[109] I am sure that I do not know what they are going to do with the troops allready here when the Hot and Wet months set in for they cannot find barrack accommodation for all and it will be the death of many to keep them out in tents. We have here in Bombay the 3rd, 8th[110] and 17th Lancers and where they are to get horses from I dont know it is sure they are getting a lot of young horses from the Cape and other Colonies but it will be some time before they get horses to complete 3 regiments and then they have to be broken in for the service, so that if we could be sent home here is a fine lot of horses ready to be mounted and take the field at once . . .

NAM 6307–60

48
Nerbudda Field Force Orders

Gulgaon

[Holograph]   19 January 1858

1. Troop 14th Lt Dragoons & 1 Company 3rd Europeans will remain behind tomorrow for the purpose of escorting the Siege Train.

2. On the march from Bhilsa and until further orders the Advance Guard will be reinforced by two companies from the 24th Regt N.I. and will be formed in front of the company of the

3rd European Regiment. When near country occupied by the Rebels they will load and form skirmishing order in front with the skirmishers of the 14th Lt Dragoons, and searching any jungle or hilly ground impassable for the cavalry. The office commanding the party will instantly send in a report of any appearance of the rebels, to the officer commanding the Advance Guard.

The Officer Commanding the 24th Regt. N.I. will be pleased to select intelligent officers and men for this duty.

3. The four Elephants passed by the committee which assembled on the 17th Instant are to be trained for drawing guns.

✤ ✤ ✤

5. The guides hired daily for the column are to be tested by the Deputy Assistant Q[r] M[r] Gen[l] 2nd Brigade as to their knowledge of the road.

✤ ✤ ✤

OIOC MSS D1007

49
Kalpi garrison orders

Kalpi
[Holograph copy]   21 January 1858
(Translation)   [5 Rajab 1274]
Parole Poona

A letter of Tantia from Chirkhari of 4 Inst. states that the battle commenced on the 3rd. On the same day we took 1 entrenchment and 14 guns. All the magazine etc. which were there were taken. Be it known to all Comdg. Officers that no one should come to report without a Commanding Officer. The news of Lucknow states correctly that many of the British soldiers were killed and the rest fled. It has been reported they are again to cross the

Ganges in 3 Brigades. The Rais of Furruckabad has again taken his country from the Nusaras [Christians] also many of them were killed there. They intended proceeding again to Furruckabad and they have encamped at Sheorajpore. On account of fear they can not proceed further. Goolam Hyder Khan son of Dost Mohumud of Cabul with a considerable army, and also the nephew of Goolab Sing with a large force left their country and are coming on to assist the Hindustanees.[111] A relation of the Rajah Sutteepershad of Sheorajpore with 4 other Rajahs and an immense number of troops is coming from the west. The five Regiments which were disarmed and doing duty with their ramrods at Achanuk were told by the Infidels that if they would swear fidelity their arms would be restored to them, and they would be sent to Lucknow, on which all the soldiers went to the Ganges to swear, and swore as follows 'Oh Ganges the English may spare us but we will not spare any while we have life'. After this oath they got back their arms, as the oath was a mystification. The sepoys having got the opportunity killed all the Infidels and marched towards Lucknow. According to Established custom the Holee Festival commences from today, all parades and drill excused but the regular duties will be performed. The Gun that is usually fired will not be fired now, but another one in its stead.

OIOC Home Miscellany 727 f. 26

50

Orders for the attack of the Fort of Rahatghur

Rahatghur

[Holograph]   26 January 1858

The Fort of Rahatghur is to be attacked on the south east [indecipherable] rear of the slope of the rock on which it stands by the 2nd Brigade of the Nerbudda Field Force at 12 o.clock this day. This attack is to be a real one and it is to be made under cover of a feigned attack of the Town. All possible use is to be made of advantages gained in the course of the feigned attack as has been

explained to Brigadier Steuart. The troops stated in the margin*
will make the real attack on the Rock of Rahatghur.

The troops as stated in the margin† will make the feigned
attack taking possession of the rising ground known to the
Brigadier & Lt Col. Turnbull in front of the Town and a little to
the North East of the Seraie, as the position for the two eight inch
Mortars and the one eight inch Howitzer.

OIOC MSS Eur D1007

51
Rose to Campbell

[Holograph copy]

Rahatgarh
27 January 1858

I hope soon to be able to announce to your Excellency the capture
of this fort, and my arrival at Saugor, which is only 26 miles from
here. All the rebels and scamps in this part of the country have
taken refuge in the fort at Rathgarh, which they have a high idea
of, on account of its strength and antiquity; it is the most
picturesque and perfect Fort I have seen.

* Lt Col. Liddell, 3rd Eur Regt Commanding[112]
  Detacht of Siege Train under Lieut. Mallock
  Two/18/pdrs – 16 men Bom. Artillery
  2 5½in Mortars – 10 men, do.do
  90 Madras Sappers and Miners
  Two 6pdr guns Artill. Hydr. Contingent
  One troop 3rd Lt Cavy. under Capt. Forbes 3rd Eur. Regt.
† Brigadier Steuart commanding
  Four Six pounder guns
  Bombay Horse Artillery
  Six 9pdr guns Bombay Light Field Battery under Cap. Lightfoot
  50 Bombay Sappers and Miners
  Detach. of Siege Train
  Two 8 inch Mortars ⎫ 26 men
  One 8 inch Howitzer ⎭ Bom. Artillery
  All the artillery under Lt Col. Turnbull
  Two Troops H.Ms. 14th Light Dragoons under Major Scudamore
  24th Regt. N.I.

This afternoon a detachment of the 3rd Europeans and 24th N.I. took a strong outwork in masonry only 70 yards from the chief gate of the fort, with only two casualties.

Your Excellency will be glad to hear that the discipline of my troops is excellent and that consequently they are very serviceable.

The Political Agents say I shall have a great deal to do in Bundlecund; that the Rajah of Banpore and others are collecting asemblages of Rebels to make a last effort.

I am strong in Cavalry and Artillery but weak in Infantry; I shall act accordingly.

I shall get to Jhansi as soon as I can and meet my 1st Brigade there.

BL Add MSS 42812 f. 21

52
Captain Orr to Elphinstone

Guna

[Manuscript telegram]   28 January 1858

I arrived here this morning with the Cavalry of my force. I am glad to be able to report the entire line of Dawk communication open to Gwalior and Agra from Indore. The country between Shahjehanpore [?and here] is quiet and insurgents dispersing on hearing of advance of troops.

OIOC MSS Eur F87, Box 9D, Letter Book 4

53
Nerbudda Field Force Orders

Rahatghur

[Holograph]   28 January 1858
Parole London
Countersign York

1. In future there is to be both a parole and a countersign & no sentinel is to allow any armed party to pass his post after dark without the countersign.

2. Advance sentries of Outlying Pickets will not allow any one to pass even tho' in possession of the Parole or Countersign but will halt all, one sentry reporting their arrival to the Officer Commanding the Picket who will not allow them to pass until he is satisfied himself of their identity & has secured a written order to permit them to pass.

3. Commanding Officers are requested to instruct their men in the proper mode of challenging persons approaching their post as the Maj. Genl. observed a want of knowledge on this point on the part of sentries who were on the night before last with the exception of those of H.M^s 14th Light Dragoons who performed their duty perfectly.

4. No one except Staff & Artillery Officers & those on duty is to be allowed to go to the Battery on the Hill without an order from the Maj. Genl. or Lt. Col. Liddell as so many crowding into it creates noise and confusion.

5. All the troops are to be under arms before daybreak until further orders.

❊　❊　❊

OIOC MSS D1007

54
Rose to Stuart

Rahatgarh

[Holograph copy]   28 January 1858

. . . I think that as soon as you have selected the pieces of the Siege Train and the Ordnance and Engineer material which I started, you had better march to Goonah, leaving orders with Major Keane Commanding at Mhow for the 86th Reg^t to follow you as soon as possible. The *whole* of the 86th with their head quarters should join you at Goonah, and the two Cos. which are to form part of the garrison of Mhow must be selected from the Companies coming from Baroda, Surat etc. and what remains of men, over and above the two companies of the 86th for the garrison of Mhow must follow you *as quickly as possible* to Goonah.[113]

56

I have done all you wish as to the prisoners and treasure at Indore; as regards the former, I enclose you a copy of a letter from Sir R. Hamilton which relieves you of all charge of them, and as regards the treasure Sir R. Hamilton says that Holkar will take charge of it so that you can move at once with your force from Mhow to Goonah, taking up Major Orr and his force at Beowra.[114] He will give you every information about the Rajah of Ragoogurh who, I should think, can in no way be trusted. We are doing very well here. I attacked the Town and Fort the day before yesterday and gained a very good position against the former, they abandoned the Town and I am now breaching the fort, which is very strong with about 1,000 men in it including your old friend the Phazadah of Mandisore[115] with many other such rebels.

BL Add MSS 42812 ff. 23–4

55
Rose to Elphinstone

Rhatgurh
[Manuscript telegram]   28 January 1858

I attacked yesterday the town and fort of Rhatgurh on the right bank of the Bena river with my second Brigade. The attack on the town was a feint to cover the real attack on the south east of the rock of Rhatgurh. I directed Brigadier Stewart to derive all the advantage he could from the feint. The rebels were completely deceived by the feint. I gained without a casualty an excellent position for the seige on the high and difficult rock of Rhatgurh and the rebels abandoned the town and went into the Fort. The prisoners say that there were 4,000 people in the fort of whom only a portion were fighting men. The Shahgarha of Mandisore,[116] Mahomed Fazil Khan and other noted rebels are [incomprehensible] and is a very strong position. I have surrounded it with my force, as well as the thick jungle and great extent of ground allow me. I have commenced battering and shelling the Fort with part of seige [sic] train and Field Artillery and at midnight the 18 pounders will open their fire on it. The conduct of the troops both native and European under trying circumstances is very good, they have to attack and guard a most difficult country, hill, jungle, and river, 10 or 12 miles in circumference.

OIOC MSS Eur F87, Box 9D, Letter Book 4

56
Kalpi garrison orders

Kalpi

[Holograph copy]   28 January 1858
(Translation)   [12 Rajab 1274]
Parole Madras

Every Comd^g Officer and Sirdar of Reg^{ts} and Artillery should inform their Sepoys that no one should go in the town nor oppress the citizens. And during the Holee Festival they should not speak obscene words, nor throw the Abeen, and half the Sepoys should be ready prepared, because the Kafeers[117] are at hand, and those at Cawnpore are in great fear from the approach of the Army from the west. It is reported that a man threw an anonymous letter in the Cawnpore Kotwalee that during the festival of the Holee rivers of blood will flow. On the 25th Instt. the Kafeers sent word that a decided battle would be fought at Lucknow and it will be decided who is to rule the country. And the King of Lucknow has sent a letter enjoining them in the name of Jesus to bring all the soldiers they can collect in this country, and in Europe and that in the name of God we will destroy them all with the sword. The troops of the Chief of Jummoo has come 6 marches from Ambalah, it is coming by double marches. Our army is under the fort of Chirkari, if God pleases they will be victorious in 3 or 4 days. One boat is going to bring shishum wood from Heerapore, and will return by evening. The Maharajah Bala Sahib Bahadur is coming from Nepaul with 12,000 army, 6 Batteries & three Regt^s of Cavalry. An order has been issued by Sreemunth Himmast Prudhan Rao Saheb Bahadur Peshwa[118] that I have always regarded the soldiers of the Moorar Contingent[119] and Bengal

Army in the same light, and will always do so, it is very improper that one party should taunt the other. The Comd^g Officers should prohibit this. Our Sepoys demand their [pay]. It is well known to every one that from a long time I became very poor, and have nothing in my possession. I am greatly ashamed and if I had any thing with me I would gladly have given them, but as long as I am alive I will not leave the Army. I have sent Tantia to the force at Chirkhari and I am sure he will settle something regarding pay. My soldiers tell me about the Holee. It is true that this is a grand festival and a time of rejoicing, but it is the will of God that we should not do so. I therefore most earnestly solicit you all that you will kindly accept the Goolal and Pan[120] which I present you, but if we are alive by the mercy of God we will have a grand Holee festival. I am in these days in a miserable state. I have settled today about the Ghauts. The sowars who came with me should attend there.

OIOC Home Miscellany 727 f.32

57
Shakespear – diary

[Typed copy]

29th January [1858] Rahatgarh. The first thing I heard awaking this morning was that the Fort had been evacuated during the night and the birds were all flown. I went up about 9 o'clock to have a look at the Fort and went all over it. There were several bodies about and lots of tattoos, horses and cattle, besides no end of papers, matchlocks, cooking pots, grain etc. etc. . . . We then followed the wall and came to the spot where the enemy had got away, it was an old postern which had been bricked up and not noticeable from the outside, in this the fellows knocked a hole and let themselves down the face of the rock by a rope which was there when we passed, the river at the foot was very deep but they crossed by two fords above and below, thence to another place where the wall had been broken away, the descent here was much more precipitous but the women are said to have escaped this way and clothes of all descriptions were in the bushes, one man was laying at the bottom dead, having evidently lost his footing, thence on the breach which was almost practicable at 8 o'clock last evening, the assault was to have come off this morning.

In the course of the afternoon, Fazil Mahomed Khan and a Pindara Chief Kamdar Khan were caught in the jungle between the Foot of the Fort Hill and the river; they were hanged up at once over the gateway of the Fort. A number of other prisoners were made during the day and on the night of the escape; some twenty five were shot.

1st [February, Rahatgarh] They had a sharp affair of it yesterday and I am sorry I was not there.[121] The General by all accounts did not reap any laurels there as a General though there is no doubting his bravery. Our Dragoons were never brought into action and we prevented the fire of our guns by constantly getting in front of them. The 3rd Cavalry are said to have made a fair charge . . . The enemy were strongly posted on a hill with a deep nullah below but they were beaten out of it, as also of the villages, but they carried off one gun . . . Today we tried 26 men of whom seventeen were hanged.

OIOC MSS Eur D 706/2, ff. 101–3

58
Tantia Topi to Nana Sahib

Chirkari

[Printed copy]   31 January 1858
(Translation)   [15 Rajab 1274]

It is very difficult to capture this fort inasmuch as the place is hilly and I have only a single body of men with me. The Rajah does not wish to side with us, as he believes very much in the strength of the English. When such is the case, whatever success may be achieved by me will of course have its origin in your good fortune.

The sepoys boast very much now but in the time of difficulty they will desert us. God does whatever is good. In the battle fought the day before yesterday our troops fled before the enemy. I hope therefore that you will be pleased to send Vilayatee men to our assistance and one hundred pieces of cloth which I will distribute among the troops as an inducement to take the field. You will also be pleased to send Kerinda[122] and the munitions for which I had already written to you.

FPP Suppl. Cons. No.627, p. 50, 30 December 1859; FSUP, III, pp. 228–9

59
Indian Officers, Gwalior Contingent, to officers of Raja of Chirkari

Raut

[Printed copy]   31 January 1858
(Translation)

We are all well and wish to know your welfare. For a long time we have received no news from you. Pray write to us from time to time.

For the sake of our faith, we and our subordinate sepoys have mutinied and encountered various difficulties. Our lives are at stake.

It was not becoming in your master to oppose us in our recent outbreak, being regardless of the next world. His disagreement with the troops however will be visited with proper punishment. Considering you as our brothers, we write this to you in order that you may have no ground for complaint in case anything should befall you. It is therefore incumbent on you to join us with your sepoys and arms. We do not force you to side with us; but come over forthwith having a regard for your faith and your spiritual welfare. We write this to you as it concerns our religion but you are at liberty to do as you like. If you do not come, we will through the divine assistance do our best to defend our faith. Consider this short statement as sufficient and reflect on the remarks above alluded to.

The pay of each sepoy here is ten Rupees[123] and that of a Subedar or other Officer of course higher according to his rank.

Send an answer to this as soon as possible.

FPP Nos.1365–6; FSUP, III, pp. 229–30

60
Canning to Elphinstone

Buckee

[Copy telegram]   31 January 1858

I hope to avoid the necessity of any change of command in Central India, at all events it cannot take place now.

OIOC MSS Eur F87, Box 9D, Letter Book 4

61
Hamilton to Edmonstone[124]

Saugor

[Printed copy]   3 February 1858

I have much pleasure in reporting for the information of the Right Honble the Governor General in Council that the second Division of the Central India Force under the command of Major General Sir Hugh Rose K.C.B. relieved Saugor this morning, emancipated the Officers and Men with their families, who had for seven months been confined to the Fort, and enabled them to return and occupy their barracks and residences in the Cantonments.

2. I have the honor to annex a list of European British subjects in, and not in, the Government Service, who have thus been relieved from all peril after an anxious and trying confinement in a Fort, during the most inclement months of the year, little adapted for the residence of Europeans, without much more than bare

necessities and deprived of the ordinary conveniences and comforts which are absolutely necessary in this country.

3. The mortality during this period has amounted to twenty two; of these some were from cholera and small-pox – which terrible diseases broke out in the Fort.

4. As we approached the Town, I may say the whole native population, in addition to the Europeans (Ladies and all) came out to welcome the Column, whose arrival spread the greatest joy and confidence amongst all classes.

5. On its march from Raatghur no opposition was encountered; but on the 31st Ultimo, information was brought to me that the Rebels had collected in some force beyond Jilla, about twelve miles from our camp at Raatghur towards Korye.[125] I immediately communicated the same to Sir Hugh Rose, who at once arranged to attack them. The result was very successful; the Rebels were driven with much loss from their strong positions in the village of Burodia, and for some distance across the river, and they evacuated Korye (which has been occupied by some of the Regent of Bhopal's Troops) as well as Nariaoli and Bhoplye, two positions from whence they had threatened and molested Saugor, stopping all communication by the direct road via Bhopal and Sehore to Indore and Mhow.

6. I trust I may be permitted to offer my congratulations to the Right Honble the Governor General in Council on this relief of the last remaining station wherein our country-women and so many children have been beleaguered. The Officers of the Native Corps, the Civil Establishments and the Europeans of the Company of Artillery who have so long held the Fort of Saugor, have well performed their duty and their conduct will, I am sure, receive the approbation of his Lordship in Council.

General Order 36, 1858

62
Rose to Elphinstone

[Manuscript telegram]

Rathghur

3 February 1858

The Fort of Ratgurh and several rebel leaders of note including the chief rebel commander in Central India the Nawab Mahomed Fazil Khan fell into the hands of the troops under my command this morning. The rebels who had declared that they would die or hold Ratgurh which is very strong, in good repair and supplied with 1 years provisions lost heart when they saw the siege artillery brought up to a position which they thought impracticable and making a breach in the curtain of the fort. Two hours before daylight this morning they abandoned the Fort precipitately letting themselves down by ropes from the rocks. Part were killed or seized, part effected their escape (across the line allotted to the Bhopal native troops). A party attempted to sally out of the main gate of the Fort but were driven back by the fire of Captain Lightfoot's 9 pounders. Yesterday morning 1,500 rebels from their fortified camp at Naraoili and Bhopal having many mutinous sepoys amongst them attempted to relieve the Fort and coming out of thick jungle attacked the Videts guarding the right rear of my camp. I had just returned from the battery. Collecting the inlaying and outlaying picquets I drove the rebels across the river, Captain Hare with the Hyderabad Contingent killing and wounding several of them. After dusk other rebels made a trifling attack on the Videt on my left flank. My second Brigade under the able command of Brigadier Stewart deserves all my thanks, surrounded by thick jungle and dangerous ground, attacked in their rear, and performing duties which according to rule demanded three if not four times their numbers, they have carried on to their front with resolution and discipline the Seige and investment of the strongest fort in this part of the country and reduced it in 3 days, bringing to justice leaders of the rebellion and relieving Saugor, so long the object of anxiety. Mahomed Fazil Khan and another rebel were hung at sunset over the principal gate of the fort. The 3rd Europeans young as they are have done credit to the Bombay Army. The women and children of the rebels were treated by the troops with the greatest humanity.

OIOC MSS Eur F87, Box 9D, Letter Book 4

63
Rose to Elphinstone

[Manuscript telegram]   6 February 1858

My force marched into Saugor yesterday and its three hundred and seventy British inhabitants are now free and at my request went the same day out of the Fort into the Cantonment. The success at Barodia has produced excellent results – in consequence of it the rebels have fled from the fort of Korrye which is 45 miles to the north of Saugor. In order to make the most of this advantage I sent with Sir Robert Hamiltons concurrence 98 men of the Bhopal troops to Korrye and I have moved Major Orrs force from Goonah and the Headquarters of the 31st and 42nd Bengal NI from Saugor to the same place. The rebels have also abandoned Bhopal, their fortified camps at Nooreowlee and Sanoda 12 miles to the East of Saugor. The rebels have devastated the country during their long occupation of it, and I regret to say that I am prevented by want of supplies from marching against Garracotta garrisoned by the 52nd mutineers[126] and rebel allies. Eighteen rebels most of them taken at Ratgurh were executed there the day after capture.

OIOC MSS Eur F87, Box 9D, Letter Book 4

64
Rose to Adjutant-General, Bombay

                                                              Saugor
[Printed]   7 February 1858

✿ ✿ ✿

I ascertained that the rock, 1½ miles in length, covered and surrounded with thick jungle, slopes from the West, where it is precipitous, to the east where it is accessible.[127] The North front of the Fort was the only one which was habited; the other fronts were merely fortifications. The River Beena runs under its West face.

The reconnaissance confirmed in all essentials the information on which I formed my plan of attack. I carried it out, by investing the same evening the rock of Rathgur as closely as the great extent, hills, thick jungle, and a difficult River would allow. But it is impossible, unless with a very much larger Force than my own, to invest completely such ground, because a great part of it is dense jungle, which, hiding all view of the Enemy's motions, enable him, by a feint, to concentrate videttes and picquets on one point, and then pass through the vacuum.

Leaving a Troop of the 3rd Light Cavalry at the foot of the slope to cover our rear, accompanied by Captain Forbes, Commanding the 3rd Light Cavalry, who is always as zealous as he is useful, I mounted with the troops in the margin,* under the command of Lieutenant-Colonel Liddell, the slope, two Companies of the 3rd Europeans skirmishing and covering the breadth of the rock, two Companies supporting and the rest in reserve, we made our way through thick jungle, and reached, without being discovered, the edge of the open ground in front of the East curtain of the Fort, which Major Boileau[128] had selected for the breaching Batteries.

I directed a road to be cut immediately by the Sappers and Miners from the foot of the slope to this Battery; our left to open a communication down the South of the rock with the Troop of the 3rd Cavalry, investing the South of the rock, our right to open a communication down the North side of the rock with the Camp

---

*   Lieutenant-Colonel Liddell, Commanding 3rd European Regiment, Detachment of Siege Train under Lieutenant Mallock, two 18-pounders, 16 men Bombay Artillery. Two 5½-inch Mortars, 10 men Bombay Artillery, 90 Madras Sappers and Miners, two 6-pounder Guns Artillery Hyderabad Contingent, one Troop 3rd Light Cavalry under Captain Forbes.

and Rifle pits to be made at night in front of our attack, enfilading as much as possible the Enemy's line of defence.

The feint against the Town drove the Enemy out of it into the Fort, and enabled Brigadier Steuart, with the Force in the margin,* to take possession of the 'Eedgah' a Mussulman place of prayer, opposite the North face commanding the Town and within range of the main gate of the Fort; on this height, and another to the left he skilfully placed Captain Lightfoot's 9-Pounder Battery, one 8-inch Howitzer and two 8-inch Mortars. These Batteries forming the right or Town attack kept up, night and day, an effective fire on the line of defences and buildings of the Fort.

On the 28th instant, at 8, the sand bag batteries of the left attack having been completed, the two 18-Pounders and the 8-inch Howitzer having been brought up to them, commenced their fire against the outer wall of the east curtain of the Fort with such good effect, that it was evident that a practicable breach would soon be made.

I had just returned to the camp from the Battery when the Rebels coming in force out of the thick jungle, crossed the River Beena and attacked the Videttes of the right rear of the Camp; another large body of them appeared at the same time on the opposite bank, the two bodies amounting to 1,500 or 2,000 men, many of them Sepoys or valaitees.

I moved rapidly with the outlying picket of Her Majesty's 14th Light Dragoons, who in less than a minute, were in their saddles against the Rebels, ordering two guns and the rest of the pickets to follow in support; the Enemy, who were skirmishing with a picket

---

* Four 6-Pounder guns, Bombay Horse Artillery, Six 9-Pounder guns, Bombay Light Field Battery, under Captain Lightfoot. Fifty Bombay Sappers and Miners. Detachment of Siege Train. Two 8-inch Mortars, one 8-inch Howitzer, 20 Men Bombay Artillery. All the Artillery under Lieutenant-Colonel Turnbull. Two Troops of Her Majesty's 14th Light Dragoons, under Major Scudamore, 24th Regiment Native Infantry.

of the 3rd Light Cavalry, on seeing our approach, fired a discharge of muskets and rockets at us, and ran into a gorge of the Beena and up its rocky banks; I directed Captain Hare, following in my rear, to move by a short line and cut off their retreat.

Brigadier Steuart, whom I had called up, advancing from the Eedgah, with a few rounds of Artillery, sent the Rebels on the other side of the River into the jungle, and the whole retreated rapidly to a precipitous ridge above the village of Chunderapore, four miles to the North-West of Rathghur, from whence they had started in the morning.

After nightfall, the rebels made a feeble and unsuccessful attack on the left of the Camp from the Saugor road. The Rebels, who had come from their fortified camp Noreonlee and from the Fort of Kooreye, failed completely in their attempt to surprise the Camp and relieve Rathghur – during the whole time of their attack, the breaching Batteries continued their fire. Colonel Turnbull reported that the breach would be practicable for an assault the next day at sunset.

Accounts now came in to me that the Rebels from the Chunderapore ridge had early in the morning attacked, in the difficult pass mentioned in the first part of this Report, a convoy of supplies coming for my force from the West, and killed Scindia's vakeel who was in charge of it.

The safety of my supplies rendered it necessary that the Enemy should be driven from Chunderapore during night. I was employed in making arrangements for attacking them, which was not easy, as my Force was already engaged in an operation for which, in former times, a Force of four times their strength was considered necessary. However, I was on the point of marching against Chunderapore, when two spies I had sent out during the night, came in and reported that the Enemy had left that place for Baroda.

Colonel Liddell reported also, at the same time, that judging from the stillness of the Fort, that its garrison were escaping, he had entered it by the incompleted breach with part of the 3rd Europeans, who, after receiving some shots from the few Rebels still there, had killed them and taken possession of the Fort. The main body fled by an ancient sally port and a hole dug under the parapet to the South-West, from which when I entered the Fort the ropes were hanging, by which they had let themselves down. The reports of all the Officers on duty state that these Rebels, crossing a ford over the Beena to the South-West, under the Bhopall Camp, passed through the Bhopall lines into the jungle, the Bhopall Troops fired a few shots at the fugitives, two or three of their dead baggage animals in this ford showed the track they had taken. The Bhopall troops have been, and are still so useful to me that I merely mention this circumstance, which is nothing out of the way amongst Oriental Troops, out of justice to my own Force.

At sunset Mahomed Fazl Khan and the Nawab Kamdar Khan, a pensioner of the British Government and a son of the great Pindaree Chief, taken by Sir John Malcolm,[129] were hung over the gate of the Fort in presence of Detachments of my Force, the next day seventeen more, most of them Rebels of note and all part of the Garrison of Rathghur were executed, two of them, brothers of the Pindaree Chief, had taken part in the murder of the British Assistant at Bereiseeah, Kishen Ram, a Secretary of Mahomed Fazl Khan, is stated to have been instrumental in atrocities committed on forty Christians. Wallidad Khan, who admitted on his trial 'that he had done all he could and three times urged Fazil Mahomed to go down sword in hand and attack the Camp', a valaitee leader, &c.

The Fort was provided with a fine tank cut out of the rock fifty feet deep; and in it were found great stores of salt and grain sufficient for a year's consumption, a few Camels, Cattle and several Horses, two of them belonging to Mahomed Fazil Khan, one with a silver bridle and another to the Shahzada of Mandesore,[130] a mould for casting cannon and shot, and an immense mass of Native Correspondence and English accounts, which I made over to Sir Robert Hamilton, one object was also found which excited indignation, the effigy of the head of a decapitated European female, which it appears these supporters of a change of rule in India carried before their Troops, as fitting emblems of their deeds; notwithstanding this, and all that has passed, far worse than this, the 3rd Europeans, when they entered the Fort, treated the women and numerous children of the rebels who were left there with the humanity which was to be expected from their discipline and their faith. I had enjoined the troops, for the honour of their Country and the Army, not to harm a woman or a child.

✿ ✿ ✿

Forrest, IV, pp. 2–8

65
Rose to Whitlock

Saugor

[Holograph copy] 7 February 1858

I received with much pleasure today your letter of the 1st inst. and I lose no time in making known to you my future movements.

I have been detained here by want of supplies but the day after tomorrow the 9th inst. I hope to have sufficient to march against Garracotta, garrisoned by the 52nd Mutineers and their Bundela and Pathan allies. I hope to take it in three or four days, and then to move via Shahghur which, I believe, will make no resistance, against Chandeeree, where Sir Robert Hamilton thinks the Rajah of Banpore will make a stand, the Fort is strong and they have a foundry for cannon, making shot etc. there.

From Chandeeree I shall move on Jhansi.

My 1st Brigade is, I believe, on the march from Mhow to Goonah.

A successful attack which I made on Barodia on the road from Rathgurh to Koraye has caused the rebels to retreat from Koraye and Kimlossa.[131]

Nothing could be more advantageous for the suppression of the rebellion than your rapid march to Saugor en route to Banda. This is not only my opinion but Sir R. Hamilton and Major Western. Your progress up to here will clear the valley of the Nerbudda and secure our supplies which is our only cause for anxiety.

The Commander in Chief, so General Mansfield says, is anxious that my force should move to Jhansi with as little delay as possible, in order to keep his left rear clear.

BL Add MSS 42812 ff. 25–6

66
Major Macpherson to Hamilton

Agra
[Printed copy]   10 February 1858

7. The Durbar considered that the Bengal Native army believed that the Government intended, through the greased cartridges, to strike at the Hindu and Mahomedan religions in favour of Christianity.

That the army, being fully predisposed to revolt, made that grievance the pretext and occasion to rise to our overthrow.

8. Enquiry must show who were their immediate instigators. The foremost enemies of our rule embraced the opportunity offered and fomented, while the King of Delhi headed, the rebellion.

That a strong and general expectation rapidly arose that our power would be overthrown and that of Delhi re-established.

9. That the army were predisposed to revolt through sharing the dissatisfaction with our rule felt by the people of Hindostan.

13. The chief causes, to the mind of the Durbar, of dissatisfaction with our rule may be comprised under these familiar and pregnant heads:-

1. The extinction of Native States, and our consequent measure
2. The depression of the Chiefs and Heads of society
3. The resumption, or conversion into life tenure, of hereditary rent-free tenures of land, or of hereditary interests connected with land or the land revenue
4. The alienation of Zemindary lands for arrears of revenue, or in satisfaction of civil decrees
5. The non-conferment of estates or honors for eminent services to the State
6. The want of conciliatory and confidential intercourse between our officers and the Native Chiefs, Heads of society, and people
7. Our system of civil justice

14. Our measures relative to Suttee and to the marriage of Hindu widows, although unnacceptable, our educational measures, unnacceptable only when accompanied by special taxation or when unduly pressed, or our missionary operations, in face of the perfect religious neutrality of the Government, did not contribute to the revolt

As to the motives of revolt included in the love of power, of aggrandisement, of licence, of rapine, of bloodshed, of fanatical excitement, however they may have activated individuals or bodies of the Troops to commit, or allow their leaders, or the ruffian masses acting with them, to commit monstrous excess, these motives had but slight weight in the production of the revolt of the army compared to their desire to exchange British for native rule.

Report on Gwalior, No. III (copy in Indian Mutiny Pamphlets – NAM '1857' 54)

67
Canning to Hamilton

Allahabad

[Printed copy]   11 February 1858

If the Nerbudda Field Force proceeds to Jhansi and if the Ranee should fall into its hands, she must be tried, not by a Court Martial, but by a Commission appointed for the purpose.

Sir H. Rose will be directed to hand her over to you, and you must put together the best Commission which your material will allow.

If for any reason it should not be possible to deal with her at once, and if there should be difficulty in keeping her in custody in or near Jhansi, she may be sent here. But it is very desirable that the preliminary inquiry into her conduct, which will decide whether there be grounds for a trial, should be completed before she arrives here. She must not come here with any doubt as to whether she deserves to be tried or not. I hope, however, that you will be able to finish her trial on the spot; what may be done with her after trial will depend upon the sentence.

I say 'if' the Nerbudda force proceeds to Jhansi, because Sir H. Rose will receive authority to pass by that place in the event of his having any doubt as to his being strong enough to deal with it. In that case the Nerbudda Field Force should be directed upon Calpee or Banda (one or both) and operations against Jhansi be suspended until additional strength can be sent from this side. Nothing would be more embarrassing and even dangerous than that the Nerbudda column should sit down before Jhansi, or any other place in that direction, and find itself unable to achieve its purpose without aid from this quarter.

I therefore wish that Sir H. Rose should not consider himself under any obligation to attempt the reduction of Jhansi against the probability of success; and he will receive instructions from the Commander-in-Chief in this sense. He is too weak in European infantry to run such risks.

Forrest, IV, Chapter I, lxxix–xxx

68
Mansfield to Rose

Cawnpore

[Printed letter]   11 February 1858

Confidential

I have the honour, by desire of the Commander-in-Chief, to call your attention to the defence of Jhansi.

You are probable aware that it is of great importance that Jhansi should be reduced with as little delay as possible; but if the defence be strong, and if there be a very large assemblage of insurgents in that city, it may be doubted whether you have a force sufficient to undertake the siege.

His Excellency observes that you have not, at the very outside, more than 1,500 of British infantry.

Sir Colin Campbell, therefore, considers that before undertaking this operation you should have made quite certain from intelligence to be derived from Sir Robert Hamilton, or other quarters, that a serious opposition, to overcome which your force is unequal, is not likely to be encountered at Jhansi, as a check might have very disagreable consequences.

If, after weighing all these circumstances, you should be of opinion that the siege cannot prudently be undertaken, your march may be directed in two divisions viz. one on Calpee, on the Jumna through Chirkaree, and the other on Banda, from each of which places you would report for the information of the Commander-in-Chief.

OIOC MSS Eur F87, Box 9D, Letter Book 4

69
Rose to Elphinstone

Garakotah

[Manuscript telegram]   12 February 1858

Last night before the Fort of Garrakotta could be invested or any arrangements for its attack be completed the rebels fled from the

Fort in a South Westerly direction circling round, I believe, to the north of Shahgarh. I had time, and no more, to invest the North West and North East which were the probable points of the garrison's escape but it is fair to state that such is the impracticable nature & extent of the ground round Garrakotta that no investment made by a force of my numbers could have been complete. 2 Flying Detachments are in pursuit of the rebels. Garrakotta is a place of extraordinary strength between two rivers with a large forest on its north side. Brigadier Watson in 1818 failed in making a practicable breach in the defences of the Fort with 28 pieces of artillery and Major Boileau Commanding Engineer is of opinion that if the garrison had made a resolute defence its capture would have lost much time and a great loss of life in Infantry; there are 12 guns in the Fort and large supplies of ammunition and grain. The left flank of Saugor is now free from danger, the villagers show a friendly feeling and come out to meet the troops. The enemy resisted our advance to the Fort but were completely driven from their positions by my artillery and Infantry.

OIOC MSS Eur F87, Box 9D, Letter Book 4; BL Add MSS 42807

70
Bonus to his parents

Saugor

[Typewritten copy]   13 February 1858

. . . I think that my last letter was written at Rahutgarh, a very short one. I will fill in a bit. On the 23rd of Jan. we arrived within 12 miles of Rahutgarh, a fort said to be full of Rohillas,[132] Bundelahs, and men of other tribes, and very strong. Orders were issued that the force would not march the next day the 24th, but this was a blind intended to deceive the enemy, for it is pretty certain that there are spies in camp. Sir Hugh Rose kept his secret so well that all save the Divisional Staff were astounded when next morning at 7 a.m. an order was issued 'March on Rahutgarh at 8 a.m.'. During the night the heavy guns had come up and at

8 a.m. we started. The march was very slow, very hot and very wearisome. We had to advance with great care, skirmishers in front and on both flanks; report said that we were to be attacked on the road. However we were not worried and we came in sight of the fort without a shot being fired; just as we neared the river which runs beneath the hill on which Rahutgarh stands, firing commenced among the skirmishers. The General was in front, I was riding with the Brigadier some way behind, when an Officer came back at a gallop with the order 'Horse Artillery and Cavalry to the front.' Away they went splashing through the river right at the enemy who were in force on the opposite bank, banners flying, a picturesque sight. But they did not await the onset, some shots were fired and then they turned and bolted into the town at the foot of the fort. We lost a Native Officer killed and three or four men wounded. No Officer was hit. Prendergast's[133] horse was shot in the neck. The fun lasted about two hours. Then we camped and had some food; we had nothing since dinner the previous evening. Next morning the General with his Staff rode right round the fort; they started at 7 a.m. and did not return till dark. I did not go. I received no orders and being very tired was glad to escape a long day on horseback. I had a look around. The fort is very strong on account of its position. It stands at the end of a spur of hill and on account of the precipitous nature of the ground, is unapproachable on three sides save by the road through the village leading to the fortified gateway. On the fourth side is the fairly flat top of the hill covered with low jungle.

On the 26th at noon we commenced business. The force was divided into two parts; one part under the direct orders of the General was to gain the hill and the other under the Brigadier was to attack the town. I was ordered to take charge of all Engineering duties with this latter part, Major Boileau and Prendergast going with the General. We advanced in line against the town and drove the enemy into the fort, they made very little resistance and did us no harm, one round shot from the fort struck the ground close to my horse and wounded an Artillery horse, nothing more. We found an excellent place for a battery and soon had two 8 inch mortars in position and we bombarded the fort till dark.

On the 27th I was rushed about a good deal. The General works his Staff pretty hard. In the afternoon he sent me to reconnoitre a round tower about half way up the fort hill, and some 50 yards from the wall; this was rather a nasty job. I had to crawl along on my hands and knees, and I was careful to remove my white cap cover. While I was looking at the place, a party of men dashed out of the town and into the tower. From where I was I could not make them out. I hastened back and reported to the general when he told me he had sent the party which I had seen. He then ordered me to wait till dark, then take a party of Sappers and make the tower into a good post to prevent escape by the gate of the fort as the tower fully commanded the gate. Accordingly I took the men, but directly I entered the place I saw that it was almost untenable. The interior was very much above the level of the ground outside and with the exception of a small patch just under the wall nearest the fort was entirely exposed to fire from the fort. The small party which I had seen was crouched in the small protected space. Nor did it seem to me that the place would be of any use for the purpose of preventing any exit from the Main Gate of the fort. However it was my duty to carry out my orders if possible. We worked hard all night trying to make an entrance into the tower from the rear facing our battery but the job proved too much. The wall was about 16 feet thick, we could work only on the outside as the inside was exposed to the enemy, and there was a bright moon. At 4 a.m I decided to report the state of things to the Brigadier, he sent me to Sir Hugh. I did not like this at all as I knew Sir Hugh would be asleep; he was, I had to wake him. After hearing what I had to say, he told me that I might evacuate the tower. I hastened back deciding to move about an hour before sunrise as at that time natives are always cold and sleepy, and the moon would have set. We got clear of the tower without a shot being fired.

On the 28th a force of Bundeelahs and others attacked our camp but were repulsed with loss; this was an effort to help the garrison which kept up a smart fire on our batteries, while the fight was in progress. On the 29th we found that the fort was empty; the rebels had made their escape by letting themselves down the precipitous cliffs with ropes: the place was so steep that

I could hardly bear to look over: two men had fallen and been killed, I saw the bodies lying at the bottom. There were several dead and wounded in the fort and a good deal of food and plunder of sorts; this is sold and the proceeds become prize money.

All next day I was busy preparing mines and other arrangements for the demolition of parts of the fort but outside other business was in progress. The General marched out and attacked the enemy who were posted in a village not far from our camp, Barodea the name. In this little fight, Captain Neville of the Royal Engineers[134] was killed by a round shot. He had joined only the day before from Mhow. We lost several killed and many wounded.

My demolitions in the fort were not very successful. Goodfellow was with me, we nearly managed to demolish ourselves. We had made a hole horizontally under the rampart, loaded it with a heavy charge, but time being short, had rather scamped the tamping. G. and I luckily took refuge behind a dwarf wall. When the explosion took place the tamping which consisted mainly of stones, shot out and pelted the small wall behind which we were crouched. But we made a fine mess of the Main Gate, wrecking the whole place.

We left Rahutgarh on the 2nd February, and marched into Saugor the next day; the people there were mightily glad to see us; they had been shut up in the fort, a very small one, since July; they must have been packed very close; all the houses and shops in the cantonments had been looted and many burned.

We had a grand parade in Saugor, in order I suppose to impress the natives. I had to ask the General in what dress he wished his Staff to appear. His reply was 'I don't believe you have a complete Parade dress among you.' I think he was nearly right; my uniform is completely worn out.

We stayed in Saugor till the 9th, on which day we started for Garahkotah, a fort about 27 miles away, said to be held by the 52nd Bengalees (they mutinied at Jubbulpore) and a lot of wild Bundeelahs. Every one seemed to think we should have hard work as it was said the garrison had been working at the defences for some months. On the 10th we did 19 miles to Garahkotah, making a flank movement to avoid a battery which was reported as commanding the direct road; by this movement we surprised a picket, the men were all shot. As soon as we came within range of the fort guns we received some shots. Sir Hugh who exposes himself without the slightest hesitation in the most dangerous places rode almost round the fort and he is such a man for 'just a little further' that we did not get to camp till 8 p.m., having been 18 hours in the saddle without any food too.

Next day, we started at 8 a.m. for a reconnaissance, our party consisted of Sir Hugh and Staff with an escort of a troop of Dragoons, two Horse Artillery guns, and a company of the 3rd Europeans; at one spot the rebels got our range pretty accurately, and sent round shot unpleasantly near; we could see the shot skipping along towards us; one went through our Infantry, without doing any harm as the men jumped to one side. We had a long ride not getting into camp till past 7. I dined with Sir Hugh that night.

The next morning, I was getting ready to go up to the howitzer battery which had been established when I was told the enemy had bolted during the night, one man whom we caught said that our reconnoitring party had frightened them into the belief that they would be surrounded and so they had gone. These men are poltroons, they had a splendid position, and might have defied our force for weeks; we could not have breached the fort wall but by mining, and that is a long and tedious operation. There were large quantities of provisions in the fort, those will be sold and should do something to swell the prize-money.

A party of Cavalry and guns were sent after the fugitives and cut up some 60 of them, the pursuit was stopped by a river which the guns could not cross.

After demolishing part of the fort, we returned to Saugor, entering on the 17th. Here we are still, this is the 22nd and we don't know when we shall move. When we do move we expect that Jhansi will be our object; but there are of course all sorts of rumours, some say we stop here a month, some say we march immediately, some say that the Queen of Jhansi has sent a letter to Sir Robert Hamilton protesting that she is always our friend, and that she intends to give herself up as a prisoner. I do not believe this yarn; the truth is, nobody knows when or whither we shall go, the General wisely keeps his own counsel . . . I must explain to you one or two things about this force; I think you confuse things a bit. The Central India Field Force is our proper title, the force is composed of two brigades, called the First and Second Brigades; the First is commanded by Colonel Stuart of the Indian Army, the Second by Colonel Stewart of H.M.'s Army, this is the Brigade at Saugor to which I belong though I do not really know whether I am on the General's Staff or the Brigadier's. Sir Hugh Rose commands, he is the General.

We have now a Sapper Mess, there are seven of us, Goodfellow, Dick,[135] myself, and four Madras Officers. The Mess is excellently supplied with stores, including wine and beer. The Mess is a great thing for Goodfellow and me; we have stepped into luxury after our late rather poor living. I find that with the hard work here I can drink and enjoy beer. I could not do this in Poona and Aurungabad.

I see by the home papers that people think Canning too lenient, we too think so, but there is no leniency here. Sir Hugh knows no native language so he pays little heed to what a prisoner says. His first question is 'Was this man taken with arms in his hands?' If the answer is 'Yes', 'Then shoot him' says Sir Hugh. By the way do not believe half what you see in the papers about the doings of this force. I have been astonished at the lies I have seen.[136]

OIOC IOR neg. 4395

71

Rose to Elphinstone

Magrone[137]

[Manuscript telegram]   14 February 1858

The Flying Detachments under Captain Hare consisted of Horse Artillery and the 14th Light Dragoons which I sent off after the rebels retreating from Garrakotta came up with their rear & killed from 70 to 100 of them many of them were sepoys of the 31st, 42nd,

52nd and 70th Bengal Native Regiments. Their English muskets and quantities of copper caps have been taken. The country people showed our troops the way. Major Boileau is demolishing Garrakotta as much as he can. Fuel and great surplus of wheat and grain, saltpetre, sulphur and 4 cartloads of ammunition have been found in the Fort. I shall be in Saugor tomorrow and as soon as my guns are repaired I march against the forts of Multhoun, Chandere and Jhansi at all of which places there are large collections of rebels. I hope that you will send me the 71st Reg^t, which has just arrived at Bombay, by Bullock train to Goonah in time for my attack on Jhansi. Sir R. Hamilton has received information that the rebels commanded by the Rajah of Banpore lost 400 men at Barodia & that the Ranee of Jhansi is much dejected by their defeat. Pray send me plans of Chandere and Jhansi.

OIOC MSS Eur F87, Box 9D, Letter Book 4

72
Central India Field Force Orders[138]

Saugor

[Holograph]   16 February 1858

The Major General has before warned soldiers and others about plundering and it is with regret that he has received a report of a soldier of the Sappers and Miners having been plundered and beaten by European soldiers of the same Brigade and that at a roll call parade taken at the time this occurred some men of the Artillery and 3rd European Regt. were absent; great suspicion must therefore fall on these men. Should such conduct again be brought to his notice the Major General will direct rolls to be called every hour and if this does not put a stop to plundering he will take even severer measures for he is determined that conduct which must disorganise any Force and reduce it in the hour of victory to a mere rabble shall not exist in the Force under his command . . . and he calls upon all officers to assist him to their utmost in its suppression . . .

The following notification is published for general information

No. 1499 of 1857 Notification

It being understood that Prize Agents have been appointed at Delhi for the collection of Booty captured by the British troops from the Mutineers and other persons in rebellion against the Government, it is hereby notified for the information and guidance of all Parties concerned that a clear distinction exists in cases of re-capture between Property of the state originally captured by an Enemy in time of war and similar property seized by Rebels or Mutineers during an insurrection. In the former case, the Property re-captured is in general property treated as Property of the Hostile State and becomes subject to the Law of Prize.

But in an Insurrection such as the present one, the Troops of the State whose property has been pillaged by its own subjects or by Foreigners aiding such subjects in their treason where they retake such Property from the Plunderers merely retake it on behalf of the Govt. and acquire no legal right of prize or of property altho' they have strong claims on the liberality of the Government. These principles apply also to the Property of Private Individuals plundered by the Insurgents and retaken by the Troops of the State. Such Private Property can in no case be deemed Lawful Prize when clearly identified and claimed by the original owner.

In accordance with these principles, the Right Honble. the Governor General in Council is pleased to direct that officers in command of British troops employed in quelling the present insurrection, shall appoint Committees of officers for the purpose of taking an account of all treasures and other Public Property, Cattle, Munitions of War, Stores etc. recaptured from the Insurgents and Mutineers in order to [?expedite] the delivery of the Property as recovered into the nearest Treasury or the custody of the proper Civil or Military officers and that copies of such accounts shall be transmitted to the Secretary in the Military Department for the information of Government . . .

In all cases of clear identification of Property restitution may be made to the owner on the spot provided that in the case of Natives they shall prove to the satisfaction of the Committee that they have not been guilty of any offence for which their property would be liable to forfeiture, and have to the best of their ability rendered active assistance to the British Government and when claims are not clearly established, or the property belongs to any persons deceased the orders of the Govt. to be awaited before delivery.

The claims of the Troops composing the Field Force by which Delhi has been nobly wrested from the hands of the Mutineers and rebels, and by whose gallantry signal punishment has been inflicted on the Insurgents there, are fully appreciated by the Governor General in Council and in recognition of their services, His Lordship in Council is pleased to grant a donation of six months batta to be forthwith distributed to all the Troops engaged in the operations against Delhi.

OIOC MSS Eur D1007

73
Field Force Orders

[Holograph]

Saugor
18 February 1858

The Skirmishing and Light Infantry drills being successful against the mode of warfare of the Rebels, Brigadier Steuart is requested to direct officers commanding Regiments in this drill in accordance with the Field Exercises. These drills are to be short and active. The Buglers and the Trumpeters are to be thoroughly drilled in the calls. The Drills are to take place every afternoon when not on the march.

OIOC MSS Eur D1007

74
Rose to Elphinstone

Saugor

[Holograph]   23 February 1858

I was rather annoyed not at your telling the Governor General the
essentials of my letter about Sir Robert Hamilton but the part of it
which I only wrote to you as a friend. I mean what I said as to the
causes or motives of his conduct. But I can assure you that I was
not *secretly* [indecipherable] that I did not quite know what to say
about the 'question Hamilton', and was besides hard up for time,
for as you know, the correspondence is very great, the day being
taken up by early marches, and their consequence, going to bed
when you are going to dinner. I am become a perfect Turkey.

There is nothing, I think, we would not do to catch Nana Sahib.
I have already brought up my men to the highest pitch, and
I really believe that almost all the poor followers would rather
catch him than receive the lac of rupees.[139]

Nana Sahib is clever and has some strategy about him; but he is
not bold, at least hitherto he has never given proof of being so.
I doubt therefore his making a run for the Deccan, which in his
point of view, he ought to have done long since. Nor will ever,
I think, shut himself up in a fort, it is too great a risk; he will,
when a beaten force, skirt about the country he knows best, the
Ganges, the Jumna, and the Doab. I think that he had better not
come in the way of the 3rd Bombay Lt Cavalry; at Barodia, they cut
down the Valiatees and Bundeelas, with an entire disregard of
caste, one Trooper cut down two or three of his own caste, and
they were almost as unceremonious with a picket of Bundeelas,
when I set them on to patrol in front of Garacota.

OIOC MSS Eur F87, Box 6G, Packet 20

75
Field Force Orders

Saugor

[Holograph]   26 February 1858

❊ ❊ ❊

1. The Major General calls the attention of the Commanding Engineer to the state of his Park which on his visiting it yesterday was neither fit for inspection or any description of military operation . . .

OIOC MSS Eur D1007

76
Rose to Elphinstone

Saugor

[Holograph copy]   27 February 1858

❊ ❊ ❊

I, and what is far worse, the cause, am a victim of the eternal and fatal question of Transport and Supply, which has saved Constantinople from Russia, and now to compare great things with small, has tied my force by the leg, nine precious days, doubly precious not only on account of lost time, at a season when every cool day saves the health and lives of European soldiers, but also because every day I lose has allowed the rebels to recover the morale which they had lost in consequence of my operations which I had made as rapidly and as efficiently as possible, knowing that any success with Orientals produces twice as good a result if you do it promptly, and follow it up with another. My men were hardly worked at Rathghur but I attacked Barodia at once, came back the same night to Rathghur, and then without a halt to Saugor, and nearly as quickly to Garrakota. The result was the 'Moofsid'[140] got into a sort of Panic, abandoning Multhone, Nurat, Marowra, Shahghur etc. But this unlucky delay on account of supply has very much done away with former good effects and all those places are now re-occupied and my movements are still encumbered by bad and scanty transport and supply. I can only go a certain distance from Saugor because I depend upon 5,500 Bullocks coming with grain from Nursingpore.

Napoleon, Souvaroff and all the great generals have said that no transport can be depended upon but one with a complete *military* agency. I am aware that a clever Contractor, with a genius for transport and supply, which are inseparable, may with a great capital supply an Army in the Field. But this is an exception. What is required is a System which will work well under common place intellects. No contractor can prevent camel men bolting or deserting at night, or keep cartmen, who have fled to the hills or jungle. Nothing requires system so much as Transport; laying supplies, as it is called, is perfectly easy in a fertile and peaceful country but this will not do, as in my case, when a country is devastated by an enemy, or the country is in the hands of the enemy; then appears all the evils of a *civil* or *occasional* system of supply.

I had a great opinion of Brinjara bullocks,[141] but they answer only occasionally, not as a system. There must be a sufficient number of them, they must not have been frightened out of the country as in the case of this district etc. Why dont you my dear Elphinstone put yourself at the head of the great question of Indian military transport? You would do your country more good than all of us generals put together. I will give you all my humble assistance.

BL Add MSS 42812 ff. 29–31

77
Shakespear – diary

[Typed copy]

Rojwass March 1st We were to have gone to Barodia a village about 4 miles further (visible from our camp is the little Fort on the end of the hill) but did not as it was reported 'occupied'.

About noon Major Scudamore went off with a party and guns to reduce it but about ½ past three sent back for a Howitzer to blow in the gate. Instead of this the General must needs go off in person with guns, Dragoons and Europeans in fact large reinforcements. Sir Robert went and I could not resist so mounted my horse all orders to the contrary notwithstanding and accompanied him. The Howitzer when in position soon knocked the wall about the doorway down and after the first shot there was no more firing from the Fort. Of course there was a postern at the back on to the Hill and when after two or three shots the Europeans went at the place they found it empty. Our generalship is certainly very defective – it would have been so easy to have thrown a line of skirmishers across the hill in rear of the Fort before anything else was done and then the fellows would never have got off.

❉ ❉ ❉

OIOC MSS D 706/2, f. 89

78
Field Force Orders

Rajwas

[Holograph]   2 March 1858

❉ ❉ ❉

4. The delays and confusion which occur in the execution of Division Orders in the Brigade Offices compels the Major General Commanding to notice and remedy them. The day before yesterday the countersign issued to the Pickets was different from the one issued by the Asst Adjutant General – and the sentries had different countersigns. Yesterday the 3rd Bombay European Regt. had not received the order to march against Burrodia when the Siege Train was actually marching to that place and the Major General had to go himself and turn out the Regt. The Major General therefore requests that the time will be noted on a

Division Order when it is issued, when it is issued from the Brigade Office, & when it is received by the Troops.

* * *

OIOC MSS Eur D1007

79
Shakespear – diary

Pipraee 3 March Major Scudamore with a Squadron Dragoons, the 24th N.I. and 3rd Cavalry moved on Malthone this morning to distract the enemy attention as it is at the head of the formidable Narhut pass which is well defended. The rest of the Force under the General moves through the Muddanpore pass which was reported to be comparatively unguarded. We were ready to move at ½ past three but did not do so till ½ past five. For some distance we moved through open country. Major Orr and the Hyd. Cont. formed the Advance Guard. About four miles from Camp our road began to be commanded by a high hill to our right along the base of which we marched for some two miles, the country to our left being quite open. Of all days today we had not a single skirmisher or flanker thrown out but we were not molested till we came in view of the pass about a mile ahead of us. Shots were then heard to our right in the Hills. We moved up to about 1,100 yards from a small hill in front of us over which our road led and which was covered with the enemy and with jungle. The Hyd. guns opened fire on it with shell and we could see the rebels getting out of the way, some light H.A. guns were now brought up with Dragoons in support and off the General went with them straight towards the Hill. I joined in and we galloped up to within a couple of hundred yards of the Hill when just as we pulled up to unlimber a tremendous volley was let into us from a nullah (ravine) which lay betwen us and the Hill and then a continuous file firing. I left the guns and joined the Dragoons in the rear about 100 paces but there the bullets were falling like hail. The Artillery men being obliged to work their guns kneeling, and to lay down, were at last withdrawn and so about we all went and *walked* away, the enemy shouting after us that the 'ghore log bhagte' (Europeans running away). We pulled up and commenced firing again at rather a more proper distance. (It was most wonderful that we had only *two* men wounded in this for the fire according to good authority was heavier than in a pitched battle. The reason of the few hits was that the enemy being in a ravine fired high.) Now came up the Hyd. Inf., shortly after that the Europeans these soon cleared the ravine and hill and the road was again open. The Column moved on and passing over the hill (not high) came down into a narrow glen and there we all formed up for in front of us was a tank (lake) and the village of Muddanpore in rear of it. To our left was a high hill sweeping up to the village and between the base of which and the edge of the tank lay our road. The enemy had their guns posted on the bend in front of us and while we were halting for some heavy guns to come up that we might shell the village, treated us to a few shots but they did no harm and immediately on our opening fire theirs ceased altogether. During this halt, Sir Robert had his breakfast party. I was to the front, could not be found and lost mine. To our left was a low range of hills, and after a few shots finding no reply, skirmishers were thrown out on both sides and on we moved and entered the village of Muddanpore without opposition and so the pass was ours with I believe only six men wounded. We lost a good deal of valuable time in the village, the General mooning about, at last he sent off the Hyd. Cavalry in pursuit – but it was no good, two hours since the enemy had ceased firing and I had little hopes of their ever catching them.

OIOC MSS Eur D 706/2, ff. 90–1

80
J.H. Carne[142] to Edmonstone

[Printed copy]

Allahabad
4 March 1858

In continuation of my letter, No.17, dated 1st Instant, I have the honour to state for the information of Government, that the city of Chirkaree fell entirely into the possession of the rebels on the evening of the 1st Instant.

2nd. During the last three days every habitation has been plundered and then set fire to. The Rajah's own residence has also been rifled of every particle of property which could be carried away, while costly mirrors, chandeliers, carpets and other valuable fittings and furniture of English fashion were smashed to pieces and otherwise destroyed by the rebel mob.

3rd. Elephants and horses with their trappings, carriages of various kinds, palanquins and other conveyances, camels and draught bullocks, all the cattle belonging to the inhabitants, besides twelve pieces of ordnance, the majority of which had been brought away from the field, but could not be conveyed up to the Fort, in the confusion of the fray, have all fallen into the hands of the enemy.

4th A large brick-built mansion, one of the Rajah's residences, but principally made use of and reserved for English visitors, was set on fire last night and every article of furniture destroyed.

5th It would occupy too much of your valuable time were I to enumerate all the mischief that has been done; suffice it to say that the total loss is estimated to be not less than from fourteen to fifteen lakhs of rupees.

6th The city was taken through the treachery of a mercenary *Thakoor* named Joojhar Sing. He had a large band of men who occupied one of the most important (in fact they were all most important) defensive posts. On the approach of their assailants they fled without offering any resistance and are now in the ranks of the enemy. This opening gave the rebels the entrée into the city, which they at once commenced setting on fire. Having become masters of this position they were enabled to make a diversion in favour of another party who were attacking its neighbouring position, by taking them in the right flank and rear. The gallant defenders of this post fought bravely, but being surrounded they were overpowered. They managed, however, to effect their retreat even under such difficulties, in an orderly manner.

7th The men at all the other posts maintained their ground unflinchingly, though hotly pressed by a strong and determined enemy, but as numbers came pouring in through those positions which had been carried it was thought advisable to order these brave men to retire into the Fort, because it became every moment more and more evident that their retreat would quickly be cut off.

8th As evening closed in it was ascertained that more than one half of the Rajah's troops had decamped towards their own homes, and during the last two or three days of truce numbers of others have also fled. In short almost all the temporarily hired troops have vanished.

9th The enemy conducted all their operations very systematically. They latterly received reinforcements from Calpee of from 500 to 800 sepoys. They could afford their relief parties; while some fought others rested; as one set was observed going away, another was seen coming to take their places, even during the continuance of the conflict. They had their bugle-calls during the last grand assault, and each separate band of matchlock-men was led on and performed its assigned task under the tuition evidently of some of the smartest sepoys who had been instructed by us in the art of war. They had their hospital dhoolies and they appeared to have a large and well-organised bazaar with abundance of supplies. They, in short, displayed all the active energies of the battlefield, while their opponents were the personification of brave but comparatively dull, bulky, dead-weight resistance.

PP, *The Native Princes of India*, Chirkaree, 1860; FSUP, III, pp. 241–2

81
Rose to Campbell

Maiaora[143]

[Holograph copy]   6 March 1858

I hope sincerely that you will approve the forcing of the pass of Mudinpore on the 4th inst. – it has had very good results, the natives thought it a sort of barrier between the Saugor and Shahghur districts which we could not surmount and the rapidity with which we got through it, and into their rear, has produced a general panic.

I hope that my advance to Tehree may be of use to your Excellency's attack of Lucknow by drawing the mutineers of Calpee and the rebels of that part of the world from the Doab towards me; if I can only get them well into the plain, I do not think many of them will escape my cavalry which is good and numerous. Hitherto my ground has been very unfavourable to Cavalry. I should have killed far more of them at Mudinpore but having so little Infantry, was obliged to guard my immense tail of Supplies, Ammunition, and baggage with cavalry as the enemy threatened it. Our forcing the pass so rapidly and with few casualties was most fortunate, for it was very difficult, far more so than I had been led to believe; if I engaged the rebels at a distance and let them feel confidence in their position, the delay, especially if night had come on, in such dangerous ground, might have been critical. An oversight of a gallant and excellent officer, L[t] Col Turnbull, precipitated, as our French friends would say, the situation and gave a little advantage to the mutineers; it was most necessary therefore to make a rapid advance and gain a decided advantage. I put the Hyderabad Contingent infantry into a glen in skirmishing order, supporting them with some of the Europeans, drove them out of it, turning their left. I gave them no breathing space, sending more of the 3rd up to the rocks in which was their right, as well as some capital men of the Salt Customs Service who, although all Bengal men, fight their brethren with the best good will. Their right was driven back as quickly as their left, and a feint by a Troop of the 14th L[t] Dgns. against their rear gave us the pass. The Sepoys have quarrelled with the rebels of the country because they say that they ran away, the whole are quite demoralised for the present, the Sepoys trying to divest themselves of necklaces or anything that shows that they are Sepoys.

I hope that my 1st Brigade will soon take Chanderee; they were to attack it today.

I sincerely hope that I shall find sufficient supplies there and that I shall not have to wait for the Nursingpore supplies; the Asst Commissary of my division is to make his report on the subject immediately.

Your Excellency will be glad to learn that my men conduct themselves very well, and treat the inhabitants in a way which inspires confidence, and forms a striking contrast with the rebels. The consequence is that when supplies are to be had the country people bring them in. I cannot say as much in favour of the Camp Followers, but I have improved their morality by invariably flogging when they loot . . .

BL Add MSS 42812 ff. 32–4

82
Bonus to his parents

Maraura

[Typewritten copy]   8 March 1858

I do not think that our General Sir Hugh Rose is at present much beloved in his force. He, however, has certainly one very good point, his pluck is outstanding. He is always to the front in the thick of the fire and cares no more for bullets than peas, but it seems to me that his place is not there.

Since I last wrote we have forced the Pass of Muddenpore, which is in the line of hills a little north of Saugor. I will give a slight account of the job. We arrived at Rugwas about 25 miles from Saugor on the 1st inst; and encamped about 2 or 3 miles from the hills. A couple of miles or so from camp we saw a small fort on the side of a hill and a party was sent out to take it should the enemy be in it. They found it occupied and the officer commanding sent into camp for an eight-inch howitzer thinking that a few shells of that size would soon make the place untenable, but to our surprise the General turned out the whole Brigade, Artillery, Cavalry, Infantry, this for a place about fifty yards by thirty, with a garrison of some fifty men, we were very sick. After about half a dozen shells from the big howitzer, the gentlemen bolted and got off scot free over the hills. When we entered we found but one dead man; thus ended the attack and capture of the Fort of Barodea; no doubt it will be made a grand affair by some people. For some not very apparent reason the General dawdled about the fort till nearly dark and before we started back a storm came down. The result was unfortunate; some men went astray in the jungle, and some guns stuck in a nullah; the confusion was great. Part of the Artillery did not get into camp till next morning. The consequence was that we were obliged to halt and lose a day so that the enemy gained time for the defence of the pass. On the 3rd at 3 a.m. a strong force started for the Pass of Multown[144] and at 4 a.m. another for the Pass of Muddenpore, the object of this plan was to deceive the enemy, for, of course, they had spies in camp; those when the first party went off would send warning to their friends. This seemed a good plan but unluckily it did not work well. The first column could not get clear away with all its impediments before the second one had to start; the confusion was dreadful, it was pitch dark, the roads and paths were blocked up with camels and carts, and no one knew his way out of the mess, we were in fact stuck till daylight, when we went our several ways. The General and I with him, as one of his Staff, went with the Muddenpore lot; the Multown party were to march until they came under fire, then to move to their flank and follow us through the Muddenpore pass.

At about 8 a.m. the first shot was fired at our advance guard and on coming to the top of some rising ground we saw a vast crowd of sepoys and budmashes about 400 yards in advance of the edge of some jungle. For some seconds Sir Hugh would not believe they were foes. When he did, he ordered the guns of the Hyderabad Contingent to open fire, but the crowd slipped into the jungle and were for a moment safe. Now comes an incident which was really funny, but might have been serious. The Artillery galloped up to within 50 yards of the jungle, unlimbered, loaded and were about to fire when a perfect storm of bullets swept over us. I say 'us' as Sir Hugh and his Staff had moved up to the guns, these opened fire, but I believe did no harm. We could not see a soul; I expected to be hit every second.

This lasted only a minute or two, the guns limbered up, and we all retired. I suppose we owed our escape to our proximity; the bullets went over us. We did not escape scot free however, three or four men were wounded. Sir Hugh's horse was hit, and two or three of the gun horses. If the enemy had been better shots, we should all have been knocked over. When we retreated our friends issued from the jungle and cheered. The General then ordered up the Infantry, they very soon cleared the place, losing only a few men wounded. We discovered that the men who fired on us were posted in a dry nullah quite safe from our guns.

We now advanced up the Pass, and soon the enemy opened on us with round shot from 4 guns which were entrenched at the village of Muddenpore, at the far end of the Pass; between them and us was a large tank. I thought we should have advanced at once and seized the guns but Sir Hugh waited for the big howitzer, after a couple of shells, neither of which did any harm, the enemy horsed the guns and withdrew. We threw out our skirmishers and advanced to the village, which we found entirely deserted, not a soul was there. After dawdling about the village some time some Cavalry were sent in pursuit. They overtook the rear guard and killed some 60 of them. It was a poor affair, we ought to have had those guns. It was about 3 p.m., the men had been out since 3 a.m. without food or drink, and the heat was very great. We thought we should camp, but Sir Hugh thought otherwise; he sat in the shade of a tree for a bit and had some lunch, then we went on for about 4 miles or so and halted. But unluckily the General selected for the camp a spot which was very unsuitable, as it was extremely difficult of access for guns and bullock carts, especially the latter; he was advised of this, but it was some time before he would give way. However, he at last gave orders for a change and the camp was marked out in a good position. It was now dark, you cannot imagine what glorious confusion and hubbub there was, baggage continued to arrive all night, the noise was deafening, but we were all dead tired, and managed to sleep.

Sir Hugh can be a most courtly and agreable gentleman, but he can also be very much otherwise. He has a fine temper of his own, I have heard him swear coarsely even at his officers, but the subject is unpleasant. Let me leave it.

We could not move the day after Muddenpore; men and horses were quite unequal to it . . . On the 5th we arrived here; Sir Hugh ordered the march at 3 a.m. but the men were kept waiting in their saddles till nearly 7 before we moved off, I am told that the General rode away forgetting to give orders about the route, and so the Brigadier had to wait till one of the General's Staff came back with orders.

The column which marched via Multown joined us to-day. There is a rather strong fort here; yesterday the Union Flag was hoisted on the highest tower and saluted with 21 guns in proof that we have annexed the territory of the Rajah of Shahgurh. There is a reward of 10,000 Rs on his head, and I daresay we shall hang him before many days are past.[145]

OIOC IOR neg. 4395

83
Rose to Somerset

Kumhari[146]

[Holograph copy]   9 March 1858

Your Excellency, who is very kind and always encourages one so much, will be glad to hear of our success at Mudinpoor, which was a more difficult operation than we have yet had. The pass was a very difficult one, the road descending all of a sudden passing through deep glens of thick jungle, and then passing under rocky heights on one side and a lake on the other; a good enemy might have held it against the best Army; the rebels had made capital rifle pits in the rocks which no artillery could have turned them out of. I cannot conceive men playing such a dismal game as the Sepoys letting themselves be driven out of such capital positions. At the end of the pass is the village of Mudinpoor protected by a sloping Bund at the head of the Lake, which no artillery I have could have breached.

Orr at 700 or 800 yards, who formed the advanced Guard, was making very good practice at them at the head of the pass with shells and spherical case, when Turnbull letting his ardour get the better of his judgement took his battery rapidly forward to cross his fire with Orr's and rake a body of rebels on the mountain side, but he had not observed only 50 or 60 yards away to his new front a deep dell full of Sepoys. Before Turnbull could unlimber 300 or 400 Sepoys opened as rapid and heavy fire as is [?not] often seen. Turnbull's guns could not keep down this fire as he could not depress his guns sufficiently, or rather the fall in the ground covered the rebels. I had followed Turnbull to see what he was doing and came in for the suffering – my best horse was wounded, and my orderly's also, luckily the rebels were too eager to destroy us and fired too quickly and too high, only 4 or 5 horses were wounded, and three men.

Turnbull is so *gallant and good* an officer that I have only given him a mild wigging, begging him never again to act without my orders, and pointing out to him that his having done so in the present instance, had been the cause of his having to retire his guns and give the enemy a temporary advantage.

However, as it turned out, the oversight of Turnbull only, as our French friends say, precipitated the situation and brought matters to a more speedy conclusion. I moved a company of the Hyderabad Infantry into the dell in double time, made them bring their right shoulders forward, drive the rebels down, taking them in flank with a company of the 3rd Europeans. It succeeded perfectly, the rebels who just before had been cheering, were driven out of their first position on the right of the road. I never gave them time to breathe, made two companies of the 3rd Europeans storm the rocks on the other side of the road, and supporting these troops with fresh ones, and always moving them forward, the pass was ours in three quarters of an hour. The great thing with these Indians is not to stay at long distance firing, but after they have been cannonaded, *to close with them, they cannot stand.*

The English advancing with a cheer, I also made a move with a troop of the 14th which disheartened them; I sent them whilst the Hyderabads were turning their left, to a rising ground in their rear to which I knew they would make. When they saw the 14th they broke. Our men the Infantry came up with them in the broken ground and caused them great loss. I had just cleared the pass when a report was made to me that the enemy were threatening and firing on my rear. I sent Cavalry to guard my rear, which was not further molested. The Sepoys all wore red jackets so that they looked exactly like the Hyderabad Infantry; we had also a few irregular infantry, who looked exactly like the rebels. This, I am sorry to say, saved the lives of a great many of the rebels, as our artillery in doubt stopped their fire. Several of the Sepoys who were killed wore medals for the battles in the Punjaub, one man had been Soubadar of the 31st reg[t], he had beautiful pistols and sword and was a sort of General of the rebels. When the man of the 3rd Europeans was going to shoot him he turned round and begged him to shoot him in the back of his head. One Sebastopol medal, belonging to a man of the 34[th][47] was found on a dead rebel. By forcing the pass of Mudinpore, I have taken the whole line of the enemy's defences in the rear and an extraordinary panic has seized them, giving up whole tracts of country without firing a shot; I should not be surprised if they did not defend the Fort of Tal Behut which is only 33 miles from Jhansi, & the strongest in this part of the world, and which as usual they say they will defend to the *last.*

Orr, whom I sent in pursuit, after forcing the pass, killed 6 only rebels of whom, I am happy to say, the Col of the 52nd was one; he clubbed his musket and tried to knock Orr off his horse, he killed him with his revolver. I had not much cavalry as I had sent part of it with Scudamore to make a feint against a strong pass to the West, whilst I made the real attack at Mudinpore, and I was also obliged to leave a good deal of cavalry with my rear guard. Fancy, what with *15 days supplies*, reserve ammunition, and *Indian* baggage[148] wh I have reduced as much as I can, without even seeing the Pass, the tail of my baggage was 10 miles off . . .

BL Add MSS 42812 ff. 38–41.3

84
Rose to Whitlock

Kumhari
[Holograph copy] 9 March 1858
No. 311 of 1858

As it is of the utmost importance that the Pontoons which I left at Saugor on my departure, for want of carriage, should join my force immediately in order to assist me in one or two difficult operations, I should be extremely obliged to you if you would have the goodness to forward them to me, together with the Nursingpore supplies of grain, and have the kindness to lend me the Bullocks necessary for their Transport. I will return the Bullocks by the first opportunity.

BL Add MSS 42812 f. 35

85
Field Force Orders

Banpur
[Holograph] 10 March 1858

3. One of the most important duties of the Quarter Master General's Department is to point out the proper road to the Troops in the Field. Confusion and delay occurred this morning – and it is not the first time – because the officers of the Quarter Master General's Department were entirely ignorant of the road to be marched and because the guides were not distributed as prescribed in Division Orders. It is superfluous to dilate on the

advantage given to the enemy if the Force had been attacked whilst changing its front in the dark; embarrassed as it was besides by being mixed with the line of baggage. It is impossible that officers can discover a road in the dark if they have not learnt it by daylight. The Major General Commanding with the view to prevent a recurrence of a neglect which is so unmilitary as it is dangerous directs that in future the Assistant Quarter Master General will make himself acquainted and take care that his subordinates make themselves acquainted with the road on the day previous to the Troops marching. The order is repeated that one guide is to be sent to the Quarter Guard of each corps and one to the tent of the Major General's A.D.C. on the eve of the march. Besides this two guides will be furnished to the leading files of the Advanced Guard.

❊ ❊ ❊

OIOC MSS Eur D1007

86

Rose to Elphinstone

Munjara

[Manuscript telegram]   11 March 1858

The capture of the pass of Mundenpoor and the total defeat of the rebels on the 3rd Instant by my force has produced results which are beyond my hopes. The rebels in their panic have abandoned firstly the Fort of Seraj with 4 guns and a rude manufactory for powder, guns and musketry shot, ordnance stores, carriage and tents; Secondly the town and Fort of Murrowra with a triple line of defences. Thirdly the Town and Fort of Multhonee.[149] Fourthly the pass of Goonah. Fifthly the pass and town of Hural and the Fort of Cornel Burh. Both these passes are most difficult and the rebels had fortified and barricaded them. Other results are our occupation of the independent district of Shahgurh which on account of the rebellion of the Rajah of Shahgurh was attached 2 days ago by Sir Robert Hamilton to the British Government, the

British flag in consequence was hoisted this morning on the Fort of Murrowra in the presence of the 2nd Brigade under a salute of 21 guns. Sir Robert Hamilton has received confirmation that Lalltirbadie one of the worst rebels whom the mutineers of the 52nd Regiment made their Colonel was amongst the killed at Mundispore. My communications are also now opened to the North with Tehree[150] and supplies for my force have just come in from that district. The dâk communications are also opened between this and Saugor.

OIOC MSS Eur F87, Box 9D, Letter Book 4

87
Birch to Whitlock

Allahabad

[Printed letter]   13 March 1858

From intelligence which has reached the Right Honourable the Governor General from Chirkaree, it cannot be doubted that the fort of that place has, by this time, fallen into the hands of the insurgents, who were laying siege to it, and who were already masters of the town, part of which was burnt.

Punnah also and Rewah are threatened.[151]

It is of urgent importance that support should be given to the local chiefs of Bundelcund as soon as possible, and as no Troops can be moved into the Bundelcund States from this side of the Jumna, the Governor General directs me to request that you will proceed at once, with the column under your command, in the direction of Punnah, Chirkaree or such other point as you may judge expedient, with the object of supporting the chiefs who may be threatened by the insurgents, and freeing them from the dangers to which they are now exposed.

You will use your discretion as to leaving a garrison at Dumoh, or elsewhere in the Saugor territory, but you are requested to bear in mind that the Governor General wishes the relief of the well-affected chiefs to be considered the paramount object for the present.

It is necessary that you should communicate your movements to Major General Sir H. Rose, in order that he may be able to shape his own course, so as to combine with yours in giving confidence and support to the chiefs.

OIOC MSS Eur F87, Box 9D, Letter Book 4

88
Rose to Stuart

Tal Behut

[Holograph copy]   14 March 1858

You cannot tell to what inconvenience you have put me and the Service by not giving me an account of your operations. I have several important operations on hand but in consequence of the entire ignorance in which you keep me as to your proceedings I can do *nothing*. When troops act together in combined operations, the first, and indisputable condition for their success is the knowledge of their respective operations. By your silence you prevent me carrying out one or two operations of vital importance for the *cause* we are fighting for. You ought not to have forgotten that your silence to the Officer in Command is most prejudicial to the great and just cause for which we are contributing.

PS I beg you not to delay the Camel Sowar with Irregular Cavalry but to send him back immediately; he will deliver your answer to another Camel Sowar, stationed with another party of Irregular Cavalry, half way between this place and Chanderee; by this means I hope to have your answer tonight.

BL Add MSS 42812 ff. 37–8

89
Rose to Mansfield

Tal Behut

[Holograph copy]   14 March 1858

I must have explained myself carelessly and incorrectly if I made the C in C and yourself think that Nana's movements in any direction caused me any alarm. I meant merely to speak of the unfavourable feeling which the approach of this wretch causes amongst the natives, with whom his name unquestionably exerts great influence. Lord Elphinstone and others, whose experience of India is as great as mine is small, were always of opinion that if he made his appearance in the Deccan or Southern Mahratta, a general uprising might ensue. As regarding myself, I wrote to Lord Elphinstone that he would skirt about the Doab like a beaten 'fox'.

I was very sorry not to be able to see your brother who gave me a very kind invitation. He is universally most highly spoken of, and by none more than Lord Elphinstone.

I wish that His Excellency would have the great kindness to allow me more staff; nothing would assist me more than a Chief of Staff. Of course a small one, for a small man like myself. But I feel convinced more than ever after experience that a chief of the staff is necessary for the quick and uniform despatch of business. I have only a common divisional staff, I have to make reports to yourself, to the Commander in Chief in Bombay, with three or more Politicals to collect and sift information about the enemy, correspondence about Supply and carriage, which unluckily is not very well organised in Bombay, the whole system being based on the country being in a pacific state. Then there are no plans of any of these Forts or positions and I do not like to undertake an operation unless I have reconnoitred the location myself. I am often fourteen or fifteen hours and more in the saddle on this sort of duty alone, so that I have not time frequently to write a private letter.

I hope under these peculiar circumstances that His Excellency will allow me an increase in staff.[152]

BL Add MSS 42812 ff. 48–9

90
Hamilton to Elphinstone

Tall Behut

[Manuscript telegram]   15 March 1858

❊ ❊ ❊

The mutineers and rebels under Balla Sahib brother to the Nana in great force are plundering in Bundlecund levying money from every one and demanding large sums from the Chiefs. The town of Churkaree has been burnt and the Rajah driven into the fort which he was still defending by the last account. Seven lacs of rupees had been wanted of the Chunapore Rajah. Sir Hugh Rose with the 2nd Brigade are at Tall Behut 36 miles from Jhansi. The 1st Brigade are attacking the Fort of Chandiree on the left bank of the Bitwa which is expected to be occupied immediately after which the two Brigades move on Jhansi. The force is very healthy and supplies are plentiful. The Tehree state has helped as well and so has Bijawar. The country in our rear is quite quiet the crops promise a good harvest. Johannes Jacob who was a Jemadar[153] at Bisseah and a Captain commanding 100 men in the Bhanpore Rajah's service has just given himself up with 4 followers and I have made him over to Sir Hugh Rose to be tried by Court Martial. All quiet at Indore and Malwa, the panic at Indore was without any foundation.

OIOC MSS Eur F87, Box 9D, Letter Book 4

91
Rose to Stuart

Tal Behut

[Holograph copy]   18 March 1858
Secret

I found the greatest good at Rathghur from placing the men with Enfield rifles in Rifle Pits, in advance of the attack in order to pick off the men on the Enemy's defences, and keep down their fire.

The rifle pits should be made at night and I should imagine from the nature of the ground, that there must be great facilities for making these rifle pits. They should be dug out of the earth in a semi-circular form and then a little parapet made of stones and earth, with loop holes for the men to put their rifles through. I have observed that our Enfields frighten the rebels as much as artillery.

If you think your force is not strong enough to take Chanderee it is much the best *for the Service* to tell me so at once, and I would reinforce you at once.

The mutineers have quarrelled with the Ranee of Jhansi, and she is in great alarm and drawing in her troops.

Sir R. Hamilton, at my request, has directed the 31st and 42nd B.N.T.,[154] now on their march to Goonah, to join you. You will find Capt Hare of great assistance.

BL Add MSS 42812 ff. 41–2

92
Captain A.B. Little[155] to Brigade Major, 1st Brigade, CIFF

[Printed copy]

Chandairee
17 March 1858

I do myself the honor to report for the information of the Brigadier Commanding 1st Brigade, C.I.F.F., that agreeably to his instruction I proceeded with my detachment as per margin* through the Kattee Ghattee[156] shortly after the Brigade had moved past my post. This morning I led my men as quietly as possible towards the point I had decided on attacking but had not reached the lower wall between the Round Bastion at the 'Corner' one opposite our mortar Battery when we were challenged by the Sentry of the Enemy on the Round Bastion and fire immediately opened from the guns and matchlocks. We however continued to

---

* 100 Rank and File H.M.'s 86th Regt. under command of Lt. Lewis
13 Bombay Sappers and Miners under Lt. Gordon Asst. Field Engineer
100 Rank and File 25 Regiment N.I. under Lieutenant Miles[157]

advance steadily and had just reached the wall when the signal for assault was fired. I saw to my joy that the wall was broken down and no impediment except very rugged and bushy ground was between us and the walls of the Fort itself, and hearing the cheers of the Columns assaulting at the breach, with a yell we charged and in a few minutes many of us had with each other's assistance and without the aid of ladders scaled the wall. The ladders were however thrown up and the remainder of my detachment all gained the Fort. The Round Bastion having been taken on our left we swept to our right and driving the Enemy before us carried with slight opposition the next Bastion. We here fell in with some of the Enemy (who were flying before our troops who had entered at the Breach), many of whom were killed. Seeing the next or Corner Bastion as I have above designated it, had not been taken by our men I could not resist the temptation of taking it also although exceeding the orders I had received in getting some men together with [?for] a rush. The object was soon gained. We then advanced towards the Palace (taking the gateway on our left) and were then joined by the whole assaulting Column etc.

The conduct of all under my command both Europeans and Natives was admirable and when all behaved so well [it] would be difficult to bring any one prominently to notice. I cannot however conclude my report without saying I consider Havildar Ramhaz Khan and Private Shaik Lall, Light Company 25th Regiment N.I. are deserving of much praise as by their aid I was in great measure guided to the point I was anxious to gain. These two men had on the night of the 15th Instant attended me on a reconnaissance in the same direction and did good service. I trust they will meet with some mark of approval for the good service done by them.

Our loss this morning I am sorry to say 1 Private 86th killed and 8 wounded.

FPP, Cons. No. 25, 10 September 1858; FSUP, III, pp. 278–80

93
Rose to Stuart

Sirasgaon[158]

[Holograph copy]

18 March 1858

I congratulate you most sincerely on your success, which will have the best results. Pray tell Major Keating how very much I am pleased with his gallant conduct.[159] Sir Robert Hamilton mentioned that he could, if you wish, send his son in law Lt Shakespeare to supply his place. Would you like this arrangement? My Ass^t Q^r Master Genl writes to you to send on to me as many of the 14th Lt Dragoons as you can spare. I intend to halt here tomorrow to await the arrival of Major Orr's Cavalry which I sent to reinforce you, as well as that of Captain Hare's for which I have sent, as my wish is to send on all the Cavalry from [indecipherable] my next halting place, on the road to Jansee, and surround the town, following myself the next day, and encamping at the position the most favourable for attacking the Fort. Pray therefore send me 70 of the 14th Dragoons if you can as I do not think that there is the slightest chance of your being attacked, an opinion in which Sir Robert Hamilton concurs. They are the greatest sneaks imaginable, and are out of their own country at Chanderee, they will not stop running for three or four days. If you could send Major Gall with the 14th I would feel much obliged. Of course you shall have him back and the 14th you send now, and those you lent to this Brigade at Mow.

Beside's Hare's detachment I had a troop patrolling 4 Coss along the road to the west in order to cut off the fugitives from Chanderee; they must have been right amongst some of them, about 60 who were seen by Sir Robert Hamilton's people. The Rajah of Banpore was present two days ago at Jhansi.

Except Cawnpore, there was no place where there was a more numerous and awful assassination of the English than at Jhansi, the horrid Ranee being at the head of the atrocities; the people assisted in hewing down the English officers, ladies & children, then dragged their *naked bodies* through the town and danced round them. I will therefore not let if possible a man escape, who was concerned in these wholesale [?butcheries].

BL Add MSS 42812, ff. 42–4

94
Court of Directors, East India Company, to Canning

London

[Holograph copy]   18 March 1858

Despatch No. 40

1. Our attention has been drawn to the following account which appeared in the newspapers of the manner in which 149 mutineers were executed by Sir H. Rose at Sehore

'When I last wrote, I mentioned that Sir H. Rose was marching upon Sehore, about the 7th of this month he reached the Station, and on the 9th called out the whole of the Contingent, and ordered the troops of all arms composing it to lay down their arms. After a little hesitation the order was obeyed, a large number of the mutineers, between 200 and 300 of them apparently, were then arrested and their trials were at once commenced. A few days later, no fewer than 149 were led out for execution at one time. The firing party was not more numerous than the Prisoners, consisting of only 150 men of the 3rd Bombay European Regiment, many of the shots failed, as may be supposed, to inflict instant death, and some even missed altogether, rendering necessary a further discharge and even, I believe, the sabres of the Dragoons, an unseemly spectacle.'

2. We have not yet received from you any report of this transaction.

3. You will probably have called for a full explanation of all the circumstances attending it, but if you should not have done so, such explanation should be called for on receipt of this letter.

BL Add MSS 42807 f. 30

95
Hamilton to Edmonstone

Jhansi

[Printed copy]

20 March 1858

I have the honor to acknowledge the receipt, at 1 P.M. this day, of your Despatch, N° 273, dated 13th March, and to state that I immediately communicated its contents to Major General Sir Hugh Rose.

To enable the Governor General to form a correct opinion on the position of this Brigade, it is necessary for me to enter into the following details:-

It, the Second Brigade, is today within ten miles of Jhansi. The whole of its cavalry under Brigadier Stuart[160] will have invested the fort and town before sunset, and Major Boileau, the Chief Engineer, will have made reconnaissance with a view to fix the site of our batteries on the arrival of the remainder of the Brigade before Jhansi early to-morrow morning. The garrison of Jhansi are aware of, and prepared for, our approach so that any cessation of operations would now be looked on as a retreat, the moral effect of which would be hazardous, if not actually fatal.

Moreover, the First Brigade has been detained at Chandeeree and could only move this morning to join this, which will take at least five long marches.

Their junction with this Brigade is essential to any forward movement, even supposing Sir Hugh Rose were now to refuse Jhansi and draw off to proceed to succour Punnah and the loyal chiefs in Bundelcund.

Again, it is important that our communications with Goonah and Saugor, from whence our reinforcements and our supplies must come, be secured and that nothing is left in our rear which would require to be watched.

If Sir Hugh Rose were now to turn off, he must pass almost within range of the guns of the fort to reach the Burwa Saugor road,[161] the ford of which must be taken for his force to cross that difficult and unbridged river, the Betwa; but this advance would entirely cut off his communications with his First Brigade and place Jhansi with its 15,000 Mutineers, town and Fort and 1,000 Bundeelas, not only in his rear, but between the two Brigades, and entirely cut off his communication with Goonah and Saugor, and consequently with his reinforcements and supplies.

Further, Chirkaree is, by the nearest route, eight marches but that place could not be reached in eight days by his Brigade with its large siege train; supposing it were to move to-morrow morning, probably not before the 31st of this month. It would be some days longer in reaching Punnah, while General Whitlock's force should reach Punnah in eight marches from Dumoh, or by the 24th or 25th; if they march from Punnah to Chatterpore it would be four marches more, and thence to Chirkaree is about 50 miles.

There is then every reason, and the hope, that Punnah and Rewa will both be relieved by Major General Whitlock's force before Sir Hugh Rose could arrive there, supposing he went at once and met with no opposition or delay.

Already has the pressure on Jhansi caused the Ranee to call in all her troops who were attacking Orcha and Mhow and it has also forced her to send and ask assistance from Tantia Topee, which, if complied with, must cramp his operations to some extent, and relieve, in some degrees, our loyal chiefs in that quarter, whom the advance of General Whitlock will effectively protect.

Under these circumstances now existing here, and the above statement of facts, I hope the Governor General will consider that it would not be politic to suspend operations before Jhansi, but rather to urge them on vigorously, until the First Brigade arrives from Chandeeree, when Sir Hugh Rose will be able to form a flying column which can move towards Begawar, Chutterpore and elsewhere, to succour the loyal states between Tehree and Punnah, by routes along which heavy artillery could not travel.

I may add that in the opinion of the vakeels in camp, the fall of Jhansi is likely to have a very great effect on the Rebels and Mutineers now infesting Bundelcund and the advance of Sir Hugh Rose's force, after its capture, will be the more effective, and greatly accelerate the rout and destruction of the Rebels.

In conclusion. I beg to state that Sir Hugh Rose desires me to express his entire concurrence in the views and reasonings above expressed, and his hope that they will be considered sufficient to allow of a slight delay in giving effect to His Lordship's wishes.

Forrest, IV, Appendix E, pp. lxxxiv–vi

96
Stuart to Assistant Adjutant-General, C.I.F.F.

Muszid Ghat[162]

[Printed copy]   21 March 1858

I have the honor to . . . report the proceedings of this Brigade in connection with the capture of the Fort of Chandairee.

2 – The 1st Brigade C.I.F.F., strength as per margin*, reached Koorasee on the left bank of the river [indecipherable] about 8 miles distant from the Fort of Chandairee on the 5th March and having crossed the river without opposition encamped there. In the course of that afternoon Major Gall Commanding Left Wing H.M.'s 14th Light Dragoons, accompanied by Captain Fenwick, Field Engineer,[163] and Captain Keatinge, Political Assistant, having proceeded on a reconnaissance was fired at by a picquet of the enemy at the Khooshee Ka Mahal, an old palace about a mile distant from the Fort of Chandairee. On the morning of the

* Left Wing H.M.14 L.D.	100	
3rd Reg[t] Cavalry, H.C.	183	
No. 6 F.B., R.A.	109	
No. 4 Light F.B.	40	
21 Co[y] R.E.	103	
2 Co[y] B.S. and M	50	
H.M.'s 86th Reg[t]	517	of these 318 joined with Hdq[r] on 16 March
De[t] 3rd Eur. Reg[t]	50	
25th Reg[t] N.I.	813	including 150 recruits
Total	1965	

6th March the Brigade marched and on arriving at the palace in question found that the picquet which occupied it the preceding day had fallen back upon a strong line of masonry defences which cover the Futtiabad outskirt of the town, and, having been reinforced held the same in strength, immediately attacked them, having previously detached 2 bodies of Infantry to turn both flanks of their works. The left flank attack, though made over most difficult ground, succeeded admirably and the enemy commenced to retreat. On moving up the main body of the Brigade to the Futtiabad Gate which was about the centre of the position I found that the enemy had all fled precipitately to the Fort. Accordingly I encamped the Brigade near to the gate in question, until a plan of operations against the Fort should be determined upon. In the afternoon of that day Captain Fenwick, in company with Captain Keatinge, P.A., made a further reconnaissance and their reports determined me on moving the Brigade the next morning near to the village of Ramnugger, possession of which they had already secured. On the morning of the 7th March the Brigade marched in two columns, dislodging the Kutty Ghutty outpost of the enemy, and clearing the whole approach to that part of the Fort against which the Field Engineer recommended that trenching operations should be commenced. The description of the Fort of Chandairee and the Field Engineer's Journal of the siege, herewith transmitted, will explain to the Major-General the difficulties we had to encounter, not the least of which was experienced in conveying the siege pieces to the Batteries. From the 8th to the 16th March siege operations were carried on, particulars of which will be found in the Journal already referred to. These operations extended over a longer period than was at first anticipated, but I beg to assure the Major-General that the delay in bringing matters to an issue was quite unavoidable. On the afternoon of the 16th March I received a favourable report of the breach from the Field Engineer and immediately ordered that the assault should take place at day-break the follg. morning, 17th March; and that the troops should attack in the order named in the margin. I also arranged that another attack on our left by escalade should be at the same time made by the troops marginally noted* under the command of Captain Little 25th Regiment N.I. at the re-entering angle of the Fort opposite to the Kutty Ghutty Pass. Captain Little I should mention had been in command of an outpost at this Pass from the time of our arrival before the Fort and had therefore good opportunities of studying the ground and making his arrangements. I also caused another diversion in our favour to be made by a small body of Cavalry under the command of Lieutenant Gowan, H.M.'s 14th L.D.[164] who moved out to the eastward of the Fort. I opened a brisk fire when the assault took place shortly after 5 A.M. on the 17th March. The troops having formed up near the Breaching Battery with steadiness and silence which no one could fail to appreciate, I gave the preconcerted signal for the assault viz. a salvo from all the siege pieces in position which had been carefully laid for the head of the breach and the enemy's bastions. The storming party commanded by Lieutenant Germe, H.M.'s 86th Regiment, and accompanied by Lieutenant Forbes, 25th Regiment N.I., Lieutenant Gossett, Ass[t] Field Engineer,[165] and Captain Keatinge, P.A., moved steadily to the front, received a volley at the foot of the trench and with a cheer only dashed gallantly up 'A'. They were warmly received by the enemy but resolutely driving all before them at the point of the bayonet they made good the assault, and their cheers soon told the

---

*   Advance party
    50 R. and F. H.M.'s 86th Reg[t] under an officer; 50 R. and F. 25th Reg[t] N.I. under an officer, the senior to command the whole.
    Column of Assault
    50 R. and F. 21 Co[y] RE under an officer, carrying ladders and various implements
    2 Co[y] B.S. and M.
    R. and F. H.M.'s 86th Reg[t] Column of Section R in front
    25th Reg[t] 25th N.I. Column of Section R in front
    Reserve
    50 R. and F. 21 Co[y] RE
    2 Co[y] B.S. and M.
    30 R. and F. H.M.'s 86th Reg[t] under an officer; 70 R. and F. 25th Reg[t] N.I. do. – the senior to command
    100 R. and F. H.M.'s 86th Reg[t] under Lieut Lewis
    100 R. and F. 25th Reg[t] N.I. under Lieut Miles
    13 R. and F. 2 Co[y] B.S. and M under Lieut Gordon RE

whole Brigade how their brave conduct had been rewarded. The Column of Assault quickly followed them and, moving steadily across the Fort, completely cleared that part of it, the enemy who fled most precipitately throwing themselves headlong from the walls in many instances. Line was then formed on the left with three Companies of H.M.'s 86th Regiment in skirmishing order. Their line being prolonged on the right flank by the skirmishers 25th Regiment N.I., also three Companies H.M.'s 86th Regiment as supports and the 25th Reg[t] as reserve, the whole Brigade swept down the plateau of the Fort, which is of some extent. On nearing the Palace where it was expected some stand would be made a gun opened on the line but the Grenadiers of H.M.'s 86th Regiment rushed to the front and instantly took the remainder. The enemy then retreated from the Fort in precipitate flight in the direction by which I had every reason to believe they would encounter Captain Abbott's Cavalry. The miscarriage of my letter however to Captain Abbott on the previous evening admitted of their escape by that road to my very great regret as the Major-General is aware. The small body of Cavalry at my disposal, and the difficult nature of the country round Chandairee for Cavalry, enabled me only to hold them in readiness to pursue as might be practicable. As, however, the enemy scattered in every direction, mostly by twos and threes into thick jungle and hilly ground, except in the direction by which I anticipated Captain Abbott would fall in with them, I had no opportunity of using my Cavalry in pursuit.

3rd – I am happy to be able to state that the left attack on the Fort of Chandairee under the Command of Captain Little, 25th Regiment N.I., supported by Lieutenant Lewis, H.M.'s 86th Regiment, Lieutenant Miles, 25th Regiment N.I. and Lieutenant Gordon, Ass[t] Field Engineer, was admirably carried out and I beg to forward Captain Little's report, by which the Major-General will be able to see how gallantly it was conducted and how well the troops concerned in it behaved.

FPP Cons. No. 25, 10 September 1858; FSUP, III, pp. 266–71

II

Jhansi to Kalpi, March to May 1858

Facing Rose was perhaps the most powerful fortress in Central India. It consisted of two elements, the city wall and the fort. The city wall had a circumference of 4½ miles; it was 16 feet thick in places and ranged from 12 to 30 feet high; round the walls at intervals there was a total of 12 massive bastions containing artillery [106]. Abutting, or perhaps more accurately imbedded in, the wall on its western side was the fort, standing on a rocky hill with precipitous sides and with equally massive walls. The most prominent feature on the south side of the city wall was a large bastion on a mound.[1] Unlike many fortresses in Central India, Jhansi reared up from a relatively bare plain, on which, to the south of the city, stood the remains of the old European cantonment. The garrison amounted to some 11,000 men, of whom some 1,500 were mutineers from Bengal regular regiments and the remainder *vilayatis*, local levies and the Rani's state troops who had recently defended Jhansi against attacks from Orcha and Datia. The garrison appears to have been commanded by the Rani in person who resided in a palace inside the city, although frequently observed on the battlements.[2] A large relieving army from Kalpi, under Tantia Topi, was at Chirkari, 80 miles to the east [104].

Rose's first action was to set up a ring of seven 'flying camps' round the city, each garrisoned by cavalry and horse artillery, to prevent fugitives escaping and to warn of enemy forces approaching.[3] His next action was to conduct an exhaustive reconnaissance since he possessed no plan of the position [99]. The main camps were then established south of the city behind

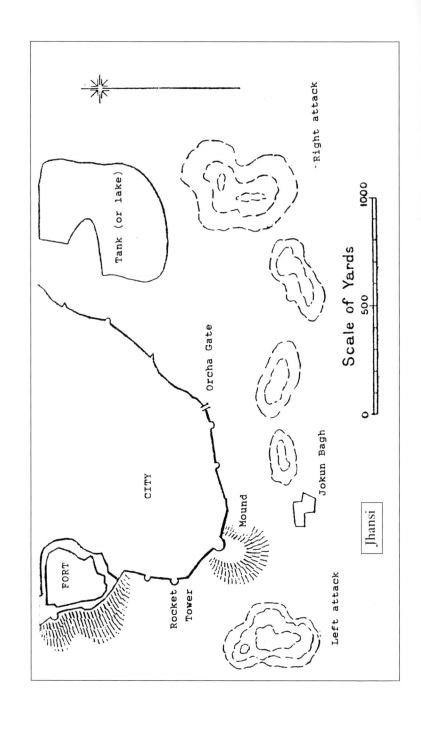

Jhansi

two hills, a mile and a half apart, which offered positions for the breaching batteries. From his reconnaissance, Rose had concluded that the fort itself could not be attacked successfully because there were no suitable battery positions. He proposed therefore to breach the city wall near the Mound Bastion, the most powerful of the city defences, and assault the city through the breach and by escalade at the Orcha Gate, further east [111]. With the city in his hands, he could then attack the fort from inside the city.

The Right Attack battery opened fire on the walls and the rear of the Mound Bastion on 23 March; the breaching battery (Left Attack) on 26 March.[4] Despite heavy rebel fire, rapid progress was made and by the 30th Rose was ready to assault. That afternoon, he learned that Tantia Topi, with 20,000 men and 28 guns, was approaching the east bank of the Betwa river, six miles south-east of Jhansi. He abstracted some 1,500 men and 19 guns from the besieging force, and marched to meet Tantia the next evening [107]. To keep the garrison's attention fixed on the siege and prevent a sortie to assist Tantia's army, Major Gall was to carry out a feint attack on the north wall of the city [108, 119].

Rose planned to lure Tantia across the river and force him to fight with his back to it. By a feigned retreat, he persuaded Tantia to move his first line across the river on the evening of the 31st. That night Rose learned that part of Tantia's force was crossing the river further north to take him in flank and cut him off from the city.[5] He was forced to split his force again, despatching Stuart with 900 men to counter this new threat. At daybreak on 1 April, Rose faced Tantia's main body with four troops of cavalry, 400 native infantry, three heavy guns, four horse artillery guns and some field guns. In the action that followed, two troops of Light Dragoons charged Tantia's right wing and a third troop, together with a troop of the Hyderabad Contingent Cavalry, led by Rose himself, charged the left wing. Tantia's force disintegrated and was pursued across the river for two miles, losing in all 1,500 killed and 18 guns; Stuart's force completed the rout [109, 116, 118]. Rose lost 19 killed and 66 wounded.[6]

The troops were back at Jhansi the same evening and after a day's rest Jhansi was assaulted at dawn on 3 April [117, 118]. That evening Rose had half the city in his hands and by the close of the next day he had the whole city and the fort in his hands, the fort having been abandoned without a fight. The Rani of Jhansi escaped on horseback carrying her adopted son, narrowly escaping capture [130] but eventually reaching Kalpi.[7] In scenes reminiscent of Badajoz and Ciudad Rodrigo, the city was sacked and plundered; the rebel loss was put at 5,000, of whom many were undoubtedly civilians [114].

Rose was detained at Jhansi for three weeks, primarily by the threat from rebels evicted from Kotah to the west.[8] Despite the need to move on Kalpi as quickly as possible, while the rebels were disorganised, he could not move with such a potential threat in his rear [121, 123, 124, 127, 129]. He moved out of Jhansi with the 1st Brigade on 26 April; the 2nd Brigade followed a day later. Left behind in Jhansi was a garrison of some 800 men under Lieutenant-Colonel Liddell, with the sick and wounded. Effectively, the Force was now down to about 4,500 men but *en route* to Kalpi it was reinforced by the Headquarters Wing of HM 71st Highlanders, bringing the Force up to about 5,000.

The Kalpi rebels, temporarily disorganised by the defeat on the Betwa, had been revived by the arrival of the remainder of the Nawab of Banda's troops after their defeat by Whitlock. At Kunch, 47 miles from Kalpi, the rebels again gave battle behind the defences of the town. On 7 May, in intense heat [136], Rose, with the 1st Brigade, moved round the north of the town, threatening the rebel retreat, while the 2nd Brigade and a detachment under the ubiquitous Major Orr, attacked the western side of the town [139, 140]. The rebels, under Tantia Topi, were dislodged but made a fighting retreat to Kalpi, screened by a rearguard of sepoys whose self-sacrifice and discipline greatly impressed their enemies [138].

Rose did not have enough men to subdue the countryside but he seized every opportunity, as at Lohari [132, 138], to break up hostile combinations within striking distance of his route. It is clear, however, that his troops, worn down by constant campaigning in hostile conditions of heat and dust, and with tenuous logistics, were nearing the end of their capacity [144, 179].

The advanced guard of the 1st Brigade reached the Jumna at Golaoli, 4½ miles downstream from Kalpi, on 15 May [141]. Next day the 2nd Brigade, with the enormous baggage train, took up position on the left flank facing Kalpi, having endured a series of attacks and lost a good deal of baggage [141, 145].

97
Shakespear – diary

[Typed copy]

21 March [1858] Jhansi. When we started in the morning the General said he would have the Camp pitched when we returned so there had been the Europeans in the sun all day long, and when it was nearly dark the Camp had to be marked out and pitched. He certainly has little regard for his men. The Camels and carts were standing laden the whole day too. I had been sixteen hours in the saddle, none of us had anything to eat the whole time, only plenty of water.

OIOC MSS Eur D706/2, f. 216

98
Field Force Orders

[Holograph]

Jhansi
23 March 1858

9. According to the Rules for Sieges, the construction of the Batteries for the Right Attack against Jhansi was effected during the night, the object being to conceal its construction from the enemy, and thereby prevent casualties, and to open an unexpected fire on the rear of the enemy's defences. This object was defeated by the greater part of the officers and men covering and constructing the Batteries (except Lieutenant Goodfellow's detachment) making themselves quite conspicuous as the Major Genl himself saw when he arrived at the Battery. The Major Genl

was also surprised to see another unmistakeable indication of a new Battery which would leave no doubt in the mind of the Enemy that a Battery had been constructed against them. An open embrasure and 8 inch Howitzer's muzzle in it – the gun was not even turned away to prevent it being injured by the enemy's fire. The Major Genl was obliged to order and superintend himself the construction of a screen for the embrasure.

✳ ✳ ✳

OIOC MSS Eur D1007

99
Bonus to his parents

Jhansi

[Typewritten copy]   23 March 1858

I began this letter thinking we should have no fighting here but now I think otherwise. We have our friends here in some force I imagine. We left the Betwa on the 19th at 11 p.m. just when we ought to have been going to bed. We did not get the order for the march till 8 p.m. I at once tumbled into bed and got some sleep. We marched all night, and arrived at our camping ground at 9 a.m. I was having some breakfast and hoping for a quiet day when an order came 'Be ready to start for Jhansi at a moment's notice.' Between 12 and 1, we started, our detachment consisting of 1,900 Cavalry[1] and 8 guns, after a very hot and dusty march we arrived before Jhansi a little before 5 o'clock, a strong looking place. The detachment was divided into four parties, these were posted at intervals round the town in order to prevent egress or ingress.

When matters were all in order we lay down on the ground, our swords and pistols beside us, our horses ready, for we fully expected to be attacked during the night. The enemy however foolishly left us alone. There are 10,000 to 11,000 of them, and a night attack might have done much harm. We slept as well as we could but loose horses and a bitterly cold wind made the sleep rather ragged.

121

At sunrise Sir Hugh arrived with the rest of the force, and I was summoned to go with him on a reconnaissance round the town. Pleasant was it not? A 20 mile ride before me, no food till evening, my last meal having been breakfast the day before. We set off and rode all day; it was frightfully hot, and we did not come across a single tree. Nearing the camp, we took a short cut which brought us within range of the fort guns. The enemy were on the watch and opened on us with two guns, they did no damage though the shot skipped through our party, we picked up two balls, one about 3lbs, the other about 10lbs. I slept that night, though it was a case of hard ground, bed not having turned up. I was so tired that I could not eat.

Next (yesterday) morning, I was awakened by a man who had a paper in his hand, the sight made me groan, I knew what it was before I read it, an order from Sir Hugh to accompany him on another reconnaissance at once. I was as quick as I could but I was obliged to get some food and Sir Hugh was off before I reached his tent. However I soon overtook him and was very much relieved when he ordered Prendergast (another Ass. Fld. Eng.) and me to make a sketch and plan of the fort and to go our own way to work. The first thing we did was to go to the nearest Picquet and get a good breakfast. Then we set to work. The enemy kept an eye on us for when we sheltered for a bit under a tamarind tree,[2] a tree which gives a good shade, they sent a round shot through the tree just above our heads; we moved on. Before evening, we sent in our sketch plan, as good as we could make it in the time. The result was that two sites were determined on for batteries, and at 8 p.m. the Sappers set to work and I went to bed. This morning I rode down to the batteries to see what had been done during the night. I found two mortars and one 8 inch howitzer in position. The enemy was making good practice from the town wall, a stone place where two roads cross; one had to gallop for about fifty yards as they had a gun laid on the spot. As yet they have done us no harm. We are reserving our fire until we can open with a good number of guns at once . . . There was picked up a long tress of woman's hair, clotted with blood.[3] You will remember the Jhansi mutiny when not a soul escaped, these devils shall remember it too . . .

OIOC IOR neg. 4395

100
Rose to Liddell

Jhansi
[Holograph copy]   24 March 1858

I have received information that there is an island in the lake to your left which ceases to be an island at the present season. The Garrison consequently could pass from the town across the lake into the wood and take the right attack in flank.[4]

Under these circumstances, I wish that you would take a small party of your Reg^t. and examine thoroughly the Wood, I mean the Wood on *your* side of the Lake on your *right flank*, in which are two Hindoo temples with spires and cupolas. Would it be better to occupy these two temples or burn the wood?

I think also that a deep Trench should be cut across the roads leading into the Fort, near the attack to prevent the advance of cavalry or guns, should they make a sortie. Some of the Orcha troops might be useful for holding points between Captain Hare's and your position. But they should have strict orders *not* to leave the Buildings in which they are stationed.

Would you like the reserve brought closer to you during the night?

BL Add MSS 42812 ff. 46–7

101
Rose to Elphinstone

Jhansi
[Manuscript telegram]   24 March 1858

On the 20th instant my cavalry invested as much as possible the Fort and Town of Jhansi. The next day the rest of my force arrived here. The rebels have fortified the walls of the town and shutting themselves up in the town and Fort, have not defended the advanced position of Jhansi. The Ranee has left her palace in the town and has gone into the Fort which fired the first. The rebel garrison numbers about 1,500 sepoys of whom 400 or 500 are cavalry, and 10,000 Bundelas and from 30 to 40 cannon. Their position is strong but

I have occupied 2 strong positions one as a Breaching, the other a flanking one. I have been delayed by the want of a plan at [?of] Jhansi and consequently have been obliged to make long and repeated reconnaissances. I opened a flanking fire vertical and horizontal[5] yesterday and hope to open a Breaching fire tomorrow or, at latest, the next day. My first Brigade joined me yesterday.

OIOC MSS Eur F87, Box 9D, Letter Book 4

102
Rose to Turnbull

Jhansi
[Holograph copy]   25 March 1858

. . . no breaching battery will be safe till the Mound be ours. I should wish two 18^{pdrs} to be placed in position *tonight* against it; they would protect the construction of our front attack. We are strong in Artillery and weak in Infantry; and the most military mode of taking the work is to knock it down.

There is probably all sorts of cover near the Mound for the Rebels. Our front fire against the Mound could be assisted by the cross fire from the *right* attack. The action of the fire of the right attack however good is not strong enough & it is too far off to clear the enemy out of the work.

PS I enclose you a note from Major Orr. I think that he could do a good deal of good by firing all night.

BL Add MSS 42812 f. 47

103
Rose to Adjutant-General, Bombay

Jhansi
[Printed]   26 March 1858

❊   ❊   ❊

My Siege Artillery was ready in a few days, on the 18th Instant. But want of supplies, caused by the devastation of the Saugor and neighbouring Districts by the Rebels, and other circumstances, did not allow me to leave Saugor till the 27th Instant.

This delay did away, very much, with the good effects of the speedy fall of Garrakota. The Rebels, not seeing any further operations or movements to the front against them, regained courage and occupied again, in force, the strong positions in the Shaghur and adjoining Districts, such as the forts of Serai and Marowra, and the difficult passes in the mountainous ridges which separate the Shaghur and Saugor Districts.

These passes are three in number. The pass of Narut and the Fort of Carnelgurh near Malthone, of Mudinpore, and of Dhamooney.[6]

My object was to reach Jhansie, against which I was ordered to move as quickly as I could; but on my road there, I wished to take up my 1st Brigade, which I had marched from Mhow and Indore to Goonah, for the purpose, as previously stated, of clearing and opening the Grand Trunk Road from Bombay to Agra, in obedience to my instructions.

I anticipated resistance to my advance to Jhansie at the passes, the forts of Serai, Murowra, and Thal-Behut, at which latter place, it was said, the Rajah of Banpore intended to make his last stand.

I determined to force these obstacles to the forward movement of my Force, and to the union of my 1st and 2nd Brigades; and accordingly gave orders to Brigadier Stuart, commanding my 1st Brigade, to move from Goonah Westwards and take Chundeyree, whilst I forced my way Northwards and crossing the Betwa, march with both Brigades against Jhansie.

An operation against the passes was more than usually difficult, on account of the great length of my line of march. For knowing the danger of a want of ammunition, I took with me abundant reserves of it, having besides to take care of a convoy of fifteen days' supplies for my Force and its Camp-Followers.

The pass of Narut was by far the most difficult, and the Enemy having taken it into their head that I must pass through it, had increased its natural difficulties, by barricading the road with abatis, and parapets made of large boulders of rock, 15 feet thick; all passage by the sides of the road being made impracticable by the almost precipitous hills, covered with jungle, which came down to the edge of the road. The Rajah of Banpore, who is both enterprizing and courageous, defended this pass with 8 or 10,000 men.

The next most difficult pass was Dhamooney; very little was known about the third, Mudinpore, except that in the Ordnance Map it was described as 'good for Guns'.

Under these circumstances, I requested Major Orr to reconnoitre these passes, whilst I was detained at Saugor for supplies.

Supplies for my Force having come into Saugor, I marched from that place on the 27th Instant to Rijwass,[7] a central point from which I could move against any one of these passes. Major Orr's Force joined me at Rijwass; with his usual intelligence, he had collected information which made me select the pass of Mudinpore for my point of attack.

In order to deceive the Enemy as to my intentions, and prevent the Rajah of Banpore from coming from the pass of Narut to the assistance of the Rajah of Sharghur, who defended Mundinpore, I made a serious feint against Narut by sending Major Scudamore, Commanding H.M.'s 14th Light Dragoons, with the Force stated in the margin*, with their tents and baggage, to the Fort and Town of Malthone, just above the pass of Narut, whilst I made the real attack on the pass of Mudinpore. Having taken the ruined little Fort of Barodia, and left a small Garrison in it, I marched on the 3rd Instant, against the pass of Mudinpore, with the Force

---

*   Major Scudamore's Force
    2 Troops HM's 14th Light Dragoons
    1 Troop 3rd Light Cavalry
    100 Irregular Cavalry
    one 24-Pounder Howitzer
    3 Bhopal 9-Pounders
    24th Regiment Bombay Native Infantry.

stated in the margin*. As the Column approached the pass, the Enemy's skirmishers fired on the Advanced Guard from a ridge of hills on our right, near the village of Noonee. I sent up a party of the Salt Customs under Mr Bartle,[8] who advancing, drove them back.

At about 800 yards from the entrance of the pass, we saw the Enemy in force on the hills, on the left of the pass. Major Orr made some good practice at them with round shot and spherical case.

The pass was formed by a sudden descent of the road into a deep glen, thickly wooded. To the right, further on, the road ran along the side of a lake. The left of the road was lined by rocky and precipitous hills.

The ardour of an excellent Officer[9] induced him, at this time, to make an incautious movement with his Guns to his right front, with the view to pour an enfilading fire into the Enemy. But he had not taken into consideration that this movement brought him

---

*   Sir Hugh Rose's Force Advanced Guard
    500 Hyderabad Cavalry
    200 Hyderabad Infantry
    4 Guns Artillery
    1 Company 3rd Bombay Europeans Centre
    1 Troop HM's 14th Light Dragoons
    Sappers and Miners
    4 Guns Horse Artillery
    Right Wing 3rd Bombay Europeans
    Three 9-Pr Guns, Captain Lightfoot
    Two 5½-Inch Mortars
    One 8-Inch Mortar
    One 8-Inch Howitzer
    Left Wing 3rd Bombay Europeans
    Siege Train
    3rd Bombay Light Cavalry
    Baggage and Convoy Rear Guard
    125 Hyderabad Infantry
    1 Howitzer and 1 Gun Horse Artillery
    1 Troop HM's 14th Light Dragoons
    50 Hyderabad Cavalry

to within fifty or sixty yards of the edge of the glen, in which lay concealed some hundred Sepoys, who, before he could unlimber, opened a very heavy fire on his guns, which he was unable to depress on them. The Sepoys fortunately fired too quick and too high, and the Officer retired his Guns out of the range of their musketry, with only a few casualties. The Sepoys hailed this little reverse with shouts. But their success had only brought on their more rapid defeat. For knowing now their exact position, and seeing the necessity of showing them that a calm retreat was only the prelude to a rapid offensive, I advanced 100 of the Hyderabad Contingent Infantry under Captain Sinclare,[10] at double time, and made them charge up the glen, bring their right shoulders forward, and sweep it down the road, following this up by a movement of a Company of the 3rd Europeans, against the front of the Sepoys, and of the Salt Customs, from the extreme right, against their rear. To still further discomfort them, I sent a Troop of Her Majesty's 14th Light Dragoons to a knoll, quite in rear of the glen, and commanding a view of the lake, and the other end of the pass. The Rebels were driven with loss from the glen, and, crossing the road, ascended the hill on its left, for the purpose of joining the large body of Rebels who occupied the hills divided by ravines on the left of the road.

The glen and hills which protected the pass having been taken, I sent Captain Abbott, with the 4th Hyderabad Cavalry to clear the pass and drive in the Enemy's front; this he did effectually.

The Enemy, repulsed in flank and front, retired to the village of Mudinpore, in rear of the end of the Lake. The village was fortified by a formidable work, in the shape of a bund of great thickness of earth and solid masonry, which dammed up the Lake. The Enemy had placed the few Guns they had in rear of the bund, and had been firing with them on the 3rd Europeans on the hill.

The pass having been gained, I sent directions to Brigadier Stewart, whom I had halted in rear of the pass, with the reserve and Siege Train to advance through it, and occupy the head of the

Lake. As soon as they arrived, I opened with the 8-inch Howitzer and the 9-pounders in advance of it, a fire on the Rebel Guns.

A few rounds drove the Enemy from their position in rear of the bund, and they retired from Mudinpore, through the jungle, towards the fort of Serai. I directed Major Orr to pursue, with the remainder of the Hyderabad Cavalry.

The results of the success at Mudinpore were as numerous as they were favourable. My Force had got in rear of the passes, and the Enemy's line of defences, of which they thought so much. The pass of Narut, considered by them to be impregnable was turned.

Mudinpore, it is true, was the weakest of the passes; but on the other hand, it had been defended by the sepoys of the 52nd and other Regiments, and by 7,000 picked Bundeelas. The Sepoys and the Bundeelas quarrelled, the former declaring that the latter had run away, and left them to fight at the pass; general mistrust and a panic ensued in the rebel Camp. . . . In fact, the whole country between Saugor and Jhansie, to the east of the River Betwa, which, since the outbreak of the rebellion, had been in the hands of the Insurgents, was now, with the exception of Thal-Behut, restored to the Government.

MDP GO 110 of 1858; Forrest, IV, pp. 20–8

104
Abstract of Intelligence

[Printed copy]

26th March [1858] On the 25th Tantia Topey and other mutineers intended to march from Jeitpore[11] and to halt at Chirwaree; from this place they propose to go to Jhansi via Mhow. The Tantia has under him about 25,000 men, among these are about 2,000 mutinous sepoys. The rest of the force is composed of the followers of the Chiefs of Shahgurh and Banpore, of Deisput, Adil Mahomed Khan and the Chief of Nurwar.[12] They have 4 English guns, one of these is 18-pounder. They have other guns, 18 in number which they took from Chirkharee, exclusive of the 5 guns brought in by the Chief of Banpore. The total number of guns, large and small, is 27.[13] At Calpee there are about 2,000 mutinous sepoys with 1,000 matchlockmen and 4 guns, one of these is an 18-pounder. Row Sahib, Nana's brother, had gone from Calpee to Jeitpoor to see Tantia. 1,000 sowars escorted him. He went back to Calpee by the same route. The Chiefs of Shahgurh, Banpore, Nurwar and Adil Mahomed are with Tantia. These Chiefs have little ammunition but Tantia and the sepoys at Calpee have an abundance.

27th March To-day Tantia with his force halted at Mhow.[14] There seems to be a difference of opinion as to their future movements. The mutinous sepoys make out plans; some say they should attack Tehree now because there is little force now at that place, and their move will prevent reinforcements coming to the British from Saugor. Others advise to relieve Jhansi. It appears they may form two Divisions, one might go to Tehree, and the other to Jhansi. Out of the 27,000 men that compose this mutinous force only the sepoys might offer resistance to the British force. The rest are not able to cope with the English . . .

FSC, No 127, 28 May 1858; FSUP, III, pp. 305–6

105
Rose to Turnbull

Jhansi

[Holograph copy]   27 March 1858

I think that yourself and Major Boileau will agree with me that the Battery on the S.E.Wall of the city (where the 8 inch Howitzer upset the gun) where the rebels are now placing a gun to enfilade our left attack and the mound, should be considered as one of the defences to be destroyed, and that artillery should be directed on it. Shall I beg Major Orr to destroy it from the height near the Orcha road? Its destruction will very much facilitate the capture of the mound.

BL Add MSS 42812 f. 50

106
Field Force Orders

Jhansi

[Holograph]   29 March 1858

❊ ❊ ❊

5. In order to save the confusion which results from the Enemies' defences, which are attacked by the Artillery, bearing no designations, the following names have been given to them, and are published for general information and guidance; 1. The Garden Battery 2. The West Tower Battery 3. The White Tower Battery 4. Black Tower Battery 5. Tree Battery 6. Two Tower Battery 7. The Western Tower 8. The Letchmen Gate Battery 9. Whistling Dick Battery[15] 10. Wheel Battery 11. Syer Gate Battery 12. The Mound Battery.

❊ ❊ ❊

OIOC MSS Eur D1007

107
Field Force Orders

Jhansi

[Holograph]   30 March 1858

❊ ❊ ❊

6. The 2nd Brigade with the exception of the men in the Batteries and the Cavalry at the outposts will march tonight with one day's

provisions and without camp equipage, reinforced by the following troops from the 1st Brigade

    30 Dragoons
    100 Hyderabad Cavalry
    200 86th Regiment
    500 25th Regiment N.I.
    50 Royal Engineers and Captain Woolcombe's 4 Field Battery.

And from the 2nd Brigade by Captain Need's[16] Troop of Dragoons from outpost duty and from Major Orr's forces by the following troops in camp and outpost duty

    50 Hyderabad Cavalry
    100 ditto from Captain Abbott under a European officer
    50 from Captain Murray under -do-
    450 Hyderabad Infantry

OIOC MSS Eur D1007

108
Rose to Gall

Jhansi

[Holograph copy]

31 March 1858

Major Boileau has the goodness to let you have an Engineer officer, Lt Bonus, to assist you in reconnoitring a good spot for a feigned attack, or in any other way which you may wish.

I send you also 30 riflemen of the 3rd Europeans, as you wished to have them and should you after your reconnaissance think that more men would be useful I shall be very happy to send you them, if your plan holds out a fair prospect of success.

I would have attended to your wishes earlier but was obliged to go out and endeavour to engage the Peishwa's Army but he would not shew.

BL Add MSS 42812 f. 50

109
Rose to Elphinstone

Jhansi

[Manuscript telegram]   1 April 1858

This morning at day break the force under my orders fought a general action with the so-called Peishwa's Army and by the blessing of God gained a complete victory over it. The rebels are stated to have numbered from 20,000 to 25,000 men, they were under Tantia Topie, Nana Sahib's relation,[17] and their object was to relieve Jhansi. I did not discontinue the Siege nor investment of Jhansi. Consequently the force with which I fought was extremely weak. The rebels amongst whom was the Grenadier Regiment and another regiment of the Gwalior Contingent fought, except the cavalry, desperately but I turned their left flank with artillery and Cavalry and after making two stands they broke and fled defending themselves individually to the last. I pursued them to the river Betwa taking all their guns 18 in number, one an English 18 pounder of the Gwalior Contingent drawn by two elephants. An 8 inch Mortar and quantities of ammunition including shells and 10 pounder shot, Ordnance Park and two more elephants and two Standards were also taken. The enemy tried to stop our pursuit by setting the jungle on fire but nothing could check the Ardour of the Artillery and Cavalry who galloped in pursuit across the country in flames. I cannot calculate the enemy's loss in killed but it must be very great as the Country is strewn with bodies chiefly those of sepoys. As I shall now be free from the attacks of a numerous attacking army, I hope to conclude speedily the siege of Jhansi.

OIOC MSS Eur F87, Box 9D, Letter Book 4

110
Kalpi garrison orders

Kalpi

[Holograph]   1 April 1858

(Translation   [15 Shaban 1274]

Parole Mooltan

The troops that have returned with Sreemunth Rao Saheb should do duty as usual. A Committee should be held and all the unserviceable horses cast out from the Cavalry Corps. In future no recruits should be enlisted unless they bring their own Arms. Where any recruits are enlisted their names should be written down in the Brigade Office and also in the Sircar's Office. Any one wishing to join his Regiment from the troops that are doing duty as Maharaja Saheb's body guard should make his application within two days thro his Officer and any one applying after the expiration of that time his request will not be granted. Today one gun from the Fort with some ammunition will be sent to Etawah and an escort of one Company of the Bengal Regiment and fifty matchlock men under the command of Raja Boopsing.

OIOC Home Miscellany 727a ff. 39–40

111
Field Force Orders

Jhansi

[Holograph]   2 April 1858

❊ ❊ ❊

Assault of the Exterior Defences of the Town of Jhansi on the 3rd April 1858

The assault will be made by 2 columns from the right and left attacks at daybreak tomorrow, the first or right under Lieutenant Colonel Liddell, the second or left under Colonel Lowth.

2. Each attack will be made at two different points.

3. The first point of the right attack will be the wall close to, and to the right and left of the Saugor small gate opposite the right of the right attack.

4. The column for this attack will be formed in the Kapoo ka tope.[18]

5. The second point of attack of the right attack will be made on the wall close to, and to the right of the Orcha Gate and on the large and open embrasures of a Battery close to it.

6. The column for this attack will assemble in the garden in front of 8 inch Mortar Battery, and in rear of the Temple on the opposite side of the road.

7. The first point of the left attack will be the breach at the Mound.

8. The second point of the left attack will be the Rocket Tower and the low curtain immediately to the right of it.

9. Each storming party will consist of 150 men and a support of 200 men in the 2nd Brigade and 125 men in the 1st Brigade.

10. The supports will follow the assaulting columns immediately.

11. Each column of attack (that is the assaulting columns and its supports) will have a Reserve.

12. The Reserves will consist of 200 men from the 2nd Brigade and 250 men from the 1st Brigade. Each reserve to be under the command of its respective Brigadier.

13. The Reserve of the right attack will be stationed at the Temple Kapoo ka and out of sight.

14. The Reserve of the left attack will be in the valley in rear of the Batteries.

❊ ❊ ❊

20. Covering parties will cover the advance of the assaulting parties.

21. Those for the right attack will be in the adjacent Temple Garden as close as possible to the walls.

22. Those for the left attack in such ground as may appear best to the officer commanding the assault column.

23. The right or first assaulting column of the right attack will at once seize the Battery called 'Whistling Dick'.

24. The 2nd assaulting column of the right attack will seize the Battery of which the large and open embrasures have been mentioned, as well as the Wheel Battery or Tower.

25. The first assaulting column of the left attack will enter the Breach and seize the Mound and the houses in front of it which cover the rear of the ridge towards the Fort.

26. The second assaulting column of the left attack will seize the Rocket Tower.

27. Generally speaking, each officer commanding a column will seize any favourable ground in the Town which may be in his front.

❊ ❊ ❊

30. The above are the real points of attack. In order to mislead the Enemy as to these real points of attack, Major Gall will make near his position, a feigned attack on the north of the Town by opening one hour before break of day, a cannonade on it, and manoeuvring 200 Goonds[19] and forty men of the 3rd Regiment Hyderabad Cavalry as he deems best calculated to deceive the enemy.

31. The signal of attack will be three shots fired in succession from the 18 Pounder in the Breaching Battery.

32. Being in entire ignorance of the inside of the Town, the Major General cannot give any precise opinions as to the forward movements of the columns after they have seized the Batteries on the walls of the Town, and he will therefore merely observe that the Ranee's Palace in the Town is visibly a position of the highest importance and that it would be highly advantageous if one, and still better, if both, Columns of Attack could take possession of it, and concentrate their forces there.

33. The following troops will comprise the attack

Right Attack
2nd Brigade
Two storming parties from 3rd Europeans Regiment
Each 100 – Total 200
Two storming parties from Hyderabad Infantry
Each 50 - Total 100

Two support parties to above from 3rd European Regiment
    Each 50 - Total 100
Hyderabad Infantry
    Each 50 - Total 100

Reserve

3rd European Regiment – 100
Hyderabad Infantry – 100

Troops remaining in camp from 2nd Brigade
    14th Dragoons
    Hyderabad Cavalry 50
    24th Regiment N.I. 307

Left Attack
1st Brigade

Two storming parties H.M. 86th Regiment
    Each 100 – Total 200
Two -do- 25th Regiment N.I.
    Each 50 – total 100

Supports to above
86th Regiment
    Each 75 – Total 150
25th Regiment N.I.
    Each 50 – Total 100

- Reserve -

86th Regiment 150
25th Regiment N.I. 100

Troops remaining in Camp from the 1st Brigade
    25th Regiment N.I. 30
    14th Dragoons – 40
    Hyderabad Cavalry 125.

OIOC MSS Eur D1007

112
Kalpi garrison orders

Jhansi

[Holograph translation]

3 April 1858
(18 Shaban 1274)

Parole Madhogurh

All the troops should hold themselves in readiness that when ordered to any place may march off without delay. The whole of the troops here should be divided into four divisions, one to remain in the fort, the second to be stationed about 1½ miles from Calpee on the Oorai & Jaloan roads, the third on the Banda & Humeerpore [roads][20] and the fourth on the skirts of the town for the assistance of the three above mentioned divisions. It is intimated to all the Commanding Officers to inform the Sircar thro their Pay Hawildars if all the troops have enough of ammunition. The sepoys that have returned from Jhansi state that the troops there have been defeated but no intelligence to that effect has been received from the Sircar.[21] Gobinpershaud sepoy of the 4th Company & Bermodhsing of the Light Company 3rd Regiment have represented that they & many others are ready & willing to go and attack the Kafirs (Infidels) any where. At this the Sircar was extremely pleased and ordered their names to be written down in his office.

OIOC Home Miscellany 727a, f. 40

113
Kalpi garrison orders

Kalpi

[Holograph copy]
(Translation)
Parole Allahabad

4 April 1858
[19 Shaban 1274]

Last night intelligence was received from Tantia Topee that he was encamped at Bhandhore[22] with 4,000 men and the Soobadar of Koonch and the Soobadar who was in charge of the

Commissariat have joined him the former with 5 Guns & 2,000 men & the latter with about 2,000. Almost every day reinforcements are coming in. Tantia Saheb has sent for four Guns, two 9 Pounders & the other two from those that were captured at Chirkharee, that he may make another attack on Jhansi. He has also stated that the troops behaved most gallantly in the last action; and has requested the Rao Saheb to persuade & keep all the men that come to Kalpi.

OIOC Home Miscellany, 727a, ff. 40–1

114
An Indian account of the sack of Jhansi[23]

Jhansi

[Printed copy]   4 April 1858

. . . Next day with the dawn began desolation. Everyone of Jhansi was feeling as if he was lying in a cemetary, bound in a litter . . . On this topic a conversation took place with Kesho Bhatt Mandavgane as well . . . He told me 'There used to be a great danger of thieves in Bundelkhand and for that reason the walls of the houses were built quite thick and the place was left between them for hiding persons and property. There is one such lurkhole in that mansion. There is no air in it and terrible darkness pervades it. But instead of sacrificing life outside it is better that we should bear such hardship.' . . .

That night I ventured to have a look at the condition of the city from the roof top. The whole city looked like a fiendish burial ground. Due to the dreadful conflagration in the city everything was clearly visible even in the darkness of the night. In the lanes near relatives maddened with sorrow were lamenting mercifully sitting by the corpses of their kinsmen. Poor people were crying for food and going a begging. Animals were also roaming about here and there in quest of food and water. In Halwaipura mansions of rich people were engulfed in the flames. The flames were almost touching the sky and there was no device to extinguish that fire. Neighbouring houses were also catching the contagion of the flames. I began to tremble and shiver at the sight of this terrible ruin and devastation of the city of Jhansi; I felt mortified and no words could describe the fear that enveloped the heart. The fear of life is always very terrible, I could not sleep the night and passed that night wide awake.

In the night we returned home from the tunnel. Just at that very time the wife and daughter-in-law of Karkarey, my neighbour, began to lament at my place. Poor Brahmin Karkarey, aged 60 or 65 years, and his young son – both had been shot dead by the cruel European soldiers. Throughout the day mother-in-law and daughter-in-law both were in hiding with the dead bodies of their husbands but when night came they began to fear; and coming to my place started begging for the disposal of the corpses.

Though at that time all of us were hungry, even then we at once got up, collected seven or eight neighbours and went to Karkarey's house. In the courtyard near the canopy of *Tulsi*[24] plant we prepared a pyre and cremated the corpses. Firewood was insufficient. Anyhow, pyre was prepared with the wooden doors, planks, cradles etc., whatever wooden material could be found . . .

Next day, remembering the previous night's happenings, we hid ourselves in the *Bakhar* even before the dawn. Innumerable men were slaughtered on that day. Even if a European was seen from a distance people hid themselves behind heaps of grass to save their lives. Europeans used to set the heaps of grass on fire and compel the persons in hiding to die in the same. If, due to their fear, anybody tried to save his life by jumping into the well, they pitched themselves at the well with loaded guns. Then, either the poor man had to die in the water in utter suffocation or forced to fall a victim to the bullets of Europeans in case he raised his head above the water. Several men took refuge in the fields. They were also searched out and shot. As my neighbour Agnihotri Ji was coming out after performing *Hom*,[25] two Europeans with four Indian sepoys entered his house. They went straight to the place of sacrificial fire, with a steel lid. They suspected some money there. When they removed the lid they found underneath only ashes. Their hands got burnt from the sacrificial fire as soon as they thrust their hands into it, suspecting some money therein. On this they got irritated, and after killing Agnihotri, his brother and sons, they took away gold and silver ornaments. Eleven persons were killed in Agnihotri's house including him. His whole family perished. Whenever the Europeans saw any Indian they quenched their thirst for blood by killing him . . .

In this way the desolation continued for three days. All available gold, silver, diamonds, rubies, pearls and emeralds on which they could lay their hands were looted by Europeans. They must have got at least more than a crore of rupees in booty. Amazing is the fortune of a man! Third day when the Europeans went into the Royal residences in the city they got a large treasure there too. There they did not leave a single rag. They also took away the books after breaking open the almirahs[26] of the Jhansi library which was very big and nicely managed . . . After removing the wrappers and opening the binding, foolish Britishers began to throw the books quickly on the road from the third storey. Leaves of the invaluable being thus strewn in the air were meeting destruction. Carpets from *Farrashkhana*,[27] cushion-pillows, tents were removed to their camps, and the war-drums were pierced into the *Naggar-Khana*.[28] Their brass corners [?covers] were taken away. The wicked Britishers did not even spare the temple of Lakshmi. They looted the ornaments, clothes etc. of the Goddess . . . As the desolation would stop next day, Europeans were busy on that day with greater enthusiasm and utmost speed. They slaughtered people after hunting them in the dark corners of the houses and cellars. Even the Darmashalahs[29] and temples were resounding with slaughter and carnage of the great sinners. The most dreadful massacre took place at Kothipur. There even the ladies were put to the sword mercilessly.

Vishnu Bhatta Godse, *Maujhar Pravas* (Poona, 1948), pp. 105–11; FSUP, III, pp. 338–41

115
Rose to Elphinstone

Jhansi

[Manuscript telegram]   5 April 1858

The Fortress of Jhansi has fallen. The Ranee and the rebels frightened by the defeat on the Betwa and the capture of the city by storm evacuated it during the night. The Cavalry forming the investment aided by infantry and cutting up the fugitive garrison in every direction. The loss of the rebels has been most severe. It must amount for the 3 days of the attack of the City and of the garrison of the City and fortress to more than 3,000 men. The Ranee was driven back at one point but effected her escape at another. Jhansi is not a fort but its strength makes it a Fortress. It could not have been breached, it could only have been taken by mining and blowing up one Bastion after another.

❖ ❖ ❖

OIOC MSS Eur F87, Box 9D, Letter Book 4

116
Rose to Campbell

Jhansi

[Holograph copy]   6 April 1858

I beg to congratulate you *most sincerely* on your signal victory at Lucknow[30] which has given all your troops here unfeigned delight. I dont see how they can recover such a blow.

I am extremely obliged to your Excellency for your goodness in appointing Colonel Wetherall to be the Chief of my Staff, he will be of the greatest use, he is an excellent steady officer.

Before the action of the Betwa on the 1st, I had gone four or five miles towards the Betwa in the hopes that the Peishwa's Force would cross the Betwa and engage; I was the more anxious that they should do so because the country is favourable for Cavalry.

When I engaged the Enemy on the 1st I had not 900 Rank and file on the field, as I had a good part of my Force investing, and another part besieging, the Fort and Town; and in consequence of information which I received during the night, I had to detach my 1st Brigade which was in the 2nd line, against a large force of the rebels who were crossing by a lower ford across the Betwa. The rebels took up as they always do an excellent position.

I intended to attack them at day break but they attacked me before it. They began with a heavy cannonade and under cover of it attempted to outflank our left. I conformed to their movement but they went too far to their right and left their left exposed, on which I attacked it with Artillery and Cavalry, routed their left and advanced in line against their front. Their flight then became general and we took 6 guns, the cavalry cutting up the fugitives, mostly Sepoys, who covered the country. After three miles pursuit we came on their reserve with the 18 pounder, the 8 inch mortar etc. After a short cannonade I turned both their flanks, when a fresh flight and pursuit took place up to the Betwa; they made a fresh stand on its right bank. The Horse Artillery and 9pdrs made excellent practice at them and under their cover I crossed over with the 14th Light Dragoons and Hyderabad Cavalry to the right bank, taking the 18 pounder, the 8 inch Mortar and several more guns in the river. We got in rear of the rebels on the bank, causing them great loss, and taking another gun, the last one, two miles on the other side of the Betwa. All this time the investment was not relaxed nor the Siege. Both were continued with the same regularity, as if the enemy had not attempted to relieve Jhansi with a very large Force. The rebels lost at the Betwa from 1,500 to 2,000 men.

The 1st Brigade fell in with the enemy as I had hoped they would do, drove them back, taking from them 5 guns and driving them back.

The town made a desperate resistance and was most gallantly carried; it was fortified with a very strong wall, which we had much difficulty in breaching, and bastions with batteries.

The scaling ladders on the right attack were too short and broke down; on the left the scaling was more successful and the 86th got in at the breach, almost without a casualty. Our chief loss was caused by the resistance made in the houses etc. and outside the Town and the gardens, after the town was taken, by small bodies of rebels or individuals, for the investment was so close that they could not escape.

I ought not to conceal from your Excellency that the Hyderabad Cavalry did not behave well on the 1st of April. Although led by a very gallant officer I could not get them to move against the left of the enemy and when at last they made an attempt to charge they did it badly; the same sort of thing occurred at Garrakota and at Barodia. This is known to several officers of my Force; I of course kept it quiet but as the question of what sort of cavalry would be the best in India will be mooted, it is right that your Excellency should know that when the Hyderabad Irregular Cavalry have had a tough job to do, they, except for a few brave men who are generally wounded or killed, do not like to face it. Just as I was writing this I received a report of Col Lowth Commdg. 86th Regt. in which he speaks of the conduct of the Hyderabad Cavalry with the 1st Brigade in the most unfavourable way.[31]

Of course we cannot expect Indian Native Cavalry to engage their countrymen with the same feeling as the 14th L[t] Dgs. but from what I have observed it strikes one that their want of zeal arises more from want of discipline and pluck than disaffection. At Barodia I and my Staff made ourselves hoarse in getting them to go on.

I would prefer a good Native Police with a military organisation to the Native Irregular Cavalry. Nothing could have been better than the Salt Customs Police at Mudinpore under Mr Bartle.

The 3rd Bombay L[t] Cavalry (Regular) have behaved well on every occasion. This looks as if discipline had a great deal to do with it. The Reg[t] is not only regular but a very well disciplined one.[32]

I should be very much obliged to your Excellency if you would allow me to command the troops in Central India. Gen Whitlock is very good natured and we get on famously together, but I am sure you will agree with me that to ensure a combined operation the Command should be in [one] hand. I was for two years a Lieut General in the Crimea.

BL Add MSS 42812 ff. 52–5

117
Captain Pinckney to W. Muir[33]

Jhansi

[Printed copy]   7 April 185

No. 83

. . . I have the honor to inform you that on the 1st April, Tanteea Topee, having crossed the Betwa from Burwa Saugor, on the previous evening, marched to attack Sir H. Rose's force which was besieging Jhansie. He (Tanteea) was accompanied by the Rajah of Banpore and other leading rebels and his force consisted of 27 guns, 2,000 mutineers, 6,000 or 7,000 Boondelahs and Villayaties and a large body of cavalry.

2nd – Sir H. Rose having got intelligence of Tanteea's movement during the night was fully prepared for him. He himself with the disposable portion of the 2nd Brigade was drawn in rear of his camp, and a portion of the 1st Brigade was sent to take Tanteea's force in flank, should opportunity arise.

3rd – The engagement opened about 6 A.M. with a heavy cannonade on the part of the enemy which was replied to by the guns of the 2nd Brigade after which an advance was ordered, and the enemy was driven from his first position, losing five guns and many men in his retreat to a second position. One of our guns was disabled early in the day by a shot from the enemy's Artillery.

4th – The enemy after a short cannonade was driven from a second position with loss and retreated to a third across the Betwa, losing six guns in his retreat. He was then driven from his third position, losing one gun, and was followed up by Cavalry and Artillery to within two miles of Burwa Saugor.

5th – The action on the part of the 2nd Brigade was chiefly with Cavalry and Artillery; the enemy kept up a well sustained fire from his guns but his Cavalry never came fairly to the front. From the extended country over which the action was fought, 14 miles long by 3 or 4 wide, it is impossible to say exactly what loss the enemy suffered, but I should think it certainly could not have been less than 6 or 700 killed.

6th – In the meantime part of the 2nd Brigade fell in with a very large body of the enemy which had separated from Tantee's main body, attacked and defeated them, killing upwards of 200 and taking six guns, making a total of 18.

7th – After his defeat, Tanteea's army fled in two bodies, one making for Calpee and the other for Mow-raneepore.

8th – During the fight the rebel Garrison of Jhansie manned the walls and kept up a rapid fire from all their guns but as Sir H. Rose still kept up the seige and investment with part of his force, they could not sally out.

9th – On the 2nd the force rested, the siege being carried on as usual.

10th – At daybreak on the 3rd April the Town of Jhansie was assaulted in three places and a false attack was also made near the Oonow Gate[34] to the right of the 3 real ones.

11th – The left assault was made at the breach to the south of, and near, the Fort walls. It was carried by the 86th Foot with little loss but the Regiment suffered in advancing beyond the breach under the Fort walls towards the Ranee's Palace in the Town. Dr Stack being killed and three other officers wounded.[35] The centre assault was an escalade by part of the 3rd Bombay Europeans who succeeded and carried the rampart with little loss, Lieutenant Fox, Madras Sappers and Miners, being dangerously wounded.[36] The right attack was also an escalade but failed owing to the ladders breaking and being too short. Lieutenants Dick and Micklejohn of the Bombay Sappers, who succeeded in mounting to the top of the wall were killed and Lieutenant Bonus wounded with a stone. The 3rd Bombay Europeans who were also the assaulting party suffered severe loss but going round to the centre attack, also entered the Town.

12th – The different assaulting parties then pressed on through the Town under a heavy street fire, Lt. Col. Turnbull of the Bombay Artillery being mortally wounded and they ultimately joined each other near the Ranee's Palace which was carried after a sharp resistance. At evening time above half the Town was in our possession, the enemy holding the Fort and the North-East of the Town.

13th – During the fight in the Town a large body of the enemy amounting to upwards of 400 broke out of the Town and tried to make off in a north-west direction but they were followed up by Infantry, Cavalry and Artillery, surrounded on a hill and all killed. In this last affair Lieutenant Park, Bombay Infantry, was killed.[37]

14th – On the 4th the remaining part of the Town was taken possession of, and very many of the rebels who attempted to escape were cut up by our pickets. The rebel Garrison retreated to the Fort.

15th – On the night of the 4th the Ranee and a large body of rebels made a dash out of the Fort, but were driven back from the direction they first took; they then changed their course and got through the picket towards Bhandere; they were followed up by Lieutenant Dowker, Madras Army, of the Hyderabad Contingent[38] with a small body of Cavalry who inflicted some loss on them, but the Ranee got off although her Fort etc. was captured. Lieutenant Dowker was beaten from his horse and cut down but his wounds are not serious.

16th – On the 5th the Fort was taken possession of and an attack made on parties of rebels, mostly Rohillas, who had taken up a position outside the wall in a suburb called the 'Nya Bustee'. These parties were entirely destroyed on the 6th but I regret to say that Captain Sinclair, 39th Madras Native Infantry, was killed and Captain Lewis of the 86th Foot and 2 other officers wounded, and several of the 86th Foot and Hyderabad Infantry killed and wounded.

17th – The enemy's loss must have been about 3,000 killed, several guns have been taken.

18th – Our loss from the morning of the 1st up to the evening of the 5th April was nearly as follows.

	European Officers	Europeans	Natives	Total
Killed	6	34	15	55
Wounded	12	132	30	174
	18	166	45	229[39]

19th – The example made at Jhansie will, I have no doubt, have an excellent effect in facilitating the tranquillizing of Bundlecund.

20th – The city has not as yet been made over to the Civil Authorities. Sir H. Rose this day informed me that he did not consider it right to do so for some days yet as there are many rebels concealed singly in the Town who shoot down any European in the street, if occasion offers.

❊ ❊ ❊

FPC, No, 55, 15 October 1858; FSUP, III, pp. 322–5

118
Bonus to his parents

Jhansi

[Typewritten copy]   7 April 1858

My last letter was from camp before Jhansi, we are now in possession of the place. The Union Flag floats over the fort. I forget up to what date I related our actions, but nothing of moment occurred after that date till the 1st inst. Rumour said that a large force of rebels was hovering somewhere in the neighbourhood, but I think that no one expected them to come this side of the Betwa river. We have a signal post on top of a high hill near the camp, we call this Telegraph Hill. Late on the afternoon of the 31st[40] signal was made that the enemy had crossed the Betwa about 6 miles off and were advancing rapidly. Sir Hugh was on the move at once, the Second Brigade turned out but darkness fell so there was no fight. During the night the troops were formed up in line and awaited the dawn. I was obliged to return to camp as I had to be on duty in the trenches at 5 a.m. I gathered afterwards the following details.

Directly it was light enough to see the enemy, who were about half a mile from our force, drawn up in line, the fight began with guns on both sides. They made good practice, their first shot killed two men, the second a horse and the third smashed the wheel of one of our guns. Then the 14th Dragoons made a fine charge, the enemy began to retreat, the retreat soon became a flight; they rallied two or three times before reaching the Betwa

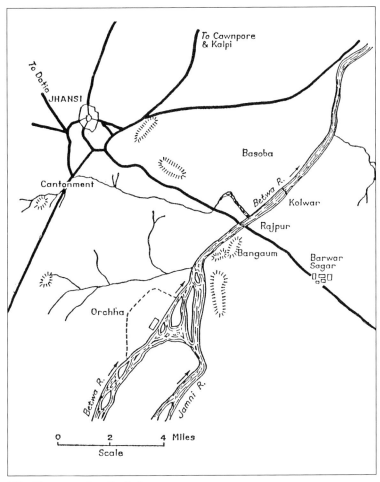

The Betwa, 1 April 1858

but our Cavalry and Artillery gave them no time and they suffered heavily. They crossed the river, and took up a position on the opposite bank, trying to protect their guns and ammunition while crossing, but our Artillery poured such a heavy and continuous fire across the river, they almost at once broke from this their last stand; for some three miles beyond the river their route was strewn with dead.

The First Brigade during the night had moved round towards the enemy's right to prevent them from throwing men into the fortress or from turning our flank; in the morning the enemy tried to do this but were repulsed with great loss. The Second Brigade took 11 guns, two of these were 9 prs, of our own make, beautiful guns, complete with limbers and wagons, one was an 18 Pr from the Cawnpore Arsenal, it was drawn by two Elephants, it was taken at the river; all their stores of shot, powder and other munitions of war fell into our hands, also a large number of camels, bullocks, and elephants.

The First Brigade took 7 guns, many stores and a large number of cattle.

The defeat was crushing. I do not think the Nana's brother who is said to have been in command will give us any more trouble here.[41] Our loss is under one hundred killed and wounded, two of the latter being Officers.[42] That of the rebels is variously stated, Sir Hugh estimates it at 1,500. One of the wounded officers is my friend Prendergast whom I have mentioned before, he was severely wounded with sword cuts, but I am glad to say is doing well. I did not take part in this fight because I had to be on duty in the trenches at 5 a.m. but as soon as I was relieved I rode out hoping to see something of the battle but I merely met the troops returning. We had a hot day in the trenches, we fully expected a sortie in force but our friends did not shew, they contented themselves with a furious and sustained fire on the batteries but killed only one man. Next day, the 2nd inst., I was ordered to go to the north side of the town and select a spot for a false attack to be made early next morning[43] as it was intended to escalade on the south side. I made my inspection and reported to the General. I took care to add that of course an Engineer Officer would be required with the false attack party. The General agreed; what I feared was that I should in all probability be sent and so miss the real business. Alas, when I got back to the Engineers camp I found that the Engineer orders were out and I was not for duty.

At 2.30 a.m. next morning the troops began to get ready but as I had nothing to do with the preparations I stayed in bed till 4 o'clock, then I dressed, took my sword and revolver and hurried down to the front. I found the Brigadier there and other Officers watching the proceedings. The ladder party was advancing to the wall. The enemy was on the alert and opened a sharp fire. There was some confusion, I thought I might be of use and so ran down to the party; I took charge of the ladder and with difficulty got it in position, then I called the men to follow and ran up the ladder, I did not see what other Engineers were doing but I was told afterwards that two more ladders were got up; the Engineers who led up there were both killed.[44] As soon as I got to the top of my ladder I was assailed by a crowd of men; I managed to protect myself with my sword but I never thought of my revolver. Had there not been a man there I doubt if I could have got over the wall for the ladder was too short. I was not at the top very long for a man to my left clubbed his musket and hit me a fine smack on my face knocking me clean off the ladder, I fell on to the rock some 20 feet below; 'the subsequent proceedings interested me no more.'

How long I lay I don't know. When I came to my senses I crawled behind a bit of dwarf wall, where I lay for some time but I have no remembrance of what was happening near me. Eventually I made my way back to the battery where I got some brandy and a man to help me up to camp, then my face was bathed and I was put to bed where I remained three days. Now I am up and fast getting all right again. I am a bit lame, but can walk about and my face is nearly healed; everyone thought I was killed certainly that tumble was a very lucky one for if I had been much longer on that ladder I assuredly should have been killed as the other two Engineers on ladders were.

The failure [of the right attack] was due to the fact that the grounds and wall had not been properly examined and that the ladders were too short, in fact the business was badly muddled. However we are in possession of Jhansi, that is the great thing. I am told that Sir Hugh's intention was in the first place to hold the corner as dotted on the sketch with the Palace as Head quarters but our men once inside the walls were not to be restrained and all the rebels who were not killed fled into the fort. The next morning, the fort was empty, the enemy cleared out in the night, but they were caught by our cavalry picquets and a very large number were cut up; in fact, the slaughter has been awful, something like 4,000. But the Ranee escaped I regret to say. Our loss killed and wounded is put at something under 300.[45] The town is in a horrid state but the dead are being burned.

OIOC IOR neg. 4395

119
Major Gall to his wife

Jhansi
[Printed]   9 April 1858

. . . I have been commanding for the last fortnight what is called 'The North Outpost', my force consisting sometimes of two, sometimes of four, pieces of Artillery, a Squadron of Dragoons, and about 290 Native Infantry. I have constantly moved out of my camp to my right, or my front, either to support the pickets near me or to attack the enemy in the city to my front and to confine him to it.

Towards the close of last month reports were rife that Naneh Sahib was marching from Charkaree on our rear, with the intention of relieving Jhansi.

A strong reconnaissance was made towards the river Betwa, but no enemy found. On the night of the 31st, however, the advanced guard of the enemy was known to be close upon our pickets.

During the night Sir Hugh Rose marched out of his camp to the eastward and met the enemy advancing upon him with about twenty guns and some 8,000 Infantry and a few Cavalry.[46] He attacked them with his Horse Artillery and Cavalry (14th Dragoons) most vigorously, defeated them and driving them back upon the river Betwa, captured their last gun, or nearly so, an 18-pounder elephant gun,[47] in the bed of the river. The Dragoons charged and took five guns, Need up rocks where no horse could keep his footing, and was in great danger, but rescued by Leith, who saw his perilous position.[48]

I was not in this action, being occupied from daybreak till seven o'clock in attacking with a nine pounder and a howitzer that part of the city wall opposite my post, and driving back into the city a party that seemed disposed to come out. When this was over I rode up to a height in rear of my post and from it in the distance saw men running away and others apparently pursuing . . . When the city was stormed, I was directed to make a false attack on my side to divert attention from the real attack. I accordingly at day-break began to blaze away at the bastion we call the North Salient angle bastion, and with 18 Native Infantry advanced close under the walls, firing into the loop holes and embrasures of the bastion, till we got so near as to be able to hear the enemy on the walls calling out Maro! Maro! but such was the strong cover which protected me in the shape of walls and houses that we could laugh at the beards of the garrison in perfect safety. Their fire slackening in an hour or two, and trusting I had not been wholly unsuccessful in my endeavour to divert attention from the real attack on the South-East, which was a most bloody one, I returned to camp.

During the day [4 May] I had been very busy with my Ghonds or Bheels Infantry and a few of the 24th Brigade[49] Native Infantry.

I had advanced up to the walls of the city to await the opening of a gate from the inside by the 3rd Europeans who were moving through the city under Colonel Liddell. I waited some time but nobody opened the gate. A gun had been fired at us from the walls, then all was quiet. This was the last gun fired from the walls of Jhansi. Suspecting that the enemy were leaving the city I ran straight up to the gate and touched it without being fired upon. I then ordered wood to be piled against it, and burnt it. It was built up from inside! Accordingly I had now no way of getting in except by a ladder twenty three feet long I had had made in the camp by our lent Lascars. This I had brought up, and putting it against the wall, I ascended with my sword in my teeth, and mounting the wall, looked into the city below, in which I could see nothing but men flying before troops I could not see. It was enough. I returned to call up all my Bheels and in less than 35 minutes we had escaladed the wall by this single ladder, and in one more I had joined the 3rd Europeans and with them captured a 3 pounder brass gun, placed so as to command the entrance by the Pheetak gateway. I soon had the gun dismounted, and a mussak[50] of water thrown over the powder box. A minute afterwards the General came up, and I told him I should have been in the city three hours sooner but for the having to burn the gate down and finding it built up inside. A great many of the enemy were killed this day in the city.

On the following day, after the night on which the ranee escaped, I moved out of my camp with about 150 Infantry and swept the ground between me and the city walls. Gowan, with a few Dragoons, did the same. Concealed fugitives who had been driven back by the fire of our sentries into the corn fields and gardens all about us sprang up in every direction and were instantly shot down or sabred. Gowan's little party got thirty of them. I, with my Infantry, killed about a hundred, amongst them many of the Gwalior Sepoys, two of them armed with Enfield rifles . . . Abbott, who was on my right on this occasion, with his Irregulars, killed 200. Beamish,[51] with some Dragoons, reported having killed about 300. Late in the day, Abbott's Irregulars, aided by some of my Infantry, attacked a party of Walaities in a garden, who were all killed, 18 in number, but not before they had killed or wounded 17 of their numerous assailants, including 2 or 3 Native Officers.

❊ ❊ ❊

Letters of the late Maj-Genl. R.H. Gall CB (Hitchin, 1881)

120
Rose to Elphinstone

Jhansi

[Holograph]   10 April 1858

You see I thought of you and your injunctions about the Peishwan's Army and Bombay. We drew his teeth and gave him a 'poisson d'Avril'.[52] An April fool would not think of becoming a Peishwan of wily Mahrattas. It really was a remarkable fight. Part of my force, the greatest part of my cavalry, closely investing Jhansi, another besieging it, and a third signally defeating & taking all their guns from an Army of 20 or 25,000 men, causing them, besides, a loss of 1,500, or 2,000 men.

The smallness of our Force and its separation made the [Moofseal] certain that they would annihilate us. Tantia Topee is an organiser and administrator, but not a General. He brought wood for replacing gun carriages, all sorts of stores; a furnace for heating red hot shot etc. But Topee left his left flank 'en l'air', and was not in the first line where he ought to have been to remedy mistakes. He had a reserve, but it was three or four miles off the 1st Line, and too far to support it, or prevent a retreat from becoming a flight. The 18[pdr], which had destroyed poor Windham, and the 8 inch Mortar, were with his reserve, but instead of retiring into a safe position, they retreated *into the River* Betwa where we took them, passing on up the height on the other bank of the Betwa under the fire of the Bundelas & sepoys, whom we cut off, taking the last gun a couple of miles on the other side of the Betwa. All the guns are brass and poor except the 18[pdr] and another one which are iron. The 18[pdr] is a better gun than our 18[pdr]

The Ranee's breakfast, milk and sweetmeats, her Elephant with her 'batterie de cuisine de voyage', her beautiful parasol, her Saree, the Elephant's bells and nosering, all in solid silver, were taken *except* herself. Dowker of the Irregular Cavalry saw her on her famous chestnut horse, her little brother in her lap,[53] thought that he had already hold of her petticoat, when he was knocked off his horse by a matchlock ball. However you must not suppose that the Gentleman rebels got off so easily as [indecipherable quotation]. The escorting Cavalry have given a very good account of them. At first it was calculated that 3,000 (besides the Betwa) had been killed: but the returns now shew that the loss of the Rebels must have been about 3,000 – at the Betwa they lost from 1,500 to 2,000, in all about 7,000 men.

As soon as I have provided for my sick and wounded, replenished my guns etc., I shall go to Calpee, via Mhow (of Bundlecund) as I believe that there are assemblages of rebels there – it would not do to leave them behind me, as they [indecipherable] Jahnsee & might reoccupy Thul Behut, or Chanderee, & cut off my communications with Saugor, Goonah etc.

I should not be surprised if the Sepoys evacuated Calpee before we came up. The Sepoys do not like shutting themselves up in Forts, and they have suffered so heavily from doing so at Jahnsee that I should think that they would prefer their chances of saving themselves and their loot to the chances of losing it, and being cut up themselves. Every Sepoy we kill has generally from 90 to 100 Rupees about him.

All the people in Jahnsee, one and all, took arms against us. They all thought, last year, that the English Raj & People were extinguished in India.

OIOC MSS Eur F87, Box 6A, Packet 4

121
Rose to Commander-in-Chief

Jhansi

[Manuscript telegram]   15 April 1858

I deferred my march today to Calpee because Sir R. Hamilton received information last night that the remnant of the Peishwa's Army and the rebel chiefs of Banpore and Shahgur had come out from Calpee to Oraye two marches from Calpee towards Jhansi with 42 guns. At the same time 4,000 rebels with 4 guns from Kotah of whom two battalions are sepoys and 800 sowars have arrived near Kolarus on the grand trunk road from Goonah to Seepree seven marches to Jhansi. This looks like a manoeuvre to draw me on to Calpee whilst the Kotah rebels, whose original destination was Jhansi, fall on Jhansi in my absence and cut up the weak garrison and the numerous sick and wounded whom I have left in the city. Today Sir R. Hamilton has received information saying that only a few thousand rebels have come out without guns from Calpee on the road to Jhansi. On the other hand the Rajah of Banpore with 4,000 rebels is at Kotah on the Betwa and other rebels are at Mhow[54] from where when I advance to Calpee they would probably combine a movement with the Kotah rebels against Jhansi. I have sent Major Orr against Mhow and shall now send him against Kotah. The rebels will make every effort to retake Jhansi on account of its great importance and it would be a great disaster if when I move against Calpee Jhansi were to fall again into their hands. I cannot move with one Brigade against Calpee because with the casualties resulting from the present hot weather I should not have men enough to do the Siege Duty. I beg earnestly that Maj General Roberts may be immediately ordered to pursue the Kotah fugitives who are encumbered with plunder, Elephants and women. An early reply is requested.

OIOC MSS Eur F87, Box 9D, Letter Book 4

122
Kalpi garrison orders

Kalpi

[Holograph copy]　　　　　　　　　　　　16 April 1858
(Translation)　　　　　　　　　　　　　[29 Shaban 1274]
Parole Lahore

A Court Martial was assembled at Calpee on the 26th Inst. for the trial of Peetum Sing and Doorga Sing Sepoys of the 47th Regiment. Charges 1st For being absent at Roll Call at 9 P.M. 2nd when he returned from Bazar he opened the wicket with his hands and assaulted the Sentry and Doorga Sing Sepoy of the same Reg[t] joined him, such conduct being breach of the Articles of War. By the evidence Peetum Sing and Doorga Sing are found guilty. The Court decides that both Sepoys are liable to be shot or imprisoned for life or dismissed and banished. The Sircar to decide what punishment should be awarded. Tantia Saheb approved the sentence passed on the prisoners and ordered the proceedings of the case to be sent to Peshwa Saheb for final orders, who passed the following orders 'As the prisoners have never before been guilty of such a crime nor any complaint made against them, therefore they are for this time pardoned, but in future if they commit a crime of this nature, they will be severely punished.'

OIOC Home Miscellany 727a ff. 44–5

123
Somerset to Elphinstone

Mahabaleshwar[55]

[Manuscript telegram]　　　　　　　　　　　19 April 1858

Referring to Sir Hugh Rose's telegram dated 15th Instant I think it very desirable that General Roberts should be desired to follow up the body of rebels from Kotah who are threatening Sir Hugh Rose's rear and line of communication. Will Your Lordship communicate with General Roberts on the subject or shall I do so.

OIOC MSS Eur F87, Box 9D, Letter Book 4

124
Rose to Hume[56]

Jhansi

[Holograph]   19 April 1858

I am much obliged to you for your communication of the 9th only received yesterday. Your messenger says he had to make a round by Gwalior which accounts for the delay. I am prevented from marching against Calpee by the arrival of 6,000 Kotah mutineers with 5 guns, besides guns on elephants, in the vicinity of Goonah and Sepree. A very weak native force from Goonah under Captain Mayne can only watch them. These rebels consist of two Regts of Sepoys, 800 Sowars and 1,500 country troops.

It is a matter of regret that they were not pursued from Kotah, as they might easily be cut up being laden with plunder, and having their wives and children with them.

My opinion that the Kotah rebels, acting in concert with the Calpee rebels, intend to fall on Jhansi when I advance to Calpee is confirmed by 500 Bundelas, the late garrison of Chanderee, taking possession yesterday of the Ford of Mayapoor four marches from here, on the road to Goonah. I sent a force last night to attack them at Mayapoor and I have in the most earnest manner begged Lord Elphinstone & Sir R. Somerset to order Maj Gen Roberts to pursue them from Kotah and fall on the Kotah Rebels threatening Goonah.

I had 340 killed and wounded in the Siege and capture of Jhansi and in the Battle of the Betwa. I can only leave a weak garrison in Jhansi, 400 natives, who are only sufficient for the protection of the Fort, not of the Town in which I am obliged to leave my sick and wounded, the greater part of the buildings in the Fort having been destroyed by our shells.

I wish particularly to learn

1st Whether guns and Mortars could cannonade and shell Calpee from the East side of the Jumna
2nd Whether I could get boats to form a bridge across the Jumna
3rd Whether the English have possession of any fords across the Jumna or any part of the banks of the river and, if so, where

4th Whether I would have any difficulty in communicating with the Force at Akbarpoor and whether that force has orders to cooperate with me . . .[57]

BL Add MSS 42812, f. 57

125
Rose to Orr

Jhansi

[Holograph copy]   20 April 1858

I am very glad to see from your letter that you have good hopes of catching the Kotra rebels. In consequence of the late Chandeyree Garrison seizing a hill Fort, Mayapoor, near here, & 500 Valaitees from Kotah or Mundasor, threatening to take Goonah, I have been compelled to send a force towards Mayapoor, now evacuated, and the 3rd L[t] Cavalry to Goonah to come back with the 71st who are encumbered with a long line of carts etc. But tonight at 12 o'clock I send Major Gall with 2 Squadrons of the 14th L[t] Dragoons, some Sappers and Miners, two 9 Pdrs and one 24 Pound Howitzer to Mote to put himself in communication with you and concert an attack. Major Gall is not to cross the River. You will not forget to send him the 200 Cavalry, as if the Rebels are at Koonah,[58] and I believe they are, he will have to make his attack on Kotra.

BL Add MSS 42812, f. 59

126
Maxwell to Rose

Akbarpore

[Holograph]   20 April 1858

I have written to Mr Hume about the boats & I presume he will put himself in communication with you. Should you intend coming down to Calpee from the N.W. I think Hummeerpoor would be a good place to pass over the ammunition as there is a good road to Calpee from that place and also a good one from

Cawnpore to the Ghat opposite to Hummeerpoor. But should you approach from Jaloun, Sherghur Ghat which is the Ghat[59] I presume alluded to by Genl. Mansfield, is about 16 miles from Jaloun, but 32 miles from Calpee by the road which is I hear a bad one. I am told that the South of Calpee is open ground, the East and West sides are a series of ravines, the North side of the Fort is a precipitous rock about 100 feet high. But I think our mortars will make it very uncomfortable for those inside the fort. I may as well mention that Sherghur Ghat has been much used by the rebels and is supposed to be the Ghat by which the fugitives from Calpee will try to escape for the purpose of getting into Rohilcund.

NLS MSS 3798, f. 160; BL Add MSS 42807, f. 26 (copy)

127
Rose to Elphinstone and Somerset

Jhansi
21 April 1858

[Manuscript telegram]

I have already reported that 4 Guns, 800 Sowars, 2 regiments and 1,500 Irregular Infantry Kotah rebels had joined the rebels of Nurwal and taken up a position threatening the grand trunk road and Jhansi. Since making that report 600 Vullaitees also retreating from Kotah had taken up a position near Goonah and have threatened to attack it as soon as the 71st leave it for Jhansi. 300 rebels also a few days since occupied a pass near Mynpore between Goonah and Jhansi they left it on the appearance of some troops from here but they are still in the neighbourhood. The vicinity of the Kotah rebels to Goonah and Jhansi prevents my advance against Calpee for if I leave Jhansi the rebels will probably try to retake so important a place. The 400 natives left in Jhansi would only protect the Fort but not the town, in which I have upwards of 400 wounded and sick. The Fort is so damaged by shelling that the Hospital could not be established there. I earnestly beg that His Excellency may be pleased to direct Genl. Roberts to pursue the Kotah rebels sending a

Brigade to Goonah which should detach a Battalion or half one at least to Jhansi during my absence. Captain Mayne is watching the Kotah rebels.

OIOC MSS Eur F87, Box 9D, Letter Book 4

128
Mansfield to Rose

Fattehgarh

[Holograph]   26 April 1858

No. 137 Confidential

Major General Sir H. Rose as soon as he can open communications with the left bank of the Jumna, will indicate to Col. Maxwell CB, H.M.'s 88th Foot Comm^{dg} a moveable column at Akbarpore when he wishes his ammunition to be crossed over. That ammunition is now waiting at Cawnpore, and will be passed to Col. Maxwell as soon as Sir H. Rose's arrival is notified.

It is probable that Sir H. Rose will find it more convenient to desire this ammunition to be passed over the Jumna at a Ghat about 10 miles to the N.W. of Calpee, but on this point he will be able to get the most valuable information from Colonel Maxwell.

In answer to Sir H. Rose's letter of the 22nd April addressed to the Chief of Staff, he is informed that there are no Guns or Artillery men available for his assistance, every soldier being at the moment in full activity in different parts of the Country.

Colonel Maxwell will be provided with Mortars for the purpose of shelling Calpee from the left bank. During the operations he will be under the orders of Sir H. Rose, but his troops must not be crossed over to the right bank of the Jumna. The Cawnpore District being very bare indeed & depending nearly altogether on Colonel Maxwell's Column. Colonel Maxwell in conjunction with Mr Hume of Ettawah will provide the boats for the operation of crossing the ammunition.

In the absence of the Commander in Chief in Rohilcund Sir H. Rose will correspond with the Sec^y to Government with regard to the destination of his Troops after the fall of Calpee.

NLS MSS 3798, f. 160; OIOC MSS Eur D174, f. 1099 (copy)

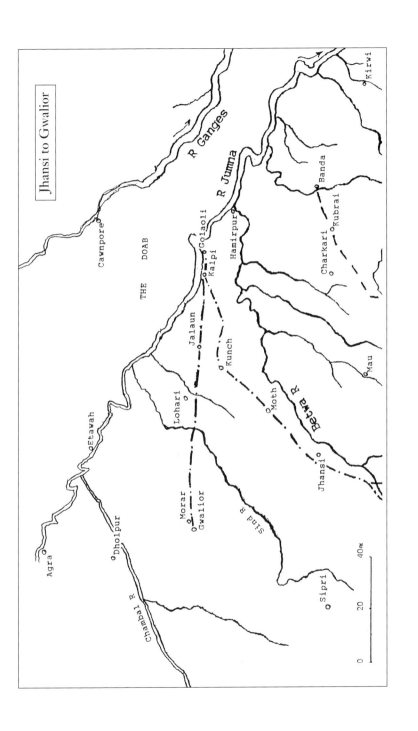

Jhansi to Gwalior

Kirwi

R Ganges

R Jumma

Banda

Cawnpore

THE DOAB

Golaoli
Kalpi
Hamirpur

Charkari
Kubrai

Jalaun

Kunch

Mau

Lohari

Moth

Betwa R

Agra

Etawah

Morar
Gwalior

Sind R

Jhansi

Dholpur

Chambal R

Sipri

0   20   40ᴍ

129
Rose to Roberts

Moth[60]

[Holograph copy]   30 April 1858

I am very much obliged to you for your letter and I hope very much that I have not put you to any inconvenience or trouble. I was in a very difficult position at Jhansie; I had a good many wounded officers & men whom I was forced to leave there. I had to move against Calpee with my Force weakened by the loss in the operations before Jhansie and in the action of the Betwa, and by the garrison I had to leave at Jhansie. On the other hand the rebels at Calpee were strengthened by fugitives from all parts. The great heat is also in their favour because siege operations in this weather will of course cause me many casualties. The arrival of the Kotah fugitives who were originally to come to Jhansie, to the neighbourhood of Goonah, stopped me leaving Jhansie. My communications by the Grand Trunk Road by which small parties of the 71st are daily coming up, of course, made it necessary to take further measures for the defence of Jhansie. I am obliged to leave as a Garrison for its protection a wing of a European Reg[t], Native Infantry, Cavalry & half a Battery besides details.

BL Add MSS 42812 f. 66

130
Rose to Mansfield

Moth

[Printed]   30 April 1858

❊ ❊ ❊

Having no plan, or even correct description of the fortress and city, I had, together with the Officers Commanding the Artillery and Engineers, to make long and repeated reconnaissances, in order to ascertain the Enemy's defences; this delayed, for some days, the commencement of the siege operations.

The great strength of the Fort, natural as well as artificial, and its extent, entitles it to a place among fortresses. It stands on an elevated rock, rising out of a plain, and commands the city, and surrounding country; it is built of excellent and most massive masonry. The Fort is difficult to breach because, composed of granite, its walls vary in thickness from sixteen to twenty feet.

The Fort has extensive and elaborate outworks of the same solid construction, with front and flanking embrasures for Artillery fire, and loop-holes, of which, in some places, there were five tiers for musketry. Guns placed on the high towers of the Fort commanded the country all round.

One tower, called the 'white turret' had been raised lately in height by the Rebels and armed with heavy ordnance

The fortress is surrounded by the city of Jhansie all sides except the West and part of the South face.

The steepness of the rock protects the West, the fortified city wall with bastions springing from the centre of its South face, running South, and ending in a high mound or mamelon, protects by a flanking fire its South face. The mound was fortified by a strong, circular bastion for 5 Guns, round part of which was drawn a ditch 12 feet deep and 15 feet broad of solid masonry. Quantities of men were always at work in the mound.

The city of Jhansie is about 4½ miles in circumference, and is surrounded by a fortified and massive wall, from 6 to 12 feet thick, and varying in height from 18 to 30 feet, with numerous flanking bastions armed as batteries with ordnance, and loop-holes, with a banquette for Infantry.

Outside the walls, the city is girt with wood, except some parts of the East and South fronts; on the former is a picturesque lake and water palace; to the South are the ruined Cantonments and residences of the English. Temples with their gardens – one the Jokun Bagh, the scene of the massacre of our lamented country-men – and two rocky ridges, the Eastmost called 'Kapoo Tekri', both important positions, facing and threatening the South face of the city wall and Fort.

❊ ❊ ❊

The attack of Jhansie offered serious difficulties. There were no means of breaching the Fort, except from the South, but the South was flanked by the fortified City wall and mound just described.

The rocky ridge was excellent for a breaching battery, except that it was too far off, 640 yards, and that the fire from it would have been oblique.

The mound enfiladed two walls of the City, and commanded the whole of the South quarter of it, including the Palace.

It was evident that the capture of the mound was the first most important operation, because its occupation ensured, in all probability, that of the South of the City, and of the Palace, affording also the means of constructing, by approaches an advanced breaching battery.

The desideratum, therefore, was to concentrate a heavy fire on the mound, and on the South of the City, in order to drive the Enemy out of them, and facilitate their capture, to breach the wall close to the mound, and to dismantle the Enemy's defences which protected the mound and opposed an attack. This was effected – Firstly, by occupying and placing batteries on a rocky knoll, the right attack, which I had found in my reconnaissance to the South of the Lake opposite the Aorcha gate and South-east wall of the town, which took in reverse the mound, and two walls running from it; Secondly, on the rocky ridge the left attack.

These batteries could not be completed till the arrival of the 1st Brigade with its siege Guns on the 25th Ultimo.

In the meantime, the right attack opened fire, from an 8-inch Howitzer and two 8-inch Mortars, on the rear of the mound and the South of the City, with the exception of the Palace, which I wished to preserve for the use of the Troops.

The Chief of the Rebel Artillery was a first-rate Artilleryman; he had under his two Companies of Golundauze.[61] The manner in which the Rebels served their Guns, repaired their defences, and re-opened fire from batteries and Guns repeatedly shut up, was remarkable. From some batteries they returned shot for shot. The women were seen working in the batteries and carrying ammunition. The garden battery was fought under the black flag of the Fakeers.[62]

Everything indicated a general and determined resistance; this was not surprising, as the inhabitants, from the Ranee downwards, were, more or less, concerned in the murder and plunder of the English. There was hardly a house in Jhansie which did not contain some article of English plunder, and, politically speaking, the Rebel confederacy knew well that if Jhansie, the richest Hindoo city, and most important fortress in Central India, fell, the cause of the insurgents in this part of India fell also.

On the 25th Ultimo the Siege Train of the 1st Brigade having arrived, batteries were constructed and opened fire from the 26th to the 29th Ultimo, on the rocky ridge, as follows, forming the left attack.

> Two 18-Pounders to dismantle the defence of the Fort
> Two 10-inch Mortars to destroy the Fort
> Two 8-inch Mortars and one 8-inch Howitzer to act on the mound and adjacent wall and City
> One 18-Pounder to breach the wall near the bastion of the mound, which was thus exposed to a vertical and horizontal fire on its right face and left rear, the 18-Pounders were changed from travelling to garrison carriages[63]

In order to prevent delay and confusion, I gave names to all the Enemy's batteries in the town, as well as in the fort; they were 13 in number.

The breaching Gun, so solid was the wall and so hard the masonry, did not produce the result contemplated on the first or even on the second day, but on the 30th the breach was practicable. The Enemy retrenched the breach with a double row of palisades, filled with earth, on which I ordered every description of fire, including red-hot shot, to be directed upon it, and the result was a considerable proportion of the stockade was destroyed by fire.

Riflemen to fire at the parapet and the embrasures and loop-holes were placed in all the batteries, with sand-bag loop-holes, and posts of Riflemen were distributed in the temples and gardens of the East and South sides of the city. I occupied also the Jokun Bagh, nearly opposite the mound with a picquet of Rifles. The Riflemen caused numerous casualties among the rebels in the town as well as in the parapets.

Our batteries had by the 30th dismantled the defences of the Fort and City, or disabled their Guns. It is true that the Rebels had made on the white turret an excellent parapet of large sand-bags, which they always kept wet, and still ran up fresh in lieu of disabled Guns: but their best guns had been disabled, and their best Artillerymen killed; their fire was therefore no longer serious. However, the obstinate defence of the Enemy, the breach, and the extent fired on had caused a great consumption of ammunition, so much so, that it was evident there would not be sufficient to multiply breaches in the town wall, or to establish a main breach in the South double wall of the Fort.

Under these circumstances, the Officers Commanding the Artillery and Engineers called to my notice the necessity of having recourse to escalade, to which I gave my consent, requiring however that the breach should form an important and principal point of attack. Both of these Officers entertained a mistrust of the breach, thinking it was mined, or not practicable.

I had made arrangements on the 30th for storming, but the general action on the 1st Instant, with the so-called Army of the Peshwa, which advanced across the Betwa to relieve it, caused the assault to be deferred . . .

On the 2nd Instant, Major Boileau reported to me that he had made all the necessary preparations for the escalade, and that a 24-Pounder Howitzer had been placed in battery in front of the Jokun for the purpose of enfilading, and clearing during the night the wall from the mound to the Fort, and the rocket bastion which is on it.

I issued a division order for the assault of the defences of the city wall, of which a copy, with a plan of attack, was furnished to the Officers in Command . . .

The left attack, ably and gallantly conducted by Brigadier Stuart, succeeded perfectly, its Right column passing without loss or difficulty through the breach, which turned out as well as I thought it would, and the left effecting, with some casualties, the escalade of the rocket battery . . . The 3rd Europeans, under Lieutenant-Colonel Liddell, did their duty, as they always have done, but they could not control adverse circumstances, arising from bad ladders, and a mistake in the road, they returned to the assault with alacrity, and fought their way through the town manfully.

Having received no reports from the right attack, composed of the 3rd Europeans and Hyderabad Contingent, I made my way to them in the South-east quarter of the City. I found them engaged with the Enemy, and making their way to the Palace; the Rebels were firing at them from the houses, which the troops were breaking open and clearing of their defenders.

The right and left attacks being now concentrated in the Palace, I gained possession of a large portion of the City by advancing the 3rd Europeans to the North-East and occupying the Burrahgong-gate, on which I rested their right flank, forming an oblique line from the gate to the palace with the 3rd Europeans and the 86th in the Palace. The two Regiments occupying with picquets commanding houses to their front. This line was a prolongation of the second line leading from the mound under the front of the Palace. This done, it was necessary to clear the large portion of the City in rear of this oblique line of the numerous armed Rebels who remained in the houses, and who were firing on the Troops. This was not effected without bloody, often hand-to-hand, combats; one of the most remarkable of them was between detachments of Her Majesty's 86th Regiment and 3rd Europeans, and thirty or forty Velaitie Sowars, the Body-guard of the Ranee in the Palace Stables under the fire of the Fort. The Sowars, full of opium, defended their Stables, firing with matchlocks and pistols from the windows and loop-holes, and cutting with their tulwars, and from behind the doors. When driven in, they retreated behind their houses, still firing or fighting with their swords in both hands till they were shot or bayoneted struggling even when dying on the ground to strike again. A party of them remained in a room in the stables which was on fire till they were half burnt; their clothes in flames, they rushed out hacking at their assailants, and guarding their heads with their swords.

The next day Brigadier Stuart and myself occupied the rest of the City by a combined movement, assisted by Major Gall, who spiritedly scaled the bastion at the Onow-gate from his Flying Camp, and capturing the Gun that was there, threw it down the rampart.[64]

The following morning, a wounded Mahratta retainer of the Ranee was sent in to me from Captain Abbott's Flying Camp. He stated that the Ranee, accompanied by 300 Vilaities and 25 Sowars, fled that night from the Fort; that after leaving it, they had been headed back by one of the picquets where the Ranee and her party separated, she herself taking to the right with a few Sowars in the direction of her intended flight to Bandiri. The observatory also telegraphed 'Enemy escaping to the North-East'.[65] I immediately sent off strong detachments of Her Majesty's 14th Light Dragoons, 3rd Light Cavalry, and Hyderabad Cavalry to pursue, with Guns to support them, as it was said that Tantia Topee had sent a Force to meet her . . . In sight of Bandiri, 21 miles from Jhansie, the Cavalry came in sight of the Irregular Horse, sent to meet the Ranee, which separated probably with the view to mislead her pursuers as to her real course. Lieutenant Dowker, Hyderabad Cavalry, was sent by Captain Forbes through the town of Bandiri, while he with the 3rd Light Cavalry and 14th Light Dragoons passed it by the left. In the town, Lieutenant Dowker saw traces of the Ranee's hasty flight, and her tent in which was an unfinished breakfast; on the other side of the town he came up with and cut up forty of the Enemy consisting of Rohillas and Bengal Irregular Cavalry. Lieutenant Dowker was gaining fast on the Ranee, who with four attendants, was seen escaping on a grey horse, when he was dismounted by a severe wound, and obliged to give up the assault.

From the time the troops took the Palace, the Rebels lost heart and began to leave the town and fort. Nothing could prove more the efficiency of the investment than the number of them cut up by the picquets of the Flying Camps; the woods, gardens and roads round the town were strewed with the corpses of fugitive Rebels. The Ranee's flight was the signal for a general retreat.

❋ ❋ ❋

MDP General Order 174, 1858

131
Rose to Canning

Moth

[Holograph copy]   30 April 1858

. . . The offer of the Banpore & Shahgar Rajas was to deliver to us Tantia Topee & Rao Sing, the nephew of Nana Sahib. I am certain of the sincerity of the person who brought the offer because he is an English officer, a clever, excellent man. Of course, I cannot vouch for the good faith of the two rajahs. As regards them & natives in general, their interests and feelings are the only guides as to their actions. The two Rajahs know that the Rebel cause is lost & that they & their sons may every day suffer a disgraceful death. They have also, like all other Indians, [?a fear] of their wives & children falling into the hands of the Enemy. They know that English troops would respect them. But still with the Connection in their mind they would rather kill their women than that they should fall into submission. Under these circumstances it is not impossible that the two Rajahs would prefer in their present state of danger & disquiet, a *life of peace* with their families in a distant part of India under a safe but not annoying surveillance.

The Chief of Goorserai,[66] at present an Ally, is the mediator between the two Rajahs & us. His motive of action is very clear – it is his hatred of Tantia Topee because he flogged him & his five sons because he took charge of Jaloun last year. If the two Rajahs *accept* the offer made by Sir Robert Hamilton the results would I think be very advantageous because 1^{stly} Tantia Topee, a rebel of first rate capacity & intelligence would disappear from the ranks of the insurgents. Tantia Topee as a connection of Nana Sahib & consequently of the late Peishwa has influence with the Mahrattas and the aristocratic and religious party among the Rebels. He is a very able intriguer & has talents for military & administrative organisation. He organised the Peishwa's Army in a short time to relieve Jahnsie, & if he had succeeded would, I believe, have marched to the Deccan & proclaimed the Peishwa, neither of which Nana Sahib would ever have had the nerve to do . . . 2^{ndly} Rao Sahib, a nephew of Nana Sahib & influential amongst the Rebels would be extinguished. 3^{rdly} the two Rajahs of Banpore & Shahgur would be neutralised. Their influence as Feudal Lords of most ancient family enabled them to convulse all the country between the Nerbudda and Jahnsie – Shahgur, Banpore, Chandery, Bundelcund have still heavily feudal institutions. The small nobility, the Thakoors, are as devoted to their Chief as the villagers to the Thakoor. The Rajah orders the Thakoor to turn out so many men for war, and the Thakoor brings his own quota of men, who very often receive no pay, nothing but grain. The neutralisation of the Rajahs would ensure that of the Thakoors & of the vassals, the villagers. 4^{thly} the delivery of Tantia Topee, Nana Sahib's relative & agent & his nephew by the two great feudal chiefs into *our hands* would cause a general mistrust amongst the Rebels & break up the Confederacy.

It remains to be seen whether the offer of the two Rajahs was a sincere one. I have not allowed it to influence military operations against them, nor have I even mentioned it to Major Orr who is now opposite Kotra preventing what is apparently a design of the two Rajahs to re-enter the districts to the south of the Betwa.

BL Add MSS 42812 ff. 63–5

132
Bonus to his parents

Poonch[67]

[Typewritten copy]   4 May 1858

We are all curious to know what at home is thought of the Betwa and Jhansi. I hope that some good and true account will appear in English papers, those in Indian papers are not good and not true being mostly written by men who have no means of ascertaining the facts, non-commissioned officers and privates.

Since my last was posted, I have had I think a more narrow escape than I had at Jhansi. Let me tell you about it. A picket of Native Cavalry was posted in a village, Loharee by name, about 6 miles from this place. One morning they found themselves beset by the enemy's cavalry, they had to cut their way through and lost two killed and several wounded. A strong force, consisting of a wing of the 3rd Europeans, a wing of the 25th N.I., a H.A. battery, a troop of the 14th Dragoons, 100 Irregular Cavalry and my company of Sappers were ordered out. We started at 2 a.m. on the 2nd. There is a fort at Lohareee. When we arrived we found this occupied by the enemy, we summoned them to surrender, they refused, so it became necessary to turn them out. But how was this to be done? Our guns opened fire and our infantry rushed the outer gate, but the next was closed. We seemed to be in a bit of a fix. I rode right round the fort to see if I could find a place where escalade would be possible but I could not see any, the wall seemed to be too high for our ladders and in good condition everywhere;

I was certain that escalade would not do. I reported my opinion to Colonel Gall who commanded the column; he did me the honour to ask my advice, I said that there seemed to me only one thing to do and that was to blow open the gate, not that I liked giving this opinion for I knew that the very unpleasant job would be mine. Colonel Gall agreed. I had not come prepared for this adventure, so I had no materials. I went into the village which of course was entirely deserted and hit upon the smithy where I found a leather bellows. The bellows of the native is a leather bag, the complete skin in fact of a goat. This I saw would answer my purpose. Then I got 50lbs of powder from the Artillery and soon had my bag ready. I took three men with me, two to carry the bag, the third, a European, to fire the charge should I be knocked over. We rushed to the gate while the Infantry poured a furious fire on the defences. I propped the bag against the gate, lighted it, and bolted back to cover. The thing was done so quickly that I do not believe the enemy knew what was up, at any rate not a man of the party was touched. After about half a minute which seemed like half an hour, the charge exploded, smashing the gate to matchwood. The Europeans rushed in, there was some desperate fighting but soon the place was ours. We had two Officers severely wounded, one man killed and about 20 wounded. All the rebels, about 60, were killed. We returned to camp in the evening after a very hot and hard day, during which we had no food. The heat was terrific, several Europeans were overcome and were brought in in carts.

Colonel Gall thanked me warmly and he mentioned me in flattering terms in his report to the General.[68]

OIOC IOR neg. 4395

133
Rose to Somerset

Punch (via Indore)
[Manuscript telegram]   6 May 1858

As soon as Jhansi and my sick and wounded whom I leave there and the road from Jhansi to Goonah were secured from the advance of the Kotah rebels and the late garrison of Chanderee which made incursions on that road after the capture of Jhansi I marched with the first Brigade from Jhansi to Poonch on Calpee. I had previously on the 21st ultimo sent Major Gall with 2 squadrons of the 14th Dragoons & 3 9 pounders on the road to Calpee to watch the movements of the enemy and to support Major Orr whom I had sent from Jhansi across the Betwa to Mow to clear that part of the country of the rebels stated to be there with orders to rejoin me on the road to Calpee. Major Orr found no rebels at Mow but beyond Gooseraj near the Betwa a little fort Goormay with 40 rebels and 3 cannon surrendered to him. I directed Major Orr to advance to the Betwa and prevent the passage of the river by the Rajahs of Bhunpore and Shahgurh and their march southwards – The two Rajahs leaving a portion of their force at Kotra opposite to Major Orr crossed the river higher up and have gone southwards with one gun and part of their force – Major Orr crossed the River at Kotra, attacked the rebels there and took one gun. I sent Major Gall from here against the garrison of Loharee, a *ghurree*[69] with one gun belonging to the Rajah of Sumpter because they had betrayed an outpost of the Hyderabad Cavalry to the rebel Cavalry in Koonch – Major Gall blew in the gate, stormed the *Ghurree* and killed the rebels in it, 71 in number. They were disguised sepoys of the 12th B.I.[70] and fought to the last. My second Brigade with the exception of the large part of it left for the protection of Jhansi joined me today. I march tomorrow against Koonch where Tantia Topee and the Ranee of Jhansi have concentrated a considerable force of sepoys from Kalpee. Sir Robert Hamilton at my request has written to General Whitelock that it is very desirable that his Second Brigade should move on and occupy the fort of Thal Behut or Mow for the purpose of opposing the Rajahs of Banpore and Shahgurh – The Brigade would also protect General Whitelocks rear.

OIOC MSS Eur F87, Box 9D, Letter Book 4

134
Birch to Rose

No. 96   Allahabad

[Holograph]   7 May 1858

I am directed to request that you will have the goodness to transmit to me for the information of the Right Honble the Gov[r] General and as soon as you can conveniently do so, the proceedings of the Courts Martial before which the Mutineers of the Bhopal Contingent were tried at Sehore. The procedings may be sent in original.

BL Add MSS 42807 f. 28

135
Shakespear, diary

[Typed copy]

8th [May 1858] Koonch. Yesterday morning about 6 o'clock after making a good circuit, we arrived at Chunnair a village about three miles west of Koonch. We halted there for breakfast and heard of the arrival of the 2nd Brigade at Oonree.[71] Major Orr with the Hyd. Field Force was with the 2nd Brigade although we had always understood that he was to march from Ait on the Oonree road so as to cut off the retreat of the rebels in that direction. The town of Koonch is not visible (beyond the old fort in the centre where there was a flag flying) in consequence of its being so surrounded by trees and gardens. After breakfast we all started, the 2nd Brigade moving direct on the North West of the town, we moved in two columns parallel with the town to the North West when after clearing a couple of villages we turned to the right and came down on the South West of the town in two lines. When we got within about ¼ mile of the trees the enemy opened fire. We replied with light guns until the heavy ones came up, seeing it was going to be a game of long bowls we took shelter under some trees where we could see all what was going on. Before this we had seen a few of the enemy's cavalry moving about amongst the trees but they never came out. The heat was intense and the wind blowing like the blast from a furnace. About 12 o'clock the General came up to our trees quite done up with the sun, he lay gasping for some time when an Officer who had been out to reconnoitre reported large bodies of Cavalry in the gardens north of the town and apparently making for Jaloun, orders were given for Dragoons and Horse Artillery to go after them, soon we heard firing, the General got up, the fire from the enemy's battery in front had been put down and by degrees the whole of our Infantry was moving on the gardens taking the flagstaff of the fort as the point to move on. When we saw the Infantry well in the trees, I and three others (leaving Sir Robert) started to see the fun, we had a little firing and the fort was gained, an old ruinous place but a capital position as from it we could see all the plain round and the town was below us. We had not been in possession ten minutes before we saw the enemy streaming away slowly from the East side. Pursuit was now the order of the day, we sent word to the 2nd Brigade of what was going on, they were near the enemy but evidently did not see them. At the same time we pushed our guns and Cavalry on but they had to pass through the whole town and the narrow streets stopped us. It was now about three o'clock. I accompanied the guns in pursuit with another officer (Captain Pinkney) leaving the General in the town knocked down for the third time by the sun. He has invincible pluck though and as I heard afterwards directly he recovered he joined us in the pursuit and went as far as anyone.

❖ ❖ ❖

OIOC MSS Eur D706/2, ff. 209–10

136
Bonus to his parents

Kunch

[Typewritten copy]   8 May 1858

We had yesterday the most trying day I have yet experienced, the hottest of this very hot weather. The night before the first bugle sounded at 9 p.m. We began to move at 10 but almost immediately we were halted and we lay down on the ground for an hour and more. Then began a most weary and trying march of 14 or 15 miles chiefly over ploughed land; about sunrise we sighted this place. There was more delay. I was not sorry for this as we were able to get a snack of food which we much wanted. I cannot explain to you the manoeuvres and fighting of the day because I have no clear idea of the General's scheme of attack or of the details of its execution. The town of Koonch was hidden by trees, but we could make out the fort, a tower of which shewed above the trees. There was a great deal of firing, both musketry and artillery. I had the excitement of a small charge with some Dragoons on a party which was grouped in the middle of a ploughed field, so rough was the ground that the horses of 3 or 4 men fell, but the rebels were all killed.

My impression is that we did not do very much harm to the enemy but we did drive them out of Koonch, they retreated along the road to Calpee. The heat was so great and our men so tired and worn out that our attack wanted vigour, at least that is my impression. Seven men of the 71st Highlanders were killed outright by the sun and others were struck down. I hear that Sir Hugh had to dismount more than once and have water soused over his head. Truly it was an awful day. We all slept on the ground quite worn out.

OIOC IOR neg. 4385

137
Bonus to his parents

Kunch

[Typewritten copy]   10 May 1858

Still here and I do not think we can start till tomorrow. Yesterday afternoon about 4 o'clock a terrific storm burst upon the camp. It came up with extraordinary rapidity and disappeared as quickly, but it wrecked the camp. The first thing we noticed was a dark haze on the eastern horizon. In a few minutes the sky was darkened and a burning blast of dust was upon us, this was followed by a downpour of rain and hail, then the air cleared and all was over.[72] But as I have said the camp was wrecked, tents were down in all directions, the Brigadier's was the only one standing in the Staff lines. When the storm broke, I was in a friend's tent, when it passed I went to see how my tent had fared. I found it standing, but hardly upright, inside there was a fine mess of papers, bath, basin, bedding, books, in fact everything I possessed strewn upon the ground in indescribable confusion.

But there was compensation, the storm cooled the air in a remarkable manner, made it quite pleasant. A move however was out of the question, the tents were soaked, they could not be carried.

OIOC IOR neg. 4395

138
Gall to his brother

Ata[73]

[Printed]   [undated but c. 11 May 1858]

❊ ❊ ❊

The same evening I was sent for and verbally instructed to proceed with

The Left Wing Bombay Europeans	210 Rank and File
Left Wing Bombay N.I., about	350
Sappers	20
	Total . . . . . 580 Infantry
Dragoons and Irregular Cavalry	220
Three 9-pounders, one howitzer	4 guns

to Loharee, bring in the Commandant Munohur Singh and all his garrison, about ninety strong, prisoners of war, or if they refused to surrender, to blow the fort about their ears and destroy them.

179

With the above force I marched accordingly, and on arriving near Loharree, halted in battle order on the plain in full sight of the garrison on the walls. Then rode, accompanied by one officer and a native official, through the village up to the gates of the fort, and summoned the Killedar – whoever he was. I was insulted by having an inferior person sent but after a while discovering that Munohur Singh, the Ranee's brother, was himself in the fort, I summoned him to come out. After many delays caused by fear, and perhaps by other causes, for he might have had a desire to destroy certain documents, he came out on foot, with an armed retinue of seven or eight, with his sword in both hands which he presented to me, at the same time his retinue laid down their arms at my feet. When he came out I upbraided him with the delay, and he exclaimed that I was dishonouring him. To which I replied 'Is it a dishonour to a Shakoor[74] holding a petty fort like this to be called upon to surrender to an army like mine?'. He then begged to be allowed to retain his sword, which I returned to him. He was in a great state of alarm. I now called upon him to make the garrison lay down their arms. This he tried to do, sending in several messengers with the order, but it was clear that he had no power over them. They positively refused to obey him, so I sent him and his retinue as prisoners to Poonch. And after vainly endeavouring to induce the garrison to surrender at discretion I proceeded to attack the place, in the full expectation that whilst engaged in reducing the fort I should be attacked from the side of Khullea, said to be occupied by 800 of the enemy. General Barr[75] will let you see a copy of the report I sent in of what followed, but I could not but leave much unsaid. To wit, that when the General heard the guns he became excited and feared I might fall, and wrote a letter in which he peremptorily forbade me to risk an unsuccessful assault, which I received just as Bonus, the engineer, was closing the powder bag, and we were in doubt whether or not it would be necessary to blow in more than one gate; and how I concealed the purport of this note from all except Thompson,[76] to whom I gave the command of all outside, while I went in. Nor could I dwell on the uncivil treatment I personally received during the assault. Once I was knocked head over heels by a rush of my own men the wrong way under the influence of an ignited bag of powder that made its appearance among them. Twice I was knocked down by stones thrown by the enemy . . . I may live many years and see many strange things but I shall never see such a fight as that again. I could never bring more than twenty men at the outside against the seventy or eighty that assailed us.

The gateways being both uncovered at the top the garrison could throw what they pleased on our heads. At the trees I had a melee with about twenty of them and then the inside of my left hand was just touched by a talwar and the sleeve of my right arm cut by another; and I had, using my sword with both hands, the satisfaction of reducing an opponent to equal terms of combat by nearly severing his left arm at the wrist. Nor could I allude in my official report to the ludicrous effect of so many dirty faces, all begrimed with the dust and smoke of the explosion.

When I got into the place the breast of my coat was drenched with blood streaming from my forehead and head, giving me the appearance of having been shot. I am still sore from the bruises I had got and can scarcely yet lift my right arm without great pain. A stone struck me upon the shoulder point and sent me reeling against the wall. At one time I thought we must lose the day, and cried out 'If you are Englishmen come on now and never come back, men'. They did come on and never returned to that gateway until every opponent had been slain.[77]

The 7th, the General with the 1st Brigade made a flank march on Koonch and gained the north side. Stewart, with the 2nd Brigade, arriving from the west, and Orr from the south-east or south. After being completely turned, the enemy was driven through the town and out of the town, and along the plain to Calpee, pursued by the General in person, for several miles with Cavalry and Horse Artillery. The enemy, chiefly the Gwalior Sepoys and Sepoys of all Mutineer regiments, retired in perfect order, throwing out a rear-guard in skirmishing order. This was overtaken by the 14th Dragoons and some Irregular Cavalry (with the latter I charged) and was cut up to a man, fighting to the last with a valour that would have done honour to Leonidas. On several occasions I saw the fearless ruffians dash with their bayonets at our Dragoons after delivering their fire at two yards distance. I have never been under a hotter fire than at one time when, among their skirmishers, my horse boggled at a drop and I became a target . . .

Gall, *Letters*, pp. 34–6

139
Rose to Somerset

Koonch (via Indore)

[Manuscript telegram]   11 May 1858

About 4 or 5,000 mutinous sepoys from Calpee, 3,000 Boondelas, 1,000 Sowars and 400 Vullaitees with some guns had occupied Konch for the purpose of opposing my march to Calpee. Konch is a large and open town but difficult to attack because it is concealed by woods and surrounded with gardens and temples with high walls – the rebels had thrown up strong intrenchments for protecting the town from the Aite and Jhansi roads by which my force was marching on it. I marched here yesterday and turned all these defences by making a flank march to the Northwest and attacking the town from that quarter with my force and Major Orr's field force after having driven the enemy infantry and Cavalry out of the woods into the town with artillery fire. I stormed the town with my first Brigade in skirmishing order covered on each flank by cavalry and artillery, my second Brigade and Major Orr supporting. The Calpee sepoys seeing they were on the point of being cut off from Calpee returned in a mass in that direction and the town was in our hands in less than an hour. I pursued the enemy with Horse Artillery and Cavalry for more than 8 miles, the former firing into them, the latter charging them. The Artillery and Cavalry were so completely exhausted by the long day's march, the intense heat and day's operations that they could go no further. Among the slain are sepoys of the 1st, 2nd, 3rd, 4th & 7th Regiments Gwalior Contingent, of the 12th, 32nd, 52nd and 57th Regt[s] Bengal N.I. and Mehidpore Artillery. We took 8 guns, quantities of ammunition and tents. I had few killed and wounded some European soldiers were killed and others as well as officers struck by the sun which was 115 degrees in the shade. March on Calpee tomorrow.

OIOC MSS Eur F87, Box 9D, Letter Book 4

140
Orr to Chief of Staff, CIFF

Etowra[78]

Printed copy   14 May 1858

I have the honor to forward the subjoined Report for submission to the Major General Commanding, of the part taken by the Field Force, Hyderabad Contingent, under my Command as per margin*, in the Action at Koonch fought with the Rebel Forces under Tantea Topee on the 7th Instant.

2. I received during the night of the 6th, the instructions transmitted to me by you, directing me to move from my Encampment at Aite[79] towards my left flank, and proceeding by Bassoop and Sunnow, align my force by its Left, with the Right of the 2nd Brigade which I should find resting on the village of Oomree. I marched during the night and early next morning (the 7th) opened a communication with Brigadier Steuart Commanding 2nd Brigade.

3. About 8 o'Clock, the Enemy appeared in force on my right flank, a large body of Cavalry supported by Infantry moving steadily down towards Daree,[80] apparently advancing with much determination, and having opened fire from a Battery mounting two or three Guns, one of them of considerable calibre. I moved

---

*   1st Cavalry H.C., 182 Sabres Lieutenant Dowker Commanding
4th Cavalry H.C., 137 Sabres, Captain Murray Commanding
1st Co. Arty., 2–6pr Guns
2nd Co. Arty., 3–6pr Guns
4th Co. Arty., 2–12pr Howitzers   } Captain Douglas Commanding
         2–4½ inch Mortars
Left Wing 3rd Infantry 333 Bayonets Lieutenant MacQuoid[82] Commanding
5th Infantry 241 Bayonets Captain Hare Commanding

forward my line, and a few round from the Guns forced the Enemy back to their original position.

4. Having received the Major-General's orders to take ground to the left, I moved in that direction to the front of the village of Oomree, from which I advanced direct upon Koonch. In my immediate front were some gardens and walled enclosures, held in force by the Enemy, and from which a heavy fire was directed upon our line. The Artillery under Captain Douglas advanced, and its fire having silenced that of the Rebels, I ordered the gardens and enclosures to be seized by the Infantry. This was very gallantly effected by a Detachment of the 5th Infantry, consisting of two Companies under Command of Lieutenant Partridge, 23rd Bengal Native Infantry, doing duty 5th Infantry Hyderabad Contingent, a very promising young Officer,[81] and the Enemy were very quickly driven out. At the same time, I directed the whole of the Cavalry under Command of Captain Murray and Lieutenant Dowker to move to the right and charge the Enemy's Horsemen, who had all this time been threatening our flank. This service was promptly and effectually performed, the Horsemen being driven quite off the field at this point and forced back within the line of their supports of Infantry, occupying several deep ravines and broken ground, and from the shelter of which a heavy fire was directed. The Enemy's Guns at the same time opened with round shot and shrapnell. The Cavalry were subsequently joined by one Squadron of Her Majesty's 14th Light Dragoons and two Horse Artillery Guns, the whole commanded by Major Scudamore, and they retained possession of the ground they had gained until the general advance, when they also followed the Enemy in pursuit.

5. The Artillery had meanwhile advanced so far as to bring it completely within range of the Enemy's Guns from two Batteries, and they were thus enabled to open upon it a double fire of round shot, shell and shrapnell from the effects of which several Casualties occurred. The Rebel Infantry also being strongly re-inforced, again suddenly came forward with a rush in great numbers and forced back the Detachment holding the Garden. I was about to advance once more at this point when I learnt that the Major-General with

the 1st Brigade had forced the Enemy's positions and was in possession of the Fort and Town. The whole Force now advanced, the Enemy was driven from the enclosures he held, and joining in the retreat of his main body, proceeded in the direction of the Orri road. I moved forward with the Cavalry portion of the Force under my Command, and joined with Her Majesty's 14th Dragoons, the Horse Artillery and Horse Field Battery in the pursuit, which continued for about eight miles, cutting up a great many of the fugitive Rebels, consisting almost entirely of Sepoys of the Mutinous Corps of the Gwalior Contingent and Bengal Army. The great start obtained by the Enemy before the fact of their retreating became known; the extraordinary great heat of the day, and the utter want of water, and the exhaustion of both men and horses from these two causes, all combined to make the loss of the Enemy heavy, though it was less so than it would otherwise have proved. The Force returned to Camp at 8 P.M. having been since 2 A.M. under arms, and in the saddle.

❋ ❋ ❋

MDP General Order 147, 1858

141
Hamilton to Edmonstone

Golaoli

[Printed copy] 17 May 1858

No. 209

I have the honour to report that the First Brigade of the Central India Field Force under the Command of Major-General Sir Hugh Rose K.C.B. arrived, and encamped on the right bank of the Jumna on the 15th, taking up a position about 4 miles below the Fort of Calpee. The Second Brigade arrived and took up its position on the 16th.

2nd – Communication has been opened with Brigadier Maxwell who came to our camp yesterday and left this morning for Bogulpore;[83] his force will take up its ground to-morrow (the 18th) and Colonel Riddell, with the Etawah Column, is at Oryah[84] and moving downwards.

3rd – The rebels are in some force, they have been joined by the Nawab of Banda and some 3,000 fighting men; they showed yesterday and attempted to get at the baggage of the 2nd Brigade, coming out with 2 Horse Artillery Guns and one drawn by an elephant, with Cavalry and Infantry, but were driven into their entrenchments suffering some loss.

4th – The following persons are in Calpee; the Jhansi Baee,[85] Rao Sahib, nephew of Nana Sahib, and the Nawab of Banda; Tantia Topi left Calpee and whether he has returned is rather doubtful.

❊ ❊ ❊

FSC, No. 89, 25 June 1858; FSUP, III, pp. 377–8

142
Note by Rose

Golaoli

[Holograph copy]   17 May 1858

The great influence of the Rajahs of Banpore & Shahghur, as feudal chiefs of most ancient name and power, in a purely feudal Country, will always enable them to convulse the country, until they and their Adherents are completely subdued by the establishment of a strong Civil power, aided by the Military.

The formidable masses of rebels composed of troops of all Arms, who were in possession not only of the Forts and Strongholds but of the whole country itself, & who carried on Military Operations on a large scale, have been completely beaten whenever they have attempted to meet the Central India Field Force – 100 guns, and all the Forts have been taken; rebel Arsenals, Foundries of Cannon, Manufactories of Powder &c have been destroyed; and the Country has been restored to the Government. But the continued advance of the Force, and the Force itself, having had no Reserve, have been the cause that the rebels, beaten & dispersed, have fled far from the Force, and then doubled back to the former scene of their rebellion. It is therefore of extreme importance for the sake of knocking revolt entirely on the head, and consolidating the peace and order of the Country, that Reserves of Troops should now quench the tinder in those places where burnt but lately the flames of rebellion.

And I beg to record my conviction, not due to any intelligence, but simply due to a constant practical experience of five months in the insurgent Districts, that it is of infinitely greater importance that Government should stifle entirely the rebellion and do the little which is now necessary to consolidate order in the Shahghur, Chandeeree, Jhansie and other Districts in Bundlecund, than send troops to Gwalior, in which, so far as I can learn, no overt act of rebellion has occurred. On the contrary, the Chief of Gwalior has been able to assist Government frequently out of his own territories – he garrisoned Chanduree; – he is constantly escorting supplies for me; – he defeated and harassed the Kotah rebels; and even captured some of their guns; all this with his Native resources.

Surely, then, it would be a matter of deep regret were a great part of the line of country which the Central India Field Force has wrested from the Rebels, to fall again, were it only partially, under their powers.

Were Saugor to be again threatened, the Forts of Jhansie, Thal Behut, Maurora & Chandeeree retaken, communication between Saugor & Jhansie cut off, the strong passes separating the Saugor & Chandeeree Districts re-occupied, the revenue again diverted from the Coffers of the State, into the pockets of the Rajahs of Banpore and Shahghur, who will apply them, as before, to founding Cannon, repairing Forts, organising Rebels, Troops &c – and I must observe that nothing is so likely to place public order in Gwalior on a sound footing, as a healthy state of the public order in Jhansie, Chanduree and the circumjacent Districts.

Every man of this Force who will be sent to Thal Behat, Lullutpore &c will be a guarantee for the peace of Gwalior.

Of course, when order is re-established in the Districts in question, or if Troops are forthcoming, it would be highly desirable to strengthen Scindia by the presence of British troops in

Gwalior. But for the sake of the welfare of the Government and the success of the Service on which I have been employed, I should seriously regret were Troops sent to keep the peace in Gwalior, where it has not been broken, and not sent to Districts where rebellion for nine months was all powerful, where it has lately been defeated, and now only requires the presence of a portion of the Force which defeated it, entirely to subdue it.

I always understood that a Brigade of Major Gen[l] Whitlock's Field Force was to be stationed in the Shahghur & Chandeeree Districts, and if this distribution were carried out, it would be better than any other. I only speak of occupying the Districts, with part of the Central India Field Force in the event of a Brigade of Gen[l] Whitlock's not doing so.

OIOC MSS Eur D174, pp. 522–4

143
Rose to Elphinstone

Golaoli

[Manuscript telegram]   19 May 1858

So great was the discouragement produced among the Rebels by their defeat at Koonch that the second day after only 11 Mutineers were left in Calpee. The arrival of the Nawab of Banda to assist them with 3,000 infantry and 1,000 Cavalry has given them fresh courage and the rebels now hold the fort and the town of Kalpee and part of the environs in force. My operations have been delayed by the sickness of my second Brigadier caused by exposure to the sun in the recent military operatins. Brigadier Stewart[86] and all his staff are on the sick list – they have been consequently inefficient and I have been obliged to protect them instead of being assisted by them. Today I march to Golowlee on the right bank of the Jumna four miles South east of Kalpee for the purpose of opening communications with Colonel Maxwell of whom I have heard nothing since I have been here.

OIOC MSS Eur F87, Box 9D, Letter Book 4

144
Rose to Canning (copies to Campbell, Elphinstone, Somerset, Harris (Madras),[87] C-in-C Madras)

Golaoli (via Cawnpore)

[Manuscript telegram]   20 May 1858

Rec^d copy of letter from Dr Arnott, Superintending Surgeon of this force which explains itself.[88] I have already requested Col. Maxwell to reinforce me with a portion of his force which he has agreed to do – intend attacking in a day or two as soon as two mortar batteries have shelled some defence which I cannot reach. I hope to have it at once – the fort of Calpee is weak but the approaches to it through a most difficult work of ravine two miles in breadth of which I had no knowledge until I came here, guarded by intrenchments and afterwards through the streets of Calpee – it may entail several days operations in the sun, which judging from the present state of the health of my force and the opinion of Dr Arnott would render it insufficient – the enemy have a strong force of mutinous sepoys, Welaitees and other rebels and from 12 to 15,000 Cavalry mutineers and several guns. The ground about Calpee is so strong that I cannot bring the enemy to a decisive action and I think probably that even when I have taken Calpee the rebels may continue operations in the country more especially as they know that exposure to the sun at this season always causes great sickness amongst Europeans. I have not merely against me the usual garrison of Calpee but they are now reinforced by the rebels from Kotah and a large force brought by the Nawab of Banda – under these circumstances reinforcements are absolutely necessary – I should think that General Whitlock could reinforce me with the utmost ease and expedition.

From Dr Arnott to Colonel Wetherall – I do myself the honour to draw the attention of the Major General Commanding the Central Indian Field Force to the health of the troops with reference to the operations which are supposed to be contemplated against Calpee – in the action before Koonch on the 8th May out of one Regiment about four hundred & twenty strong, lost 7 men sunstroke and admitted 35 into hospital and whenever it has been exposed has suffered very severely – though the rest of the troops have been heavily [?affected] and the admissions to Hospital very numerous from the overwhelming effects – temperature from 100 to 117 degrees in tents and seldom falling under 100 at night, but to illustrate better the state of health I may mention that we now have 310 Europeans in Hospital, having lost in the week 21 by sunstroke and there is scarcely an officer of the Staff fit for duty – The Quarter Master General and Brigadier Second Brigade sick – several of them and many other officers will have to go to Europe, and others will [?have to go] elsewhere for change of climate. [indecipherable] the rest enfeebled and worked out by their long arduous campaign. I cannot refrain from mentioning my apprehension should the operation before Calpee be protracted and exposure great that the force will be completely prostrated.[89]

OIOC MSS Eur F87, Box 9D, Letter Book 4

145
Bonus to his parents

Golaoli

[Typewritten copy]   22 May 1858

I ought to add a great deal to this letter but it must be posted to-day. We, that is the Second Brigade, left Etowra at dawn on the 16th and almost at once the enemy appeared on our flank. My company of Sappers formed part of the rear guard, I cannot imagine the reason for this, I think a mistake had been made as Sappers are not of much use in such a position. Our rear guard was composed of all arms, Cavalry, Infantry, Sappers and Artillery (2 guns),[90] it was not too strong for the enemy was in great force; they had 5 guns, about 1,500 Cavalry and a 1,000 Infantry. If they had had the pluck to push this attack home, they might have done a great deal of damage. You see, our business was not to fight an action but to protect the baggage and stores. The stores and supplies are nearly all in bullock carts, these move about 2½ miles an hour under ordinary conditions, in our case the conditions were by no means ordinary; the cattle were half starved, the loads heavy, the heat extreme, and the road a mere cross country track deep in dust. Very soon after our start we came to a nasty nullah which badly throttled the traffic. I took my position here with my men in order to help the carts across; it was a wearisome job, a few carts broke down and had to be abandoned. We moved on slowly across the plain, the enemy following us closely, and keeping up a continuous fire from their guns but their horsemen did nothing, they funked. Our guns of course were worked steadily. The affair was indeed rather a pretty sight. We lost several men. In the afternoon, the General sent us some assistance and the enemy drew off. We halted at a village called Dipoora.[91] It was a hot, tiring but exciting day. I do not want to be a rear guard again. But I must end.

OIOC IOR neg. 4395

146
Mayne to Elphinstone

Goonah

[Manuscript telegram]   23 May 1858

An Express from Deputy Commissioner at Jhansi dated yesterday states that all communication with Sir Hugh Rose has been cut off 5 days by rebels in some force in Koonch. The Police Thana at Lulitpore cut up, the fort and Thana Tal Behut evacuated and the whole of the Chanderee districts again [?not] in possession of the English – Jhansi threatened on all sides and the garrison too weak to move into the field.

The Rajahs of Shahgur, Bhanpore, 7,000 strong with some guns moved to assist the rebels at Chanderee – Colonel Smith will reach Chanderee on 25th Inst. but there is a call for him at Jhansi – I have ordered Sindeah's force about 650 strong to hold Chandereee but they are not to be depended on – When Colonel Smith leaves them, more troops are wanted – natives will do – I have quite sufficient here – One hundred and fifty Europeans besides my own horse.[92] No great resistance anticipated from these rebels but morally they effect great harm.

OIOC MSS F87, Box 9D, Letter Book 4

III

Kalpi to Gwalior, May to June 1858

With the fall of Lucknow, Kalpi was the last rebel fixed base in India. It contained a garrison of some 20,000 men, including many sepoys of the mutinied Bengal and Gwalior Contingent regiments, as well as a large arsenal, powder manufactury and gun foundry [152, 154]. Its defensive strength lay less in fixed defences, though these existed, than in its position resting on the Jumna and particularly on the network of ravines which covered the south and south-west approaches [144]. These offered excellent covered ways for sorties by the garrison while providing a baffling maze to attackers.

Close to finishing his campaign, Rose was determined not to be lured into an immediate frontal assault against powerful defences with a force greatly weakened by fatigue, constant fighting and disease, particularly sunstroke [179]. He therefore took up position four miles or so south of Kalpi, with his 1st Brigade resting on the river and his 2nd Brigade prolonging the line westwards towards the Jhansi road. Campbell had despatched a force under Colonel Maxwell to co-operate from the opposite bank of the river, with strict orders that no troops were to cross the river to join Rose; Maxwell would assist by shelling Kalpi and by preventing any escape across the river. This force arrived opposite Kalpi on 18 May [148].[1] The pontoons that Rose had dragged all the way from Poona were now used to ferry fresh supplies of ammunition from Cawnpore [180].

The rebels under Tantia Topi, the Rani, the Rao Sahib and the Nawab of Banda,[2] were conscious of the importance of Kalpi, both as a symbol of resistance and as their last stronghold. Defeated by Rose on every previous occasion, they appeared determined to fight to the last. They therefore pursued an aggressive policy, attacking the rear brigade of the CIFF as it struggled towards the Jumna [149] and, when the Force was finally in place, launching a series of attacks between 18 and 20 May against Rose's left.

Maxwell opened fire on 19 May and quickly created havoc in the town. Rose appears to have been aware that the rebels intended to make their major assault on the morning of 22 May. When it came it showed signs of careful planning and good co-ordination, and was driven home with a vigour not seen before. Making effective use of the ravines, the rebels first attacked the British centre and left, to lure troops away from the right where the main attack would be made. Despite Maxwell's instructions, Rose had brought the Camel Corps across the river to strengthen his infantry since the country was unsuitable for decisive action by cavalry [144, 148]. Rose claimed not to have been deceived by the rebel diversion but the violence of the attack on his right was unexpected [149, 150].[3] Stuart's troops were forced back and he and his staff had to draw swords in self-defence.[4] As at the Betwa, Rose now intervened decisively, leading a dismounted charge of the Camel Corps which finally broke the rebel attack [180]. The rebel army now retreated rapidly on Kalpi but Rose's infantry was too exhausted by the heat and fighting to follow up. Gall with some of the cavalry managed to cut up some of the fugitives but the major part of the rebels succeeded in escaping northwards. Rose occupied Kalpi the next day and despatched a properly organised pursuit under Robertson [147]. The line of retreat of the rebels was not immediately clear although it seems to have been assumed that they would head northwards along the Jumna in order to cross over into the Doab [150].

The CIFF had reached now the goal set for it seven months before and was entitled to assume that the campaign was over. Rose had been pressed to accept command of the troops to be stationed at Gwalior and Kalpi, with the status of a divisional commander. He refused this, ostensibly on grounds of ill-health, and, handing over command to Brigadier-General Robert Napier[5] and putting his horses up for sale, he prepared to return to Poona to resume his command there. The Hyderabad Contingent Force had already commenced its march to Ellichpur, its nominated peacetime station in the Deccan, when news reached Kalpi on 4 June that the rebel leaders, with the remnants of their forces, had seized Gwalior, defeating Sindia and enlisting many of his troops. With its famous fortress, its stores of treasure, munitions and other materials, the rebels had once more a base and an army, and the nightmare of a rebel invasion of Central and Southern India had revived.[6]

The magnitude of the crisis was readily apparent [186] and Rose immediately reassumed command,[7] Napier becoming second-in-command and brigade commander, and started despatching all available troops towards Gwalior, halting Robertson until these troops could catch up with him. The Hyderabad force was halted and directed across country to join the rest of the troops. Rose himself left Kalpi on 6 June but the last of his troops was detained until they could be relieved by troops from Cawnpore [164].

The Gwalior campaign differed in one significant way from the campaign which had gone before. From Mhow to Kalpi the CIFF had fought its way without assistance. At Kalpi it had linked up via Maxwell and Cawnpore with the main theatre of operations in Northern India. Rose was now able to call upon assistance from a number of sources and to conduct a co-ordinated campaign. Nothing more vividly illustrates the change in the overall situation in India than this ability to concentrate a number of forces. From Agra, a moveable column under Colonel Riddell moved southwards, escorting siege artillery.[8] From the west a brigade under Brigadier Smith,[9] which had been pursuing a largely aimless course through Gujerat and Rajputana, and had reached Sipri, was directed northwards on Gwalior, linking up en route with a force under Orr which had been operating round Jhansi. From Cawnpore, troops moved to relieve Rose's units still garrisoning Kalpi.

Rose reached Morar, the former cantonments of the Gwalior Contingent, four and a half miles east of the city, on 16 June where he fought a sharp engagement against the rebels and re-occupied the cantonments. Next day Smith's brigade occupied Kotah-ki-Serai, three miles south of the city, fronting a line of hills occupied by the rebels which protected the city.

The Gwalior position consisted of two basic elements – the celebrated fortress, reputed the strongest in India, which occupied the top of a great hill directly west of Morar, with the old city clustering round its northern end,[10] and the 'new' city of Gwalior (the Lashkar), one and a half miles to the south east.[11] If the rebels had chosen to occupy the fortress Rose would have been in serious difficulties since he hardly had enough men to invest it, and because of its height above the plain, it could not be breached but only taken by escalade. The rebels had however learned the fatal consequences of standing behind fixed defences and their army was concentrated on the southern flank of the city where a huge parade ground provided room for deployment and manoeuvre.

On arriving, Smith seized positions on the hills in front of Kotah-ki-Serai, and a squadron of the 8th penetrated a pass in the hills and charged almost as far as the city [176, 179, 182].[12] On the 18th he was joined by Rose with one brigade, Napier being left to hold Morar. Riddell was expected to occupy the former British Residency seven miles north of the city and cut off escape that way. Rose planned to seize the hills in front of Kotah-ki-Serai and then assault the city.

On the morning of the 19th he occupied positions on the hills, intending to attack Gwalior on the 20th. His troops however swept all before them on the 19th and Rose wisely seized the moment to bring forward his main attack [186]. By nightfall on the 20th, Rose had effectively occupied Gwalior. Riddell had failed to obey his instructions and the fleeing rebels escaped that way [195]. The fort was occupied next morning when a picket of the 25th Bombay Native Infantry discovered that it was virtually deserted and seized it in a daring assault.[13] Napier was despatched in pursuit of the rebels the same day (21 June) and caught up with them at Jaora Alipur some 45 miles to the north-west where he soundly defeated them on 23 June [186]. Tantia escaped, to roam Rajputana and Central India until April 1859 when he was betrayed and hanged at Sipri.[14]

The executions at Sehore pursued Rose until 1859 but the matter disappeared when he became Commander-in-Chief [192, 194]; Clyde's jealousy lasted longer [193].

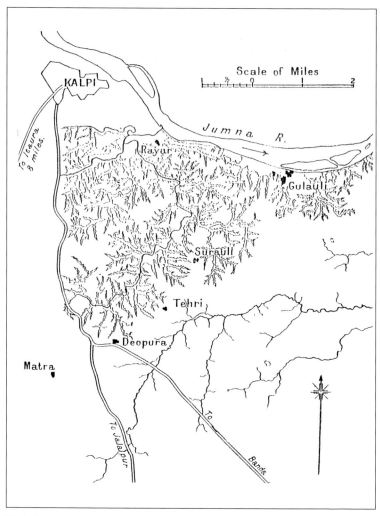

Kalpi

147
Field Force Orders

Kalpi

[Holograph] 23 May 1858

Parole [indecipherable]

Countersign Jhansi

1. The following troops will proceed in pursuit of the Enemy tomorrow morning marching at 3 o'clock under the command of Major Robertson

Two Troops 3ʳᵈ Bom Lᵗ Cavalry

150 Hyderabad Contingent Cavalry (to be selected by Major Orr)

No. 18 Lᵗ Field Battery

3 companies 25ᵗʰ Regᵗ N.I., leaving four companies behind, two of which are in the Fort

These troops will take their Camp Equipage and Commissariat with them.

OIOC MSS Eur D1007

148
Lieutenant-Colonel Maxwell to Chief of Staff, CIFF

Kalpi

[Printed copy] 24 May 1858

I arrived here on the morning of the 18th instant, with the force as per margin* and broke ground the same night. On the following

---

* 4 Guns, Major Blunt's Battery.[3]

266 Towana Horse[4]

578 of H.M.'s 88th Regiment

682 Camel Corps

458 Sikh Police

4 10-inch Mortars

4 8-inch Mortars

morning we had three 10-inch Mortars in position opposite the Fort of Culpee, and a fourth on the next day.

2. On the morning of the 19th, I received an urgent requisition from Sir Hugh Rose for a Wing of Her Majesty's 88th Regiment, a Wing of the Sikh Police Battalion, and the whole of the Camel Corps to join his force on the opposite side of the Jumna; the demand for this amount of Troops from my column was made upon the supposition that a patrol of three Companies of the 88th Regiment, 200 of the Sikh Battalion, and 100 of the Towana Horse and 2 guns which I had sent to Sherghur had rejoined me, but as that patrol had not returned, and I had no reason to expect it back for some time, I did not consider myself justified in complying to the full extent with Sir Hugh's request, and I sent across the Jumna on the night of the 20th, two companies of the 88th, the whole of the Camel Corps, and 124 of the Sikh Infantry, informing Sir Hugh that as soon as I could hear of the approach of the patrol I would send the remainder of the men asked for by him.

3. By Sir Hugh Rose's orders, I sent on the morning of the 21st two 8-inch mortars and two field guns, with a company of the 88th Regiment to Russoolpoor, a village about 3 miles below Culpee on the left bank of the Jumna, and opposite the village of Rehree, where the enemy had a battery which commanded the road by which Sir Hugh purposed advancing on Culpee.

4. During the night of the 21st, two 8-inch mortars were put into position in the village of Diloule opposite the Kutcherry and Town of Culpee.

5. Under instructions from Major-General Sir Hugh Rose, the three above mentioned Mortar Batteries opened fire at noon on Saturday, the 22nd. The well-directed fire of the mortars and guns from the Russoolpoor Battery, under Lieutenant Hare,[1] of the Bengal Artillery, soon cleared the village of Rehree, and the Rebels withdrew what guns they had there. The practice of Major Blunt's four 10-inch Mortar Battery was beautifully accurate, and that from Captain Turnbull's[2] at Diloule was most effective and well sustained until the occupation of the town by Sir Hugh Rose's force.

6. The river Jumna being between my force and the enemy, the Infantry and Cavalry under my command had not the opportunity of giving that active co-operation to Sir Hugh Rose that I could have wished, but they performed their picquet and battery duties much to my satisfaction, the Enfield rifles of the 88th Regiment annoyed the enemy very much and prevented them having the free use of the river in front of the town.

❊ ❊ ❊

Forrest, IV, Chapter 1, pp. 110–11

149
Bonus to his parents

Kalpi

[Typewritten copy]

24 May 1858

Since I posted my last on the 22nd, we have had a lively time. But I must go back to Dipoora; we halted there on the 17th and 18th; I think it was Sir Hugh's wish to keep the Brigade there as a protection to his left flank, but the water gave out and on the 19th we joined the camp on the Jumna to our great relief. The enemy attacked us each day at Dipoora but we had no difficulty in keeping them off.

By the way, did I tell that I lost my groom that rear guard day? He was with me at that unpleasant nullah but I did not see him afterwards, and when he did not turn up in camp I feared he was killed. But he came in the next morning, I questioned him, he said that at the nullah he was nearly overtaken, so he hid in a hole in the bank of the nullah until it was dark. I was very glad to see him for he is a good fellow and an excellent groom. The way in which our servants have behaved in this camp is really a marvel, they do their business as quietly and regularly as they do it in cantonments and make no complaints.

Our men and followers of all kinds were very glad to be on the river; water had been a great difficulty all the way from Koonch; we had only wells and as they were very deep the labour of watering all the animals was excessive.

A column from I believe Cawnpore met us on the Jumna to co-operate in the attack on Calpee. This column was composed of the 88th Connaught Rangers, a Camel Corps and some Sikhs. It was commanded by Colonel Maxwell. Part of these troops came across the river and joined our force. The Sikhs camped near me; on the evening of their arrival I was surprised by two men coming to my tent to ask for some food for their 'Sahib'. I was much impressed by their good manners and by their offer to carry food, by great luck I had some roast mutton that evening; I gave the men some and said I would come across to see their Sahib. I went and found a Warrant Officer was in charge of the party, quite a nice fellow but very weak from an attack of fever or sunstroke. However he had eaten the mutton and was very grateful. There was fighting every day at Galowlee and on the day I posted my last there was a regular battle, that was the 22nd, the enemy came on in great force and really pressed us hard, one or two of their round shot came right into camp. My men and I with them were left as part of the camp guard, we were simply spectators. The ground between Galowlee and Calpee is a mass of ravines running down to the Jumna, the enemy came along these on both flanks and were completely hidden; at one time I thought they would get into our camp, they were very close indeed. Eventually they were driven back and pursued for some distance, but the battle had lasted all day and our men were greatly exhausted. It was I think lucky we had received the reinforcements from Colonel Maxwell.

This battle gave us Calpee, for when we advanced the next morning the enemy scarcely offered any opposition; they fired a few round shot at an absurd range and then fairly bolted. For some reason not apparent to this subaltern, the column halted for nearly two hours, then the Horse Artillery and Cavalry were sent in pursuit. Calpee was not defended, the fort was evacuated and the whole crowd fled in rout toward Gwalior. In the pursuit a great many were killed. I rode along the route for some distance in the evening, there seemed to be a very large number of dead.

OIOC IOR neg. 4395

150
Hamilton to Edmonstone

Kalpi

[Holograph copy]   24 May 1858

I have great satisfaction in reporting the town of Calpee was yesterday re-occupied by British troops, the rebels having been driven out, & totally dispersed with the loss of their guns, ammunition, stores & baggage.

2. About 9 a.m. on the 22nd the rebels made a most determined attack from the town on the outposts, pressing on with great boldness under cover of the ravines; they were however met & repulsed at all points. Their Cavalry, which they had brought out – a very considerable body – were routed, pursued and cut up. Our loss, from the effects of the sun, were severe; but from the fire of the enemy, trifling.

3. On the following dawn (the 23rd), Major Genl Sir Hugh Rose advanced on the town with his whole force, clearing the whole of the intermediate ravines; the rebels were soon seen streaming out in great numbers & disorder; they were evidently taken by surprise. A few rounds were fired from a two-gun battery, constructed across the Jullalpore road,[5] but it was deserted before our troops could reach it. The pursuit of the rebels was kept up for some miles, during which they lost all their guns – 6 Elephants, Camels, stores, etc., & about 400 killed.

4. The Fort was evacuated; an 18 pounder, which they had attempted to carry off, was left at the entrance; the space within was covered with accoutrements, baggage, stores, cooking utensils, in utmost confusion – everything indicated the precipitation of their flight, & their utter discomfiture.

5. The fugitives proceeded by the Jalaun road, from which they have diverged towards Chowki, & will, I think, make for Jugmohanpore.[6] No certain information has yet reached me, & all the pursuing Detachmnts have not yet returned.

6. It is to be regretted that none of the leaders have on this occasion been arrested. Tantia Topee left Calpee some days ago, after his return from Koonch, the Jhansie Ranee went off before

mid-night of the 22nd, having been driven out by the shelling from Brig[r] Maxwell's Mortar Battery, on the left bank of the river. The Rao Sahib, and the Nawab of Banda fled on the morning of the 23rd. The nature of the country greatly favored their flight; our troops had to cross the heavy belt of ravines which encircle the town, before they could get on to the road by which the rebels were flying. However our success has been very great; we have full possession of their stronghold, with its vast supplies of military stores & ammunition; and the rebels are flying without guns or organisation, driven from the country in which they have for months exercised uncontrolled authority & power; the confederacy between the Boondela Rajahs and the Mahrattas broken up, & the mutinous Sepoys divided, disheartened & thoroughly routed, no longer acknowledge the Mahrattas as their chiefs.

7. I trust I may be permitted to congratulate His Lordship the Gov[r] general on the completion of the operations chalked out for the Central India Field Force. I am satisfied the conduct of all Arms of the Central India F[d] Force, since its formation at Indore on the 1[s] Dec[r], will meet its reward at the hands of the Gov[r] General. I do not think one point has been left undone that we were expected to do. Had the Force had a reserve, or any Troops to hold the country we had cleared, our work would have been more complete; but even with the small number of the Force of which it was comprised, the vast extent of the country over which it had to act, all the difficulties have been overcome; we have met with no check; we have relieved the garrison of Saugor; taken every Fort that offered any resistance; beaten the whole rebel force in the open Field; and swept the country from the Nerbudda to the Jumna, by the valley of the Betwa; and opened up the communications between Agra & Bombay; and destroyed the compact between the insurgent Boondelas & the Mahrattah party . . .

OIOC MSS Eur D174, pp. 524–5

151
Bonus to his parents

Kalpi

[Typewritten copy]   29 May 1858

This place is really quite delightful after the discomforts of the march from Jhansi; trees and water delight us all. We have captured immense supplies here, large quantities of ammunition and over 50 guns of all sorts, including those taken in the pursuit on the 23rd.

We were all under the impression that after Calpee, the force would be broken up for we have cleared our country and are now in touch with the Bengal armies. But yesterday orders came from Sir Colin Campbell which have shattered this hope, the force is to remain intact, one brigade at Gwalior, the other at Jhansi, Sir Hugh to remain in command; he will not like this, I think, he had fully expected to go to Poonah for the rains.[7] I am afraid I shall have to spend another rains in tents as there are very few houses either in Gwalior or Jhansi.

It is rumoured that the Ranee of Jhansi promised three months pay to her army if they beat us in the battle on the 22nd, after the fight she fled with Tantia Topee, her General, and the Nawab of Banda, a small column has gone in pursuit to prevent any rally.

The troops on the other side of the Jumna which came under Colonel Maxwell from Cawnpore have returned in that direction. I went across the river and saw some Addiscombe friends who were in that force. Some of our fellows have been over to Cawnpore to see it. Quite a large number of sick and wounded have been sent away, among them Brigadier Stewart, who commanded the Second Brigade, he completely broke down at Koonch, as I think I told you. Among other sick, Captain Leckie has gone, he was Deputy Assistant Q.M.G. of the Second Brigade.[8] To my intense surprise and gratification, I have been put into Captain Leckie's place. This is, I think I may say, no slight mark of Sir Hugh's approval of my work. He has been good to me in various ways. He has asked me to dinner several times, this however is not all bliss because one has to go in uniform with sword on thigh and he always goes to sleep immediately after dinner, and one cannot leave till he wakes, though one may be dog tired.

OIOC IOR neg. 4395

152
Shakespear, diary[9]

[Holograph]

May 15th Gulowlee on right bank of Jumna. About 10 miles. Fortunately a cold wind all the morning for we did not get in till late. On arrival went straight down to the river, how the old grey did enjoy the water putting half his head into it. A body of the Enemy's Cavalry supported by Infantry appeared on our left apparently watching our movements. Orr with a Reg[t] Hyd. Cavalry and some guns left behind to keep them in check and protect our long line of baggage. Some however managed to steal away to the rear without being noticed and cut up five or six of the 25th who were accompanying the baggage, they had not capped their muskets and so were surprised and did not fire a shot in defence. I have not heard of our losing any baggage. Some few straggling Dragoons came to the rescue. The ravines are so deep and come surging up from such a distance close to the road that the enemy are down on one before you know it. Last night some of our water carriers were cut up at a tank not far from Camp, some bullocks and an Elephant carried off, the latter recovered afterwards.

16th Sunday. Halt. This is the point from which we shall attack as we command a ford here by which our communication with Cawnpore is kept up. By going to the front of the Camp we can see the town of Calpee quite plain about four miles off. Orr is about three miles to our left and the 2nd Brigade has moved up to within about four miles of his left so covering the Julalpore and Hummeerpore roads, the whole of the country towards Koonch and to the north is open to the rebels if they are inclined to bolt, but we can't help it if we are not strong enough to invest the place at all. There has been a good deal of firing in Orr's direction and I hear the 2nd Brigade baggage was attacked by the enemy with a large body of cavalry, two H. Artillery Guns and one drawn by Elephants. They were said to have manoeuvred well but were beaten off, rallying two or three times. We are said to have lost neither Europeans nor baggage.[10] Col Maxwell came over from the other side this morning. His Brigade will be opposite Calpe on Tuesday.

18th Hear today that on Sunday the 2nd Brigade lost thirteen carts. Maxwell's Brigade arrived opposite Calpee the other side of the Jumna this morning. Reported that the 3rd Bombay and some Hyd. Cavalry bolted this morning before the Enemy knocking over nine gunners in their flight and leaving the guns to their fate, fortunately the enemy did not press us and the guns were brought off. Reports that the enemy from Humeerpore and Julalpore have advanced up to Kindoura.[11]

19th Maxwell's mortars opened on the town and fort this morning. The 2nd Brigade and Orr joined us this morning, scarcity of water drove them in to the banks of the river. The Hyd. Cavalry did not bolt yesterday only the 3rd Cavalry. No post for the last three days. Enemy occupy villages with a few cavalry and have cut off our communication with Jhansie. Nothing being done apparently. Time wasted.

20th Went to pay the old 2nd Brigade a visit. A great many officers done up. The Brigadier amongst the number. Heavy fire of musketry and guns to the front all day. The enemy steal up the ravines and bother us. Some seven of the 86th knocked over by sunstroke, and five wounded, the enemy not retiring till the evening. Abbott went out foraging, covered by some Dragoons. These latter brought 17 men back in dhoolies out of 36 that went! All sun.

21st Went to the front of Camp today to see where the fighting had been yesterday, they never reached our advanced pickets. 300 of the Camel Corps came across us today, they are all rifles[12] and each man mounted behind a driver. They can go fifty miles on end. Talbehut, Chandeeree, Banpore are all in the hands of the rebels again and Shahghur is likewise reported to be.

22nd Seven of the Camel Corps died yesterday of sunstroke, we are losing men daily and doing nothing, a great pity the General does not go in at once. Maxwell's mortars playing all yesterday and at it again today. Firing commenced to the front. I hear the enemy had quite made up their minds to attack us the day before yesterday. Today they attacked us in great strength and in all directions but were beaten off with great loss and all was over by 12 o'clock. Three of the Staff had horses shot under them. The Enemy very nearly succeeded in taking three of our guns which were supposed to be strongly enough posted to do without support but the rebels managed to get up within 60 yards of them, throwing themselves on their faces when the guns were fired. Some of the Camel Corps arrived just in time, went straight at the blackguards with the bayonet and accounted for them all. The 86th made a good bag too. They surrounded a party of some two hundred on the top of the bank and forced them all over at bayonet point into the river and even following them up to their waists in water did not allow one to escape. Our guns did great execution amongst their Cavalry. We have lost I fear a good many by sunstroke. Tomorrow morning we attack in two Columns, the right Column being composed entirely of Infantry beating through the ravines, their right resting on the river and the left Column of Cavalry, Horse Artillery and Camel Corps going to the left outside the ravines. The start is at two. The whole camp to be struck and collected. The right Column under Brig. Stuart, the left under the General, the camp collected under Capt. Hare.

23rd Sir Robert and I started about daylight, much wounded but we heard no firing to the front and shortly after not less surprised at finding ourselves up with the right Column and the dust of the left visible, in fact the whole thing had only just commenced. We accompanied the right column beating in lines (of about two miles) through the ravines, it was very pretty but there was no enemy, we surprised a picket and in truth the whole of them, they never thought that after yesterday's hard fight we should be down on them so soon. Not half a dozen shots were fired when we arrived at the limit where we were to remain till the left column came up. Unfortunately the General had never calculated on our getting through the ravines so easily and quickly and there we had to wait within sight, quite close to the town and then *horribile dictu* we saw the enemy stream away out of the town, elephants (18 we counted), numberless camels, carts and people all streaming away on the road to Jaloun, the identical one the left column was to have stopped up. Our orders against advancing beyond a certain distance were so strict that the Brigadier did not dare move, in truth there were two of the enemy's guns about 500 yards beyond our extreme left and rather in rear of it which we allowed to play on the General as he came up although the 71st who were close to the guns were most anxious and could have easily taken them in five minutes. Was not all this most trying to us, before the General reached this position we exchanged a few shots with these two guns but they soon limbered up and were carried off before our noses, and with all the rest got clear away leaving the town and fort perfectly empty. Two of Sir Robert's orderly Sowars were the first in the town and reporting it empty were sent off to the General who then ordered the Cavalry in pursuit who succeeded in capturing six guns, all the enemy are believed to have had, seven Elephants and a lot of cattle. We all put up in sundry little temples for the day and amused ourselves principally by abusing the General. I never saw anything so disgusting as that stream of fighting men etc. all passing before us without our pulling a trigger when a short advance would have given all into our hands. We got into tents by the evening.

24th Queen's Birthday. Royal Salute. We went up to see the Fort, such quantities of stores of all kinds, red jackets of all regiments, brass shells numberless and beautiful wood. The enemy had got their last 18 pounder English out of the fort but a wheel of the limber having been smashed by a shell they could not carry it off. There were three other large native guns in the fort and two sham wooden guns overlooking the river! Two underground magazines have been discovered with 500 barrels of

100 lbs of powder each besides no end of muskets and small arm ammunition. We (politicals) recovered an English nine pounder left in a village near by.

25th Major Macpherson, Pol. Agent Gwalior arrived in Camp last evening. Such a dust storm yesterday it was no use trying to keep one's face clean! Today I have got the whole tent shut up. Fanny's letters of 31st March and 16th April received today! Our first post since the 17th having been received.

26th A tremendous dust storm with rain, thunder etc. yesterday evening, drizzling rain all night and a cool morning.[13]

27th Last evening our *outgoing* dawk of the 17th brought in from Etowa, a village a few miles off. The runner had been murdered by some of the Enemy's cavalry having been betrayed by the villagers and the whole bag was one pulp except just in the heart of it where was found a letter I had posted that day for Henry! – almost the only letter recovered, it was re-despatched at once. Paid the Fort another visit and had a look at the guns we have captured here, 21 in number all drawn up before the General's tent, one 18 pounder and two nines (English) seven large brass ones (native) and eleven small ones.

29th Nothing particular, except that we are all tired of stopping here doing nothing for this last week when we might have been well on our way to Gwalior by this time.[14] Robertson who moved out with the 25th N.I. on the Queen's Birthday to prevent the rebels going south towards Jhansie seems to have gone in the Gwalior direction after them.

31st Orr with his Brigade gone off towards Jhansie to punish some refractory Thakoors who have been burning and plundering. I hope he is on his way to the Deccan too for I think the Hyderabad troops have been quite long enough away from their homes and I really do not think it is safe keeping them any longer, they are evidently getting discontented.[15]

OIOC Home Miscellany 725

153
Rose to Mansfield

Kalpi

[Holograph copy]   30 May 1858

. . . With reference to the return, I beg leave to observe that the Brigade at Mhow, that is the 3rd Brigade of my Force, under Brigadier Honnor C.B., is only under my orders in so far as any Order I may give him respecting the distribution of his Force does not interfere with the distribution of it which the Bombay Government may think necessary to make, on account of the state of the Country, about Mhow or elsewhere.

I ordered the Left Wing of the 71st Highland Light Infantry and a Wing of the 3rd Bombay Light Cavalry to join my Force; but neither of these Orders were carried out, on account of orders from Bombay, directing these Troops not to leave Mhow.

Colonel Smith C.B.'s Brigade of the Rajpootana Field Force, was only lent to me for the protection of Jhansie, whilst I was at Calpee.

Colonel Smith, as I had the honor to report, marched from Goonah to Chandairie to retake it from the Rebels. This Force may be recalled to Rajpootana any minute, either by Major Genl Roberts, Commanding the Rajpootana Field Force, or by the Bombay Government.

In consequence of the assistance of Colonel Smith's Brigade to my Force being merely temporary, I ordered up from Mhow the 19th Reg^{t} Bombay N.I. to Poonah,[16] in order to move it from thence in co-operation with Troops from Jhansie, against the rebels in the Chandairee district. But it is very likely that the Regiment may receive counter-orders from Bombay.

I go into these details in order that His Excellency the Commander in Chief may see that neither the Troops forming the Brigade at Mhow, nor Colonel Smith's Brigade can be counted upon for cooperation in Gwalior, Jhansie, Chandairee or Bundlecund.

I beg also to draw your attention to the fact that the Hyderabad Contingent Field Force was merely lent to me by Sir Robert

Hamilton, who succeeded Colonel Durand, to whom the Force had been lent by Colonel Davidson, Resident at Hyderabad.[17]

It was always understood that this Force was required in the Deccan, & was to return to it after the fall of Calpee. I cannot therefore count on the co-operation of this Force, which may be re-called at any time.

Consequently the only Troops on whose services I can reckon with certainty are my own 1st and 2nd Brigades, of which latter, part was left to garrison Jhansie.

In order to make known to His Excellency the services which will be required from this Force, on its return from Jhansie, I enclose a copy of a note of observations which I wrote at Sir R. Hamilton's request, on a Note he had drawn up on the subject.

The Shahghur District is occupied by small Detachments of the 31st and 42nd Reg[ts] Bengal N.I. from Saugor. The important passes through the mountainous ranges which divide Saugor from the Shahghur & Chandairee Districts, are merely held by Police. The Rebels, besides re-taking Chandairee, have re-taken Lullutpore, a British Cantonment before this mutiny, in the Chandairee District, driving out and killing some of the Government Officers, Police, & a Detachment of troops of an ally, the Ranee of Tehree.

If the spirit of revolt in the Chandairee District is not quickly crushed by the appearance of Troops, it will spread; the small Detachments of native Troops holding posts in the Shahghur Districts; and the Police occupying the passes, above mentioned, will very likely be over-powered, Saugor will again be threatened, and all that part of Central India will be afresh the scene of disorder & rebellion.

In a telegram which I wrote after forcing the Passes above mentioned, I had the honor to say that I required Troops to occupy the Country which I took, as I went on. I am quite aware that if there had been Troops to send for the purpose I stated, they would have been sent. But the continual advance of my Force, without any Reserve, has been the cause that some of the country I left at a great distance behind me, has been partially re-occupied by the Rebels.

The only Force which can now send Troops to the Chandairee District is my 2nd Brigade, when it returns to Jhansie. Brigadier Wheeler[18] at Saugor complains much of the fewness of Troops at his disposal.

To garrison Jhansie, & to send a significant Force to Chandairee will be all, and even more than the 2nd Brigade ought to do, weakened as it is by sickness, and casualties of Officers and me in the Field.

I should not, under the circumstances, do my duty if I did not assure His Excellency that it would be fatal to the interests of Government, as regards the Chandairee District, Jhansie, and Calpee were my 2nd Brigade to garrison both Jhansie & Calpee. Both these garrisons would invite attack by their weakness. The Rebels, if they did not actually besiege, would invest both these places, humiliating our power by calling into evidence our weakness and inability to assist the surrounding Country, which they would ravage, cutting off our Daks, Supplies &c.

In a communication which I received today from Major General Whitlock, he tells me that he expects immediately his 2nd Brigade under Brig^r MacDuff;[19] that he would then re-inforce me with a Brigade efficient in all Arms. General Whitlock wrote this, not knowing that Calpee had fallen; and he thought he should have to assist at its Siege. I had already written to General Whitlock that I did not require his assistance as Calpee is ours; – he had not received this letter.

May I be permitted to suggest that the difficulties as to garrisoning Calpee & Jhansie, and sending Troops to Chandairee, could be solved if Brigadier MacDuff was to garrison Calpee, leaving a Detach^t at Humeerpore, which could be supported by the troops of its own Division in Banda & Calpee on both its flanks. Brig^r MacDuff's Brigade is quite fresh.

General Whitlock's Division could then guard the line of the Jumna & his rear, with a Force imposing by its numbers, its efficiency, and the complete state of its several Arms, including Siege Train.

The garrisons of Calpee & Jhansie would be strong enough to keep up mutual communications, & to clear the roads.

There is only one further suggestion, founded upon my practical experience, which I would venture to make, & that is that Saugor should be included in Central India; the Betwa – it is almost impassable in the monsoon – intervenes between Jhansie & the Chandairee District; consequently the officer Comm^g the Central India Field Force cannot put down, efficiently, disorder in the Chandairee District, unless he can direct the operations of the troops in the Saugor District, which surrounds the Chandairee District.

Saugor is now under Genl Whitlock, but as nearly the whole of his Force is concentrated at Banda, it would be far better that the very few troops he has left at Saugor, which is about 180 miles from Banda, should join him, and that Saugor should be placed in Central India, to which, as being North of the river Nerbudda, geographically & strategically it belongs.

Saugor has a garrison composed of a Bengal Battery, Detach^mts of the 31st & 42nd Reg^ts Bengal N.I. and part of the 3rd Bengal Irreg. Cavalry. Jhansie could reinforce this garrison if necessary; but the best protection for Saugor is the tranquillity of the Chandairee & Shahghur Districts.

Since I wrote the note enclosed in this report, Chandairee has been retaken, the reason therefore therein stated for promptly putting down rebellion in the Chandairee District requires additional strength. And it is clear that the growing disturbances in that District, and the near approach of the Monsoon, which will made the roads between Jhansie Calpee & Gwalior impassable, renders it advisable that the Central India Field Force should march as quickly as possible from Calpee.

Since writing the note I have had a long conversation with Major Macpherson, which has caused me to change the opinion, which I expressed in it, regarding Gwalior, because he states that the Government made a promise to Scindiah to send a Force to Gwalior as soon as Calpee was taken, and that he would have great cause to complain of breach of faith if this were not done.

This being the case, of course, there can be no doubt that a Force ought to go to Gwalior as soon as possible. But still I venture to think that the reasons for the presence of Troops in the Chandairee District are as urgent as ever. The Rebels are mere Bundilas without guns;[20] but if Troops are not sent after them, Rebel rule will usurp the authority & revenues of the Government.

In the margin* is the Force which I propose to send to Gwalior.

OIOC MSS Eur D174, pp. 526–31

154
Rose to Elphinstone and Somerset

Kalpi

[Manuscript telegram]   31 May 1858

The troops sent by me in pursuit of the Calpee sepoys and rebels took 8 guns of which 2 are English 9 pounders of the Gwalior Contingent and two other Horse Artillery guns of the rebels. Fifty guns were kept in the Fort of which one was an 18 pounder of the Gwalior Contingent and two were mortars made by themselves – four standards were taken one of which is the Colour of the Kotah Contingent and another a Vilaitee standard and most are the colours of the different regiments of the Gwalior Contingent. The subterranean magazine contains 10,000 pounds of English powder in barrels, 9,000 shot and empty shells, a quantity of 8 inch filled with shrapnell, a case of shot, siege and Ball ammunition for small arms, entrenching tools, tents new and old, boxes of muskets quite new flint and percussion, all sorts of ordnance stores in great quantities. The contents of this Magazine are supposed to be

* Batty 6–9 p[drs]
    "   4–9 p[drs]
Two 18 p[drs]
Two 8in.Mortars
½ Co. Bom. Sap & Miners
3 Squad. 14th L[t] Dragoons
150 Hydr[bd] Cavalry
86th Regiment
Rt Wing 71st H[d] L[t] Inf[y]
25th Reg[t] Bom.N.I.

worth 2 or 3 lakhs. There are 3 or 4 foundries for cannon in the town with all the requisites of a wheel and gun manufactury. A box has been found containing most important correspondence belonging to the Ranee of Jhansi, which throws great light on the revolt and its principal authors. Everything proves that the rebels considered Calpee and arsenal a post of great importance which they intended to keep to the last and they only abandoned it in consequence of the severe defeat which they sustained at Golowlee on the 20th Instant and the panic caused by the unexpected appearance of my force before Calpee on the following morning.[21] Five or six hundred sepoys were killed at the pursuit which was checked as usual by the intense heat of the sun which knocked up men and horses. The Sepoys are quite disturbed and disorganised, they threw away their arms, have left their red jackets and disguised themselves in order not to be known as sepoys.[22]

OIOC MSS Eur F87, Box 9D, Letter Book 4

155
Mansfield to Rose

[Holograph copy]
No. 81

Futtehghur
1 June 1858

I have the honor, by desire of His Excellency, to inform you that the various subjects treated of in your letter have been matters of consultation between the R[t] Hon. the Gov[r] Gen[l] and himself from the month of October last, when your share in the general combination of the Campaign was determined, until the present date. He is acquainted with the consolidation and strength of the various Forces alluded to in your despatch, & he is also but too well aware of the numerous demands made on them from many quarters at the same time; – a part of the subject with which no one is conversant but His Lordship the Governor General & His Excellency.

His Excellency is much obliged to your suggestion with regard to the arrangements necessary in your opinion for the Central

India Command. This is a subject on which Government can alone decide, & it has not escaped attention.

❊ ❊ ❊

OIOC MSS Eur D174, pp. 534–5

156
Mansfield to Hamilton

Futtehghur

[Holograph copy]
No. 82

1 June 1858

An order has already been sent to Sir Hugh Rose prescribing the disposal of his force. Unless the R^t Honble the Governor General should be pleased to order another arrangement, the Brigades lately denominated to the Central India Field Force will be distributed between Gwalior, Jhansie & Calpee. Colonel Smith CB will provide for Jullalpore, and in all probability the European portion of that officer's Brigade will proceed to Saugor. For the present, it is not the intention to draw on Maj. Genl Whitlock's Division, which has marched an immense distance, almost without halting, will be the only moveable Column left, beyond the right bank of the Jumna. when the Force, with which you are associated, shall be placed in the various Stations assigned to it.

The importance of maintaining a moveable Division to prevent the chance of investment by the Enemy of any of our Posts will not have escaped you.

I regret to say that many parties of Insurgents have crossed the Doab since the fall of Calpee. It is to be lamented that a portion of Colonel Maxwells Troops, including the Camel Corps, was estranged from the duty imposed it; the intention of the Commander in Chief having been to use them for the guard of the Doab, which was much threatened in consequence of the Trans-Jumna operations on the one side, and those in Rohilcund on the other.

It was always the opinion of His Excellency that the co-operation by means of mortar practice from the left bank of the

Jumna would ensure the speedy fall of Calpee without much resistance. He cannot but think that his anticipation has been justified by the result.

To ensure the safety of the Doab, His Excellency entered Rohilcund with a reduced force.

That the final operation in which you were engaged should be marked by the assistance rendered to the Force under Sir Hugh Rose, which had marched from the Nerbudda, by Colonel Maxwell's Column, which was organised in the Gangetic Doab, is evidence of the large combination arranged under the orders of the R^t Honble the Governor General during the last autumn, and of the great success which has attended it in every Province of India, from the boundaries of Bombay & Madras, to the extreme North West.

OIOC MSS Eur D174, p. 533

157
Rose to Hamilton

Kalpi

[Holograph copy]   1 June 1858

I will send off the remainder of the Force to Gwalior tomorrow.

I was afraid the Rebels w^d made a dash to Gwalior; they have numerous friends there with whom they are in understanding and it is every thing for them to make Gwalior replenish their coffers with a heavy ransom, from the buildings prepared for one man etc. But you & Major Macpherson both thought that it was only Scindiah's wishes to get our troops there.

It was most fortunate that I sent Colonel Robertson in pursuit and that I afterwards reinforced him.

You should inform Scindiah without a *moment's delay* that Colonel Robertson with a British force of all arms was at Bangra[23] yesterday and that he has orders to push on, and attack the Rebels in the rear, whilst he attacks them in front. This will encourage him & his faithful troops, and discourage his unfaithful troops and subjects.

BL Add MSS 42812, f. 82

158
Rose to Elphinstone and Somerset

Kalpi

Manuscript telegram   2 June 1858

The Central India Field Force having been disabled on the taking of Calpee I have received the permission of the Governor General to return to Poona to resume the Command of the Division there. My health has suffered so much from attacks of the sun and over fatigue that I could not stay in this part of India and was obliged to decline Divisional Command at Gwalior. A wing of the 3rd Europeans and a wing of the 24th Regiment Bombay N.I., the company of the Royal Engineers, the 1st troop Horse Artillery, one squadron 4th Lt Dragoons, the Madras Sappers and part of the Siege Train are to remain until further orders. I despatched on the 24th Inst. a moveable column under Lt Col Robertson in pursuit of the Calpee fugitives who after making a flight towards Shahgur took the road to Gwalior – rebels from Bareilly[24] joined the Calpee fugitives near the river. Scindia has written to me for troops to assist him against the rebels – Sir R. Hamilton has made a similar application. I sent off remainder of first Brigade [?supported] by a wing of the 71st with siege guns to Gwalior, Sir R. Hamilton accompanied the Brigade. Scindia is going with two Regiments of Infantry, 1,000 artillery and eighteen guns to meet the rebels. If his troops are faithful he ought to beat the rebels with the greatest ease.

OIOC MSS Eur F87, Box 9D, Letter Book 4

159
Mansfield to Secretary, Military Department[25]

Futtehghur

[Holograph copy]   2 June 1858
[forwarding despatches from Rose and Hamilton]
No. 83

It is obvious from the tone of the former, that Sir Robert Hamilton & Sir Hugh Rose do not appreciate the calls made for troops in other parts of the Empire, beyond the sphere of their immediate observation. This is very natural, and not a subject of remark, excepting that the attention of Government should be drawn to the circumstance.

Sir Hugh Rose dwells on the fact of his having no Reserve. This is hardly an accurate statement. The troops at Mhow, & the Rajpootana Column, gave him an effective support on his left flank, kept his direct communications by the Agra road free – as shown by the Detach[mt] of one of Major Gen[l] Roberts' Brigades to Jullalpore, under the orders of His Lordship, when Sir Hugh Rose became alarmed for his rear.

On his right flank he was in like manner assured by the laborious march of Major General Whitlock's Brigades, which actually operated at Banda in time to render the capture of Calpee, aided as Sir Hugh Rose was by a column formed in the Doab, to co-operate with him on the left bank of the Jumna, comparatively easy of accomplishment.[26]

His Excellency is glad to see that the aid afforded Sir Hugh Rose by Sindia is now acknowledged. Had it not been for the known fact that many of the Rajahs and Ranees of Central India and Bundelcund were friendly to us, it would of course have been imprudent to cause such Columns as those of Sir Hugh Rose and Major General Whitlock to advance as they have done from the Nerbudda to the Jumna, and His Excellency would not have recommended such a proceeding. But in truth it was known from the first that no real risk would attend their advances, and that the obstacles the Generals so happily overcame were not beyond the strength of the Forces placed under their commands, while at the same time being over their means of supply.[27]

The Commander-in-Chief has not answered the reasoning of Sir Hugh Rose, the subject of which more properly belongs to the Governor General's Agent in Central India, and to the Supreme Government, than to the purely military authorities, but he conceives it to be his duty to submit it to His Lordship with this remark that although much of it may be correct as regards the particular Districts referred to, total disregard is exhibited as to the resources available to meet the numerous requirements of the State, beyond the area of Sir Hugh Rose's immediate observation.

This is not said in blame. Sir Hugh Rose and perhaps Sir Robert Hamilton are influenced as all great authorities must be who are properly anxious for the welfare of the interests with which they are charged.

OIOC MSS Eur D174, p. 551

160
Rose to Orr

Kalpi

[Holograph copy]   3 June 1858

I am extremely pleased with your success against the Thakur of Bilowah;[28] it will have an excellent effect as the number of men killed, captured and wounded & the taking of the Fort, to say nothing of the disgraceful flight of the hero of Bilowah are unmistakeable facts which will teach the people of the country that we have strength enough to take Calpee and put down rebellion at a distance from it at the same time. I hope you will tell your Force how much I am pleased with their gallant conduct. I begged Wetherall to write to you an official approval. Yesterday I received a Telegram from Lord Canning at the end of which he says your Force is to go to Ellichpore[29] and today I received from the C in C instructions that your Force is to return home. I will send you instructions. I am sure that if on your return you can 'Bilowah' any other Thakurs you will; it will have an excellent effect on all the country you traverse. I am writing a despatch begging that you may receive your due for the Malwa campaign . . .

BL Add MSS 42812, f. 83

161
Secretary, Military Department, Allahabad to Colonel Smith[30]

Allahabad

(via Calcutta and Bombay)

[Manuscript telegram]   5 June 1858

Urgent. The Governor General requests that you will immediately advance on Gwalior to cooperate with Brig[r] Stewart. This is very urgent.

OIOC MSS Eur F87, Box 9D, Letter Book 4

162
Rose to Elphinstone and Somerset

Kalpi

[Manuscript telegram]   5 June 1858

The following telegram I sent this morning to Sir Colin Campbell. I have received your telegram of the 3rd June from which I learn that Gwalior is taken. Under these critical circumstances perceiving from His Excellency's approval of my services that he would be glad that I should retain the command of the Central India Field Force[31] I carefully put aside all considerations as to health and march immediately to Gwalior with a squadron 14th L[t] Dragoons, a squadron 3rd Bombay Light Cavalry, a troop of Horse Artillery and siege pieces. The wing of the 3rd Europeans and the company of the 24th Regiment Bombay N.I. to follow when relieved by the 5th Fusiliers from Cawnpore.

OIOC MSS Eur F87, Box 9D, Letter Book 4

163
Rose to Stuart

[Holograph copy]   [no place or date]

You had better close up to Robertson. He had better remain in his present position till we close up, unless you have cause to change his or your position. With respect to crossing the River you must use your own discretion as to this. I do not think that there is a chance of the river rising till we join you. Major Orr's Force & Brig. Smith's from Sippree are to advance.

BL Add MSS 42812 f. 86

164
Rose to Hamilton

near Ataria[32]

[Holograph copy] 6 June 1858

Many thanks for the sight of your despatch to the Govr General. I have written to Brig^r Smith at Sepree (the Com^{dr} in Chief and Govr General say he is there) and to Major Orr to take the route you indicated and join me below the Pass unless they should meet with insurmountable difficulties. But this route and their positions do not suit me, because I shall take up my position at the Cantonments,[33] and make Agra my base, as on account of the rising of the waters of the Scinde our communications with Jhansie & Calpee will be cut off. I fear Major Orr's & Brigadier Smith's [forces] will not be able to join me at the Cantonments. Could you take one of any other road for them. I should be very much obliged if you could.

I have asked the C in Chief to give me reinforcements in Cavalry, as our European Force of Cavalry only amounts to [blank] and that of the Enemy to 3,000 – that besides I shall require any Infantry he can let me have – the Siege in the Monsoon and there being no cover but tents in consequence of the burning down of the Cantonments, the loss of life will be considerable.

I have begged that the reinforcements may be sent from Agra and that a party be sent to protect the Ford or bridge over the Chumbal on the Grand Trunk Road near Dholpore.[34] Is it a Bridge or a Ghat? And how much of the road from Agra to Sepree is Macademised?

The rest of the Siege Train & the portion of the Force left at Kalpee cannot leave it till the morning of the 8th because they will not be earlier relieved by the 5th Fusiliers from Cawnpore.

Have you been good enough to prepare the transmission of supplies to our Force during the rains before Gwalior, altho' I sincerely hope the Siege may be a short one. Were Scindiah's two batteries of 9^{pdrs} taken? Does the Fort hold out?

Dont you think that Scindiah and Dinkar Rao ought to come to our Camp and rally all their friends, if they have any.

I have written to Brig. Honnor to keep open the communication from Mhow to Goonah.

Have you written to Mayne to do the same, they had better meet half way – Is Mayne at Sepree?

It is no use my moving up by forced marches as it is much better the whole Force should move together, not piece meal.

BL Add MSS 42812 ff. 84–5

165
Mansfield to Brigadier Showers[35]

Meerun ka Serai

[Holograph copy]   7 June 1858

1. Brigadier Showers C.B. will have 4-24^{pdr} Guns, 2-8 inch Howitzers & 4-8 inch Mortars (if possible, six) with their ammunition in readiness to move with Colonel Riddell.

2. Colonel Riddell,[36] in command of the 3rd Bengal Europeans, will not halt at Agra, but will be instructed by Brigadier Showers to pursue his march to Dholpore, with the whole of his Regiment, the three companies from Allyghur have been ordered to march on Agra.

3. On arriving at Dholpore, Colonel Riddell will call on the Officer Commanding the Puttealah Sikhs[37] to detach one thousand of them to accompany his Regiment.

4. Colonel Riddell will await at Dholpore any orders which Sir Hugh Rose may be pleased to send to him.

5. In addition to the ammunition for the Guns above stated, 1,000 ten inch shells will be sent to meet Sir Hugh Rose's wants.

6. Brigadier Showers will detach 2 Squadrons of Mead's Horse[38] with Colonel Riddell.

7. There being reason to suppose that Sir Hugh Rose's force is very short of shoes, Brigadier Showers will take measures to have 4,000 pairs of large size got together as rapidly as possible. If they are not to be had at Agra, he will send to Meerut for them, and request Gen[l] Bradford's assistance.[39]

8. Brig[dr] Showers will inform Colonel Riddell that Sir Hugh Rose expects to be before Gwalior on the 19th of this month. On his arrival therefore at Dholpore, he must lose no time in collecting the means of crossing the Chumbal.

9. The Commissariat & Ordnance Departments at Agra must be ready to meet all the requirements of Sir Hugh Rose.

10. Captain Light's Field Battery will accompany Colonel Riddell.[40]

11. Major Le Mesurier's[41] Company of Reserve Artillery has been ordered to Agra from Futtehghur, therefore whatever Reserve Artillery is now at Agra will accompany Colonel Riddell.

OIOC MSS Eur D174, pp. 558–9

166
Mansfield to Rose

Meerun-ka-Serai

[Holograph copy]   7 June 1858
No. 88

By desire of the Commander in Chief in India I have the honor to call your attention to an error of Military discipline into which you have fallen.

Although requested by the Governor-General, at the instance of the Commander in Chief, to retain the Command of the Troops to be stationed at Gwalior, and in the trans-Jumna country, you declined to do so on the ground of ill-health, and you formally laid down your command, your resignation having been accepted.

Without authority you re-assumed that Command. Such a proceeding is quite unprecedented, and I am to inform you by desire of His Excellency that a step of this nature cannot be overlooked in any one, whatever may be the rank & previous deserts of the Officer, who permits to himself such a departure from the rules of the Service.

The Right Honourable the Governor General having been pleased to acquiesce in your re-assumption of the Command of the Central India Field Force it is not for His Excellency to contravene the wishes of His Lordship. But His Excellency considers you departed from your Duty in addressing the Governor-General on the subject, seeing that you were in direct communication with the Commander-in-Chief.

No time would have been lost had you asked permission before re-assuming the Command; and in such a matter it was for you to look to His Excellency.

His Excellency is about to establish himself at Allahabad. Any further deviation from the usual course of Military Correspondence is unnecessary on your part. You will therefore have the goodness to conform to the practice of the Service in this matter, for the future, and to cease from all direct correspondence with the Government of India.

OIOC MSS Eur D174, pp. 560–1

167
Rose to Hamilton

Ataria
[Holograph copy]   7 January 1858[42]

Many thanks for your most kind letter. I did not answer it by your remaining Camel man because I wished to send the answer off to the Brigadier without delay; and I wished also to have a little time to give you information about our supplies. You say that you can furnish us with supplies for Europeans from Cawnpore, Calpi and Jahnsi. But I suppose that you only mean *before* the Monsoon[s] because after they have begun the Scinde and Pohooj[43] will rise so that our communications with these three towns will be completely cut off.

Pray have the kindness to give me an answer on three points for it is of very great importance. Can you supply from those three towns after the rains, and if so in what way?

and

2ⁿᵈ Pray tell me, if you *cannot* furnish us with supplies for Europeans from Cawnpore, Calpi and Jahnsie, will you be able to supply us when we have crossed the Scinde and are besieging Gwalior.

I do not like your plan of bringing up Major Orr's Force & Brig^dr Smith's force to the foot of a difficult pass, 20 miles from Gwalior. I hear that from there to Gwalior it is a network of ravines, and besides they are quite separated from me.

I *understand* that on the opposite side of the Cantonments the ground is much easier and then we have our rear to Agra, which must be our base.[44]

Pray tell me, how much of the road from Agra towards Goonah is *made* or Macademised? I asked you also yesterday is there a Bridge over the *Chumbal* where it crosses the Agra & Goonah road? Pray have the kindness to tell me. There is another point of importance respecting which I should feel very much obliged if you would give me exact information.

You advise that Brig Smith should move direct to Chandpoor, Secroree on the Jhansi & Gwalior road, & so form a junction by the Antree Pass.[45] If you look at the Map, you will see that the road crosses the Scinde River *twice*, passing, besides, through the Town of Nurroni, of which, I believe, the Rajah is our enemy.[46] Can heavy artillery go over these two fords?

BL Add MSS 42812, ff. 86–8

168
Birch to Rose

Allahabad
8 June 1858

[Holograph]
Nᵒ 181

Having laid before the Right Honble the Governor General your letter of the 14ᵗʰ ultimo regarding the disposal of the Mutineers of the Bhopal Contingent, I am directed to inform you that His Lordship would be glad to meet your wishes and to publish your letter, if this could be done appropriately, but as there is no reason for printing in the Gazette the other papers connected with the Bhopal Mutiny the insertion of your letter singly would not in His Lordship's opinion answer any good purpose.

2. I am desired to state that the reference was made to you in the belief that the proceedings of the Court Martial, shewing the evidence adduced against the Mutineers, were in your camp but as this is not so they will be called for from Bombay.

3. The Governor General considers the course taken by you to have been perfectly regular.

BL Add MSS 42807, f. 57

169
Rose to Robertson

Jalaun[47]

[Holograph copy]   8 June 1858

I am very much pleased with all your doing, and your letters are full of useful and important information; the only thing I was put out about was your not saying on which side of the River Scinde the Fort at Indoorkee was.[48] [indecipherable] and Sir Robert both wrote largely about the Fort, leaving me, equally, in the dark as to which side it was on.

I have directed Lt Col^l Hicks to march with Major Orr's Force & the reliefs of the different Corps at Jahnsi, straight to Gwalior, and Brig Smith to march from Sipree. It is six marchs from Jahnsie to Gwalior, it is seven marches from Sippree to Gwalior, it is seven marches from here to Gwalior. I sent these orders the day before yesterday; Major Orr ought to have received the order today; from there he will arrive just about the same time as this Force at Gwalior. Brig^{dr} Smith is a day later, but I hope that Brig Smith and Orr may unite, as Orr's Force is weak, & all native.

I hope that the whole of my Force may be *united* before Gwalior on the 17th. Under these circumstances it would not be desirable that you should move beyond Amayin,[49] to which place I beg Brig Stuart to close up, gain information, collect supplies etc.

I am perfectly alive to the advantage of striking *quick* but I am as much alive to the disadvantage of an isolated movement which even if it succeeded could not pursue or reap the fruits of a success, and I know also the great advantages of a *combined* and *concentrated* movement which takes the natives in flank & rear, which they dread, and enables you to pursue, which they dread still more. You see your informant cannot be relied on. The day before, they were going to attack you with 10 Reg^{ts} of Infantry, 20 guns and 2,000 Cavalry; the next day they were not going to attack at all. The only success the Rebels have ever had is by Treachery, [?hovering] on a weak force and then falling on them with overpowering numbers.

I believe that the Rebels are disheartened & divided – three or four days more will neither heal their dissensions nor improve their spirit, more especially when they know that three columns with a formidable resource of Artillery and Cavalry are surrounding them on every side. I am coming up with 2 Troops of the 14th, one Troop Horse Artillery, 350 Hyderabad Cav^{ly} and 200 H^d Infantry by forced marches.

In conclusion I beg you to halt at Amayin till I come up. Pray get all the information you can about the best place to attack the Fort and the Town.^{50} I hear from some that [indecipherable] hill is fortified, others say that it is not so. Pray like a good fellow ascertain the truth.

I feel confident that by the help of God we shall gain one *more laurel*, an unfading one, by a General and concentrated attack. But we must not give them a chance.

BL Add MSS 42812, ff. 88–90

170
Rose to Stuart

Jalaun

[Holograph copy]   8 June 1858

I send you, for your perusal, a letter to Robertson in which you see I beg him to halt at Amayin. You had better close up to him and look out for *Treachery* for that is the only way they can hurt us by;

pray have patrols sent out in every direction night and day. I am making forced marches to come up to you, and intend to cross the Scinde River on the 11th so that I shall be close to you then. I think you had better halt till I come up, as the other columns, Orr's and Brig Smith's, cannot be up before the 17th, or at earliest the 16th. Of course, if you wish to move to the front a little, or to the right or left for water or supplies pray do so. You may employ the time till I come in getting the best information about the best point for attacking the Town & Fort, getting all sorts of supplies etc.

I have with me Hare & Abbott all very flourishing. All our details will join with Co^l Hicks[51] who comes up with Orr from Jahnsee.

BL Add MSS 42812, ff. 90–1

171
Rose to Mansfield

Bangra

[Holograph copy]   9 June 1858

I was aware that His Excellency had had the goodness to order the Brigade under Colonel Smith CB to cooperate with me, and I have sent him directions to Seepree to march to Gwalior, effecting a junction on the road with Major Orr, who I also on the same day directed to move from Mansee with the part of his Force he has still with him, as well as two 8-inch Mortars and one 18 ^{pr}, which I gave him at Calpee to undertake his successful expedition against the Fort of Belawar, an inveterate rebel of Bundelcund, who was attacking the Calpee and Jhansie road.

Sir Robert Hamilton was good enough, at my request to show me the point of juncture for Colonel Smith and Major Orr, which is below the pass of Antri. Colonel Smith has only 6-p^{drs}, and Major Orr has purely a native force; this union will, consequently, be, I venture to think, advantageous to both.

I have directed both Colonel Smith and Major Orr to open communications, at once, with each other, and with Brigadier Stuart.

There can hardly be a doubt that Major Orr has received these instructions; but I am not so certain as to those sent in Despatch to Colonel Smith; through Jhansie, as Seepree is four marches from Jhansie, and the road between the two places is very much under the control of the Duttiah State, of which Captain Pemberly, Commissioner of Bundelcund,[52] says to me in a letter of the 4th inst. as follows:

'This news [of Gwalior] is well known at Duttiah and I hear the people there are, as might be expected, a little shaky' – and he adds 'that he has no doubt but the Districts will rise, and that we shall have but little more territory than our Troops can cover until we again get Gwalior for Scindiah'.

Lieutenant Colonel Liddell, commanding at Jhansie, in a letter received by me from him today, says also that the Bundeelas are rather encroaching from the Westward (the Seepree side) and that he had sent out a strong Patrol of Contingent Cavalry last night which cut up twenty out of a Picquet of twenty five they had placed at Dinora.[53]

Lieutenant Colonel Liddell wants Horse Artillery, 200 Cavalry, and Camels for Infantry, which, of course, under present circumstances, I cannot give him.

I hope an Order, sent in triplicate through Sir Robt Hamilton, will reach Colonel Smith, who by a report received today from him, arrived at Seepree from Chandiree on the 7th inst.

I am very much obliged to His Excellency for the re-inforcement of one Regiment of European Infantry, some Irregular Sikh Infantry, and a detail of heavy guns, which is to move to Dholpore.

I hear that the road from Agra to Gwalior, via Dholpore, is macademised or metal, but it requires repairs in some places.

May I suggest that it would be advantageous that the bad parts of this road, as far as possible, should be repaired by laborers under an Engineer from Agra . . .

I am much obliged to His Excellency for the shoes for such of my troops as require them – I have directed requisitions for shoes, required by Brigadier Smith's Brigade, as well as the Force under my Command, to be sent into my Head Quarters immediately, when I shall make the necessary application to you.

P.S. I have just have the honor to receive your Memo, of the 7th June, for the guidance of Brigadier Showers CB, Agra, giving details of the re-inforcements which His Excellency the Commander-in-Chief has been pleased to give me, for which I return my best thanks . . .[54]

OIOC MSS Eur D174, pp. 563–4

172
Private Wood to his mother

Indurki
[Holograph]   11 June 1858

. . . I hope that before this reaches you you will have heard of our engagement at Koonch and the attack of the enemy upon our camp on the 22nd May, and our turning out and driving them back with great loss and of our capture of Calpee on the 23rd May and the cavalry giving chase to those [who] were making their escape and cutting up some hundreds of the enemy and capturing Guns and Elephants and hoisting the British flag on the fort of Calpee on the 24th being the Queens Birthday, for the whole of these particulars I sent home by the last mail to Cousin Charles. And it was expected that this would finish up our campaign for this season, and a number of the officers got leave to return home and others to the Presidencies, even Sir H. Rose was going to leave us and go to Bombay and he published his thanks to the Army before leaving us. But even he is obliged to stop and we are now on our road to Gwalior for it is rumoured that the Rebels are assembling there from all quarters and that they have succeeded in taking the town and fort from Scindias new levies and the Rajah of Gwalior himself made his escape to Agra. Mind this is only a rumour for we are now within three days march of that place and every part of the road that we have come we find traces of the enemy in such things as cutting up the roads and blocking up passes etc. and I shall not be at all surprised to find some of them at this place but not so many as it is reported – at least I hope not for we have got to take up quarters in Gwalior for the wet months and should the enemy be in force we will have to remain in tents until we can get them out which I expect would take us some time for the fort is a very difficult place to get at. You say in your letter that you think it is nearly all over. I am afraid that it will be some time before it is all over and the Country quiet. I only wish that it was settled so that I could return home for I am quite tired of this Campaign as we have been at it now for the last 12 months. Dear Mother I am very happy to say that I am in good health and have been so the whole of the season. We have lost a many through the effects of the sun it being 120 in tents so that you may guess that it is very hot.

NAM 6307–60

173
Bonus to his parents

Dagaon

[Typewritten copy]   12 June 1858

. . . In three days we shall be at Gwalior but I gather that it is by no means certain how we shall find things. There are so many contradictory rumours. The politicals say that there will be no fighting, but they said the same about Jhansi. Then we hear that fighting is still going on between the rebels and Scindiah's men, that the magazine is still held by the latter. No one seems to know the facts.

Sir Souba, Scindiah's C. in C., came into our camp a day or two ago disguised as a fakir, he had been hiding in a hay-stack for 24 hours, so it is said, but I do not know where he found a hay-stack in this country. Scindiah will, we hear, join us from Agra, his presence will be valuable.

OIOC IOR neg. 4395

174
Rose to Smith

Morar

[Holograph copy]

17 June 1858

In case you should be pressed, and to bring in Lt Colonel Hicks & the details he has brought in with him and stores, I send Lt Colonel Robertson Com^g 25th Reg^t B.N.I. with 3 troops H.M. 14th Lt Dragoons, 100 Hyd. Cavalry and the 25th Reg^t BNI to you at Kote ka Serai. Colonel Robertson will communicate to you further instructions.

BL Add MSS 42812, f. 93

175
Shakespear, diary

[Holograph]

1st June. Twelve years today since I left England on board the Bucephalus. I wish I were on my way back. A Telegram from Gwalior today saying the Maharajah had moved out with 18 guns to meet the rebels, who having been rallied by Tantia Topey and joined by some of the Bareilly rebels were advancing with some guns on Gwalior. There is no fear if there be no treachery but it will be awkward if these 18 guns fall into the rebels' hands and the bungalows now all ready for us be burnt down. A Telegram to the same effect was received yesterday but little attention was paid to it. However this one with a strong letter from Sir Robert has had an effect on the General and he has ordered the remainder of the troops intended for Gwalior to march tomorrow so we are off at last. Robertson with the advanced party is at Indoorkee and reports no enemy. Orr has given the Thakoors who burnt down Moth[55] a good thrashing.

2nd Sursela. About 7 miles. How glad I am to get away from Calpee with its dust, horrible ravines and impure air. One feels a different being here. We shall have a very pretty Brigade by the time we reach Indoorkee and join Robertson. H.M.86, Wing H.M.71st, 25th Bom.N.I. two Batteries European and three

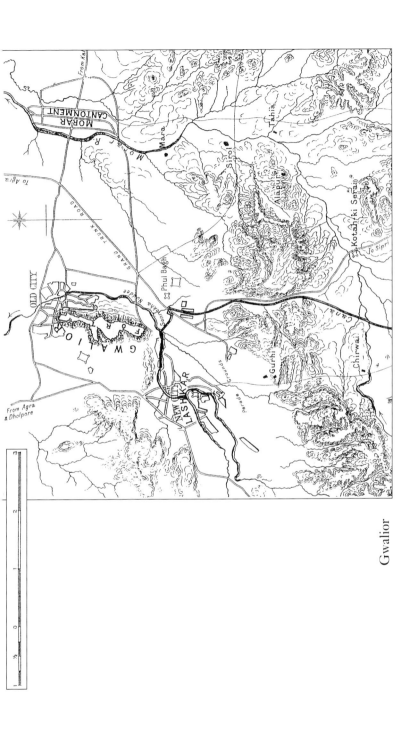

Gwalior

Squadrons of the 14th Dragoons. There are also 150 of the Hyd Cavalry but they go home from Gwalior. The General I am thankful to say remains behind as the Central India Field Force is now broken up. Brig. Stuart commands. My birthday today I am getting an old man 30 years of my life gone now cui bono!

3rd. About 8 miles. Dined at the 71st Mess last night. A very nice set of fellows I hope to become an Hon[y] Member of their Mess at Gwalior. We came a short cut this morning and never saw the baggage or troops the whole way. It was very pleasant galloping along without dust or hindrance but not the wisest thing as we were not sure of the road. English mail off.

Mail in today but no letters yet for me. Report today from Robertson that Scindiah's troops have given way before the rebels and Scindiah himself taken refuge in the Fort, but it cannot be true as we have a Camelman in Camp who left Gwalior on the 1st and all was well and this is said to have occurred the 1st. I don't half like any report being about.

4th Jaloun. 12 miles. Came along by the road today. Another report today from Rampoora stating that Scindiah's troops had deserted him and that some said Scindiah was killed, others that he had gone with the Dewan[56] to Agra and that all the Bungalows prepared for our troops were burnt down. I cannot help thinking there must be something in it. If Scindiah is killed we shall have a hard fight for it but we have a very nice Brigade rather weak though for the work.

5th Bungra. ten miles. Received letters from Mother and Jane dated the 19th April and from Fanny the 6th April! The news of Scindiah's having been beaten by the rebels turns out to be true, his troops turned against him and joined the rebels. He fled to Agra, all his ladies to Punniar,[57] the Dewan to Agra. His bodyguard alone appears to have remained true. The rebels have deposed him by beat of drum and proclaimed Nana Ruler. A telegram from Cawnpore received today says that owing to the state of affairs at Gwalior the 5th Fusiliers had been directed to relieve the portion of the C.I.F.F. left at Calpee which was to march at once to join us. This getting past a joke, we all thought Calpee finished the Campaign in these parts. We have now been close on five months in tents and the prospect of passing the rain in one is not pleasant, moreover there is no knowing where this will stop. I fear much for the Bombay troops when it is known and for Indore. I am most anxious too, poor dear Connie I wish she had gone to England last January as I advised. The rebels have now some fifty good guns, plenty of ammunition and money and Gwalior and its Fort in their possession. I don't see how we can move against them without reinforcements. Nous verrons.

If there were no ladies at Indore and Mhow I should not care, for if the Bombay army are not true it is better they should go at once and the matter be settled.

6th Mahona. About nine miles and cross the Pahooj River. Frightful ravines. Robertson expects to be attacked hourly. He is across the Sind and has been ordered back to Indoorkee where we shall join him most probably tomorrow. Letter from Sir Hugh this morning, he started last night with a troop H. Art. one troop Dragoons and some heavy guns, the remainder to follow directly they are relieved. I thought he would join us instead of going to Poonah directly he heard how matters were at Gwalior. He has ordered Orr over from Jhansie. I hope the Hyderabadees will come quietly and not turn nasty. Brigadier Smith's Column at Seepree has been ordered to advance direct on Gwalior. He will not be able to do it, he must join us. We are in for it in tents. Wrote to dearest Mother a few lines via Calcutta to quiet her lest she hear the news and nothing from me.

7th Jaitpoor. About nine miles. Here Kam Rao Soobah of Esanghur who had assisted the 1st Brigade when acting against Chandeyree came in to us from Gwalior, he escaped with great difficulty and had passed through the country dressed as a Jageer.[58] Rs 10,000 had been put on his head. Scindiah and the Dewan both got away to Agra. The Baiya Bhaie[59] and all the ladies of Scindiah's household have taken for Seepree it is said, it is likewise reported that the Mahranee gave birth to a son and heir on the road, fancy Scindiah's son being born to him whilst bolting from his capital! These good people will have some idea what it is to become wanderers.

8th Left bank of Sind River opposite Indoorkee Fort. Said to be six miles but not that I think. The ravines though for some three miles before reaching the river are frightful and as there is but one narrow road through them, of course the baggage is very much delayed. This Brigade is once more all together and I think we might easily march on Gwalior straight and without any fear of the result could we but get some troops to take care of our baggage, the dreadful impedimenta of every small force. The enemy are so strong in Cavalry that it would take half our Brigade to protect the baggage.[60]

9th Halt. How the men enjoy this River and the bath of a morning. Note from Agra saying that a Force will start shortly to cooperate with us, moving as far as Dholpore or the Chambul. Sir Hugh is coming up to us by forced marches and will join day after tomorrow. Brigadier Smith's force has been ordered by Gov[r] Gen[l] to move direct on Gwalior from Seepree and Orr comes up from the Jhansie direction. Sir Hugh hopes to be before Gwalior, all forces concentrated on the 17th. I do not expect more than one good fight and if we only had Scindiah in our Camp I doubt whether we should have that for any troops that were good in Gwalior would join us at once and all the petty Chiefs round would likewise come, as it is supplies are being collected for us ahead without any trouble.

10th June. Still opposite Indoorkee on the Sind. I could not resist the temptation so went down and had a delightful bathe in the river tho at the risk of bringing back my earache. Great fun in the evening as to who should go in first alligators having been seen about.

11th Stuart with his Brigade went off this morning to Amayoon to support Robertson. We remained as the General came in with his small party soon after the Brigade left and Sir Robert wanted to speak to him. This morning there being only two of us to bathe I sent down a couple of Elephants and made them swim about the place to frighten away the alligators before we went in.

12th Amayoon. 9 miles. First Brigade gone on again. People at Indore in great alarm. Can't hear anything of Scindiah's coming. Ear rather painful

13th Sunday. Dehgaun.[61] 10 miles. Joined the first Brigade. Such pain as I was in this morning riding I thought I should never reach camp. Obliged to have a dozen leeches round my ear, they say it is an abscess.

14th Sapowlee.[62] 12 miles came all the way in a palkee this morning in great pain.

15th. Halt. My ear has been so painful the last three days that I have been unable to sit up or do anything in the shape of work. Today the abscess has burst and relieved me much but my jaws are so stiff and muscles so tender that I literally cannot get my teeth through a piece of potatoe even.

16th Morar Cantonments. 12 miles. We intended to have halted at Burragong a village three miles short of Cantonments but just on arriving at our Camping ground Sir Robert got intelligence that the Cantonments were held by only one Regiment and two guns with a lot of Cavalry, the rebels having during the night withdrawn six of the guns and one Regt having thrown down its arms and bolted! The General being told is determined to advance at once. We accompanied the right. The enemy fired uncommonly well shot coming unpleasantly close, the first they fired knocked three of the Hyd. Sowars over. We on the right after firing some rounds advanced into Cantonments. Sir Robert got hold of the General with a Horse Battery, and led away at a gallop through Cantonments to the Bridge (the only one over the Morar River) and crossing it we emerged into the open just opposite the Fort and between us and the Fort right in front were some 1,200 Sowars at least. We had no support to the guns but we unlimbered and fired away into the blackguards. If we had only had a squadron of Dragoons we might have cut them off from the City towards which they were going, if they had only had the pluck to stand, they would have given some trouble as we had been upwards of an hour before a few men of the 86th came straggling up the river and we kept them. I was so regularly done up that I got under the Bridge for shelter from the sun, the first time I have felt it I suppose from weakness from medicine and not having had any solid food for some days. The firing soon ceased on our part as the cavalry got out of range. We then took up our position in the verandah of a roofless bungalow close to the river. Morar was ours. The action commenced at 20 minutes to 7 and we were taking tea at 9 minutes to nine! When we had been about ½ an hour in our verandah all of a sudden shots were fired at the Bridge and all the

Artillery horses which had gone down to water came galloping past at a furious pace with cries that the enemy Cavalry were on them. We ran to our horses and mounted, the Dragoons came up at a trot and for ½ an hour the panic in Cantonments was complete! After this we took refuge in a shop consisting of one good large room and two smaller ones. The General was in a fine large Bungalow but as there are only four of them with roofs in the Cant⁵ we preferred not running the risk of having to turn out for troops which we should have had to do if we had taken one of them. About two o'clock when I was very comfortable on a bed just about to take a nap there was another panic that the enemy Sowars were down on us, all a false alarm again, but it was most annoying as we had just got our tents up and taken down again considering it better to go and sleep in Camp in rear of Cantonments than run the chance of being turned out of our beds in the night because of course at first you can't tell whether the alarm is false.

The General ought in truth either to have occupied the Cantonments strongly or have had his camp covering them instead of which it was in rear of them. In the evening we went to Camp dined and slept there. On the left of the line this morning the 71ˢᵗ had a sharp encounter with some of the enemy (a part of Scindiah's own Grenadier Regt.) who had got into a narrow deep ravine, where our fellows could not see the enemy till they got to the edge of the ravine. Seeing this they just jumped down into it and bayonneted every man, 86 in number, having themselves four or five wounded and an officer who was shot by the only man who got out of the ravine. He did not escape though. The Dragoons and Abbott cut up some sixty between them and the 71ˢᵗ got another batch on a hill.

17ᵗʰ The whole force moving into Cantonments today and so did we and found it very pleasant to be under a roof again such as it is. All the Bungalows that were repaired have been again burnt down as also the sheds that had been built for the men. Only four bungalows in the Cantᵗ with roofs to them. There are however four large hospitals tiled and one or two other places. Our information is very poor from the City, the whole of Scindiah's force appears to have joined the rebels. Heavy firing all the morning in the direction of Brigadier Smith's force. Sir Robert sent out a Sowar to see what it was. He brought a note back from Smith saying that in the morning on arriving at his ground (Kota Ka Seraie) he found the enemy strongly posted on the heights in his front and that he was obliged to attack them and had succeeded in occupying the heights but was hard pushed and required reinforcements. This was received at three and Col Robertson with the 25th N.I. and a Battery was sent out to help him.

OIOC Home Miscellany 725

176
Diary of Lieutenant Crealock, 95th Foot[63]

16th (June) Marched on Antrie at 2 a.m. there we found encamped Major Orr's Brigade with the following details 71st Highlanders 5 officers – 50 men, 86th Regiment, irregular cavalry. No sooner were we on the ground than the music we had so long waited for sounded and as I write it still continues. Heavy guns and now and then rattling of muskets, some hundred reports I have already heard – it makes ones heart beat again[64] – excitement is a grand thing especially when historical events hang thereby. Over the hill lies Gwalior we have lots of shot and shell from Mhow – the men have brightened up and all seems jolly.

17th Marched on Kotah se Raio saw no enemy but we reached the banks of the river,[65] reconnaissance forward – Brigadiers horse bowled over – in 15 minutes the guns advanced to the left supported by the cavalry and my company – regiment went straight on. The enemy have been driven from their position in the tops of the trees by artillery. We then found the whole front was defended by a 'nullah' full of water impassable for artillery or cavalry[66]– seeing 2 companies skirmishing I pushed forward over the Nullah shooting 4 men as we reached the crest. Skirmished on the hill and connected with the companies in advance – the heights on the left of the pass were now all in our possession except the very distant one but as we were neither supported by cavalry or artillery we retired to the nullah and formed up the rear of the remainder of the Regiment – 2 other companies went with the guns to the mouth of the pass for some reason. We then retired about ½ a mile only to return again – by this time Foster had fallen out, Ewing also,[67] officer of the Lancers, shot thro' arms, and upwards of 60 struck by the sun – the enemy had again advanced to the Nullah and were firing thro' us and the cavalry – we advanced thro' the pass and piled arms – still under fire we had nothing to eat and drink since 2 a.m. never having stuck with the same place 15 minutes and all of us very dozy and faint – no doolis so the sick lay as they fell – at 2 o'clock or 3 some bread and meat came up – we all got ½ a loaf and a few had got some arrack – when message came 2 companies would be cut off by some enemy cavalry – we doubled over 2 hills, 8th Hussars keeping on our left by the road. With a yell we reached the crest under a cross fire from hills on flank *I was hit* here and gave them *one* volley in their flank – they turned – cease fire and 8th Hussars charged as we cheered, chasing them up and thro' their camp a mile off taking 8 guns[68] – we advanced in support and guns and cavalry formed up on the road 900 yards beyond the pass – the pass was ours – thro' camp and had we had another regiment we could have taken 'Gwalior' but it was 4 o'clock and the men were done – we lay down being under a tremendous cross fire and shortly afterwards returned to the place we had piled arms and when we reached it we had upwards of 160 sick and 3 officers struck down by the sun – at dusk we bivouacked on the crest of the hill.

Sherwood Foresters Museum

177
Bonus to his parents

Morar

[Typewritten copy]   18 June 1858

We are now in the cantonment of the late Gwalior Contingent, but the rebels have destroyed nearly all the houses, so that very few men will be under cover during the rains, if unhappily we should be here then. The cantonment is the prettiest I have seen in India, it has been very well laid out, the roads are wide, with trees on both sides, so that shade is plentiful.

We arrived here the day before yesterday and found the rebels in possession. Did I tell you that on return to the Force I was permitted to resume my appointment as D.A.Q.M.G to the Second Brigade? It is part of my duty to mark out the camping ground; in order to do this I generally ride ahead towards the end of the march. On the 16th the order was to form camp some distance short of Morar cantonment. I was engaged on my duty when on looking towards the cantonment I thought I saw people moving; I had with me an excellent telescope (an Addiscombe prize); with it I made certain the rebels were in the place. I sent back a man at once to tell the Brigadier and very soon he and the General were both on the spot. Sir Hugh decided to attack at once, the fight was really rather a stiff one, the work was done mainly by the 71st Highlanders, they lost an officer I am sorry to say.[69] About 150 of the enemy were killed, the most of them got away with their guns and made for Gwalior.

Brigadier-General Napier of the Bengal Engineers now commands the Second Brigade in place of Colonel Stewart who was invalided at Calpee. I like him very much indeed but he works one pretty hard; yesterday I was in the saddle at 5.30 a.m. and was riding till dark. In the morning we heard guns on our extreme left, Brigadier Smith had come up from Sipri, he drove in the enemy taking two guns and established himself on the high ground near Gwalior; we can see part of his force about 5 miles away.

Scindiah came in this morning, he is a young man and rather fair for a native.

Just at present we are expecting to hear some true particulars of Brig. Smith's fight. A report is going about that the Ranee of Jhansi was killed, and that the rebels are leaving Gwalior. I hope I shall soon again be on my way to the Deccan.

OIOC IOR neg. 4395

241

178
Shakespear, diary

[Gwalior]

[Holograph]

[June 1858]

18th Early this morning reports received that the Ranee of Jhansie was killed yesterday in the attack on Smith, her body had been burnt and the rebels were in full flight but nothing certain was known. Napier was ordered in pursuit at two o'clock but was fortunately delayed for about ½ past five we heard that Tantia and all the rebels had turned back and again occupied the City determining to die there and as the General had started at five with the whole of the 1st Brigade to join Smith and attack the City tomorrow, if Napier had gone we should not have had a man in Cantonments. Scindiah came in this morning escorted by Meade and his Horse, they came 60 miles in 12 hours from Dholepore having made a long detour to avoid the enemy's Cavalry.

19th We expected to have heard heavy firing this morning as we thought the General would go at the City the first thing but there has been hardly any. Letter from the General of one o'clock directing Napier to attack the City from the Cant[t] side tomorrow morning, explaining the cause much to our disappointment, however about five o'clock a telegram from the General to the Gov[r] Gen[l] was received stating that the whole place Fort and all was in our hands and that Cavalry and Artillery were in pursuit. This and Barodia are the only two fights in which Sir Robert and self have not been present but in this case we could not go as Scindiah was most anxious to go, of course this would not have done and to stop him Sir R. was obliged to promise that neither should go.

20th Sunday Went out the first thing this morning to bring the Baie B., the Maharanee, Scindiah's wife, and other ladies to cantonments. Immediately on arrival found Sir R. had received a note from the General saying the Fort was evacuated and that Scindiah should come to his palace at once. Sir R. went to Scindiah and I had a cup of tea very comfortable. When Sir R. not returning I asked where he was and found he had gone off with

Scindiah and an Escort to the City. I got on my horse and went as hard as I could the four miles but saw nothing of the party till I got to the Phoolbagh. I consider it providential my having been left behind for several shots were fired from the Fort and one of them just missed Scindiah and Sir Robert falling within six feet of them and upsetting but not hurting a Jemadar riding close behind just about where I should have been riding had I been of the party. The shot being fired from such a height fortunately did not ricochet. Not a shot had been fired all night or in the morning, the fort was reported empty and it was only when the troops were all drawn out to receive Scindia that a shot came amongst them and all had to bolt under cover. Directly after I joined the procession formed Hussars leading, Dragoons bringing up the rear and so we passed through the main street of the city up to the Palace where we dismounted and went up to a Durbar, the street a very fine one was crowded and I never before saw natives show any enthusiasm but here their delight was most marked, they shouted, salaamed and as eagerly cheered as natives could do. After the Durbar Sir Robert and I returned home. There was not much of a fight yesterday, the General in fact did not intend to take the place but the 86th brought on the fight and they say it was splendid seeing the 86th and the 95th taking battery after battery, turning the guns on the enemy. On the 19th Brig Smith lost two officers one of the 95th and one Lnt Mills of the 1st B. Lancers.[70] The fort was held by only a dozen Wullayties who returned to it when they found it was not occupied by us and who fired those guns this morning. On the 17th the 8th Hussars made a splendid charge, one man killed and one man missing, both these were found hanging by their heels.[71]

On the troops entering the place yesterday a Sergeant of the 86th was found in a Bamboo cage stuck all over with pieces of [indecipherable] having oiled rags at their ends which evidently been lighted and a man of the 71st was found horribly mutilated, of course this did not improve the temper of our troops and it is a wonder to me that the city etc escaped being sacked. The Baiya Bhaie and ladies all went to the Palace this evening.

21st Last evening some of the 25th under young Rose (not the A.D.C.) went to assist Scindiah's people occupy the Fort, they found the gate quite open. Scindiah's people attacked the Wullayties and killed all as they supposed, some eleven men, losing themselves more than that number, and young Rose was going about the streets with his men when a Wullaytie rushed out of a house and shot him through the back with a horse pistol being of course himself killed instantly. The poor young fellow died this morning, melancholy after going through the whole campaign to come to one's end in that way. Heavy firing has been heard all last night and this morning to the west and a note has been received saying we had come up with the enemy and wishing the Agra Force had moved up from Dholpore, which they may have done as we heard a party had started from Dholpore. On the 17th Smith took two guns and spiked two,[72] on the 19th we took seventeen guns and I don't know how many there were in the Fort.

22nd The General went off this morning with the remainder of the Dragoons and the 86th to reinforce the pursuing party under Napier. The 3rd Europeans have also gone somewhere and we have nothing in Cant[ts] but a wing of the 25th N.I.! Nothing particular till the afternoon when news was received of our pursuing Column having taken twenty five guns from the enemy and cut up a great number of men.[73] I suppose we shall hear all about it soon. This I should think would bring the General back again.

OIOC Home Miscellany 725

179
Captain Robert Poore[74] to his mother (Mrs M.A. Saurin)
Gwalior
[Holograph]   21 June 1858

My last letter to my Father was sent on 6th May, next day we remained at Seepry, as also on the 8th and 9th, on the 10th we started for Gwalior & marched on without incident till the 14th — on which day we had a smartish shower, so we halted the next day tho' not absolutely necessary as the tents were supposed to be wet. On the morning of the 16th as we were coming into camp (I was on rear guard & so was later than the rest of the Column) about 8½ or

9 a.m. we heard some firing which we found out afterwards was an attack of part of Sir H. Rose's column.

On the 17th we marched about 3 a.m. & halted about 7 a.m., the Brigadier, after some time spent in talking etc., took a division of the Right troop of the 1st Squadron (Montague[75] was with it) to reconnoitre a long line of intrenchments that were on our right, they went rather too close & a long line of fire opened on them, they of course galloped back, but the Brig. had a horse shot, & one of our men had a round shot just above the knee (he died after his leg was cut off),[76] the Infantry advanced after this & then as bad luck would have it Stiggs[77] got the poor Brigadier to retreat tho' they had driven the enemy out of the intrenchments & up the Hills, of course they came down again after, so there was a second advance of infantry & guns which sent them back again. Our squadron advanced after this & halted under cover of the intrenchments & about a couple of hours or perhaps more we advanced along a sort of pass, as we came near the mouth of it we halted again & they were not quite sure whether they would send a troop or squadron out, however the squadron went eventually, covered till we got out of the pass by the fire of the 95th, when we got clear we front formed & went at them, the Brig. leading for a short way, the enemy cut when we came up & we pursued for a mile or perhaps ½, & then turned & came back & got in among a lot of very deep nullahs during which time it was precious lucky the enemy did not come down on us, but we got back with few casualties, & when we formed up about 300 yds in front of the pass we had come out of, Heneage (commanding the Squadron) and Reilly (the right troop)[78] with a lot of the men fell out – done up by the sun, & poor Reilly & 2 or 3 men died: I was ordered after this to take the squadron round a bit of ground (where we should not have been under so hot a fire as we were standing still) but soon after we had started Stiggs came up & ordered the squadron back to where we had started from & tho' we did not lose any men we had to stand under fire while the Artillery were taking away the 2 or 3 guns we had taken, & were removing the wounded, there was at this time a Squadron of the 1st native Lancers who stood the fire as steady as could be. I can tell you I was uncommon glad when we got out of it, we went back to the position behind the intrenchments that we had started from & put up there for the night, it was by a well of splendid water. A squadron of the 14th L.D. came in before dark & put up on our left, they are a fine looking lot & they had been turned out so quick that nearly all were in their shirt sleeves. The next day we stayed by the well all day, and toward evening went along the pass with Stiggs but of course did nothing.

On the 21st[79] about 2 a.m. the greater part of Sir H. Rose's Force passed by us; & about 4 p.m. we turned out with a squadron of the 14th & some Hyderabad irregulars & went to a place about ½ a mile to the left of where we had been taken on the 17th (on our way we passed 4 or 5 guns which were being served & had been taken by the 86th) we had a great deal of advancing & shooting at a gun that I suppose was only served by 3 or 4 men unsupported, however they were afraid that some buildings near were occupied (which was not the case). We put up for the night at a place called Pool-Baag,[80] as we came up to the gun we saw 3 men hanging from a tree by their legs & one of them was certainly one of our men that had been wounded on the 17th, he had his head cut off, was cut about the body, but the most brutal thing I saw was a Sergt. of the 71st who had lost his way & been cut off, they had tied a torch lighted to his back & cut him about in the most fearful manner.

The next day we went off early (by this time all the enemy had cleared out of the town & there were only about 20 or less in the fort which was taken a little later in the day, there 20 men having bayoneted their wives & children, killed about 16 of the Sepoys who attacked, also the officer who commanded them)[81] to escort some artillery in dragging away 2 3pdr guns, as we were coming back we stopped at a Roman Catholic Chapel (there were a gun & some limbers in front of the courtyard wall which the Artillery carried off) where we actually found 3 ladies & a child or so, with some ½ caste people, it seems a miracle how they could have escaped, it was owing to the fidelity of their servants who when the rebels came to plunder their house hid them, their husbands having gone off at the first outbreak, as for some reason or another there was more danger for them than for the ladies, in fact their escape completely puzzles me, they told me the story once or twice but I can't make it out.[82] We moved into camp towards evening found most of the tents pitched. Today we heard some firing in the distance, in the direction the rebels had taken, which it was said was Brig. Napier's force which had been sent in pursuit, & a force from Agra which were supposed to have met the rebells, & if they have managed to give them a good mauling there will be little more of this war but as an order has come this evening for our 1st Squadron to start in pursuit I suppose they are not yet settled, however I'll tell you the news before I close this letter tomorrow.

You had better go to young Reilly's wife & break the news to her. I've got a ring of his which I'll send with his medal 1st opportunity. There is no doubt that drink finished him up, his wine bills were more than any other officer of the regt.

My Troop has been uncommon lucky as we have only lost one man since we left England (that was on the 17th) & I have at present only 1 in hospital, the other troop of the squadron in 2 days have lost 7 men from the sun & action, have 7 in hospital, and the 1st Squadron is as bad. I only hope it may continue . . .

[PS]I've lost 6 horses killed and 2 wounded & the other Troop the same killed.

22nd Our Squadron has just got the order to start in pursuit as a support. I fancy they are so anxious to surround these fellows that they are sending everybody from all quarters, the Ranee of Jhansi & her sisters were killed in our charge,[83] they were dressed as men, and the Ranees fought like bricks but now she's dead the whole thing seems disorganised . . .

NAM 9504–22–1

180
Rose to Mansfield

[Printed copy]

Gwalior
22 June 1858

In reporting to you, for the information of the Commander-in-Chief in India, my operations against Calpee, it is my duty in justice to the unvarying devotion and discipline of the Troops under my Command, to state the new and very serious difficulties which beset them after leaving Jhansie. They had to contend with, not only against the Rebel Army, fighting as usual with all the advantages on their side of very superior numbers and knowledge of the ground, but they had to encounter also a new antagonist, a Bengal Sun, at its maximum of heat. This formidable ally of the Rebel cause was more dangerous than the Rebels themselves; its summer blaze made havoc amongst Troops, especially Europeans, who already exhausted by months of over-fatigue, and want of sleep, by continual night-watching and night-marches, were often exposed to its rays, manoeuvring or fighting as at Koonch, from sunrise to sunset.

At Koonch, the thermometer was 115°; before Calpee 118° in the shade, and on the march to Gwalior, it burst in an Officer's tent at 130°.

Her Majesty's 71st Highland Light Infantry, less inured than any other Corps to Sun, because just arrived in India, suffered the most from it. Besides the 12 men, of a weak Wing of this Regiment, killed in their ranks by the Sun, at Koonch, a great many more had to go into the Field Hospital, sick from sun-stroke; and the whole Wing was more or less affected by it.

The number of Officers and men in the sick list, all of whom had to be carried, on the march, in Dhoolies, increased with each day's operations, and in proportion as I was deprived of fighting men, the difficulties of taking care of the sick, and transporting them in continued marches increased. Whilst my Force suffered so much from sun-stroke, they were deprived in a great measure of its antidote, water. Between Jhansie and Calpee, we found no streams; all was well water; the wells, which were neither numerous nor abundant, being of extraordinary depth, as we approached the Jumna, which increased the difficulties of obtaining water.

Forage also was as scant as water.

The scarcity of these two essentials hurt the efficiency of the Cavalry and Transport, at the very time that they were both urgently required – the first against the Rebel Cavalry, whose numbers and organization made them unusually enterprizing; and the latter, for the numerous and daily-increasing sick.

The scarcity of water had another disadvantage; it prevented concentration of my Force, when the strength of the enemy, and my difficulties rendered it necessary for a rapid advance on Calpee.

The Enfield Rifles had made up a good deal for my inferiority in numbers; that advantage, however, no longer existed. The heat and other causes had such an effect on the ammunition of the Rifles that their loading became difficult, and their fire uncertain, the men lost confidence in their aims.[84]

The above were some of the Military disadvantages of my position. They were increased by Political causes.

The inhabitants of the valley of the Jumna were the most disaffected my Force had yet met with. They had been under Rebel rule, and had never felt the influence of British Power since the commencement of the Insurrection. Every village had its one or two Mahratta Pundits,[85] who had made a most successful propaganda in favour of Nana Sahib as Peishwa. The villagers did good service to the Rebels, by betraying to them our Daks and movements, as well as some carts, when the drivers, on account of the exhausted state of their cattle, could not keep their place in the Columns, or sought water at a distance from the road

The Rebels had another great source of strength. They fought their best because they were defending Culpee, their best fortified stronghold in Central and Western India and only Arsenal full of war-like stores and ammunition. Culpee, on the right bank of the Jumna, in the hands of the Rebels, prevented the concentration of the British Armies of the West, with those of the East of India; exposed to attack, from the line of the Jumna, the Army engaged in operations against the insurgents in the Doab, the line of the Ganges; Oudh; and Rohilcund; and so long as Culpee was Rebel, so long had it the Enemy in their power to say that the East and West of India might be British, but the pivot of its centre was theirs.

Whilst so many drawbacks weakened me, the Enemy physically speaking, was unusually strong. They were under three leaders of considerable influence, Rao Sahib, a nephew of Nana Sahib, the Nawab of Banda, and the Ranee of Jhansie. The high descent of the Ranee, her unbounded liberality to her Troops and retainers, and her fortitude which no reverses could shake, rendered her an influential and dangerous adversary. The Rebel Army was composed of the Gwalior Contingent, the finest men, best drilled and organized Native Troops of all arms in India; other mutinous Bengal Infantry Regiments, such as the 52nd; Rebel Cavalry from Kotah and a chosen band of Valaitees, the whole reinforced by the Force of all Arms of the Nawab of Banda, comprising a great deal of mutinous Bengal Cavalry, of which the 5th Irregulars, dressed in their red uniforms, formed a part. All the Sepoy Regiments kept up, carefully, their English equipment and organization; the words of command for drill, grand rounds &c., were given, as we could hear, in English.

The numerous difficulties of my situation above recited, were rendered more grave by a series of accidents which occurred in the 2nd Brigade, over which I had no control, and which embarrassed my operations.

I could not have concentrated a force, on account of the want of water, against these defences [Kalpi]. I determined, therefore, to turn them, to break off to the right, from the high road from Oraye to Culpee, march to the Jumna, to the village of Golowlee, about 6 miles below Culpee, effect a communication from thence with Lieutenant-Colonel Maxwell, and then, my right wing resting on the Jumna, and covered by the flank fire of Colonel Maxwell's Batteries and Riflemen from the other bank of the Jumna, advance up its right bank against Culpee. The Fort of Culpee, and the part of the Town facing my advance to be well shelled before the attack. The Jumna is fordable at Golowlee; it stands in the Nullahs running down to the Jumna, just outside the dangerous labyrinth of ravines which surround Culpee.

I also ordered two Pontoon rafts, which I had brought with great trouble from Poona, to be floated by sun-set, on the Jumna, for communication with Lieutenant-Colonel Maxwell, and transport of the ammunition for my Force.

The prostration of the whole Force had become a matter of arithmetical calculation. So many hours of sun laid low so many men. I had, weakened by every sort of difficulty, to conquer the greatest stake in the campaign, against the greatest odds; half of my troops sickly; every man of them ailing, to say nothing of a very numerous and daily increasing Sick List, crowded into tents where the Thermometer stood 118° in the shade. To compare small things to great, myself and my Force were suffering under two evils, which have overcome the greatest Armies, under the most successful Generals, sickness and climate. This view of the case was borne out by an official letter which I received at this time from Dr Arnott, Superintending Surgeon, a Gentleman who is distinguished by his cool and correct judgement.

I beg leave to apologise for the length of these details. But it is right that His Excellency the Commander-in-Chief should know the reasons in their fullest extent which compelled me to reinforce myself with part of Lieutenant-Colonel Maxwell's Force.

The result proved its necessity. A day or two after the arrival of the reinforcements in my Camp, the Camel Corps, the principal reinforcement, saved, by their timely aid, my right, the key of my position, from a disaster, in a desperate and general attack on it, on the 22nd May; and that success was followed by a conquering advance of my whole line from the Jumna to my extreme left; the total rout of the enemy; and the capture, next day, of Culpee, with all its Artillery and rich Arsenal.

On the 21st Instant I received information that the Rebel Army intended to make a general attack on my position, at Golowlee, at 8 a.m. the next day; that they had sworn a religious oath on the waters of the Jumna, a sacred river, that they would drive my Force into the Jumna and destroy it, or die, and that afterwards, they would move Southwards against General Whitlock; that large quantities of opium had been issued to the Troops for the purpose of making them fight desperately.

Shortly after 8 o'clock a.m. on the 22nd May, the enemy who continued their tactics of forcing my Troops to fight in the heat of the day were reported . . . to be advancing in great force from Culpee and its environs towards the belt of ravines on my right and along the Jullalpore and Culpee Road against my left. Their left manoeuvred so skilfully that they got under cover of broken ground into the ravines, without being perceived on the right; and Brigadier Stuart reported to me as I was posting the Siege Guns that my right was no longer threatened . . . I still felt the conviction that the enemy's real object of attack was my right; and that this ostentatious display of force against my left and the perfect stillness in the deep ravines on my right, were ruses to mislead me and induce me to weaken my right by sending reinforcements from it to my left, when they would have attacked with all their energy my right, endeavoured to take the Mortar Battery and the camp, their right falling at the same time on my left and cutting me off in combination with their left, from the Jumna. Whilst therefore I protected my left against a feint, which might become a serious attack, I did not take a man away from my right.

The situation of Brigadier Stuart's position was very critical. Volleys of musketry, which killed or wounded every horse of my

Staff but one, were coming over the crest of the rising ground from the Sepoy Troops, who had debouched and were debouching in great numbers from the gullies leading into the ravines, and were advancing rapidly, firing heavily with yells of triumph, their faces distorted by opium and fury, across a small piece of level ground against the Mortar Battery and guns, to which they were close. The guns had ceased firing. Brigadier Stuart was on foot at the guns ordering the few Artillerymen who served them to draw swords and defend their guns, his lines of defence had been driven in, the men having been struck down to the ground by sun-stroke where they lay, and the fire of the rest rendered insufficient by the defective ammunition of their Rifles. Without halting on the crest I charged down it with the Camel Corps, the dense lines of the mutineers, who were ten times superior to us in numbers, the gallant Soldiers of Her Majesty's Rifle Brigade and Her Majesty's 80th Regiment giving one of those cheers which all over the world have been the heralds of British successes. The rebels wavered, turned and fled, pursued by the Camel Corps, with all their energy, through the ravines where numbers of them were bayonneted or killed by musketry fire.

My whole line was now advancing and driving the enemy from their positions . . . The Rebels were so completely beaten and disheartened that broken parties of them did not retire on Culpee but were seen flying across the ravines in a Westerly direction towards Jaloun . . . The complete defeat and serious loss which the enemy sustained this day, despite their having displayed tactics and an energy of attack which I had not previously witnessed in them, convinced me that an immediate advance to Culpee which I had some days back fixed for the next day, the 23rd instant would with the prestige of this day's victory make me master of it at once. I therefore only gave the Troops the time which was indespensible for their rest after the long day's combat in the sun, and dividing my Force into two columns of attack, marched the next morning long before break of day against Culpee.

❊ ❊ ❊

From information furnished by Lieutenant-Colonel Gall, it was clear that the principal part of the Rebels had retreated by the Jaloun Road; and Sir Robert Hamilton was of opinion that they would make to the North for the Sheer Ghat, a ford across the Jumna, or another ford higher up the River. Colonel Riddell, with a moveable column, was guarding the former ford. It was of vital importance to make a fresh pursuit of the enemy in order, either to catch him between Colonel Riddell's and my fire, to meet him if he turned, or to ascertain the real line of flight. Notwithstanding therefore the exhausted state of my Force, I detached, without delay, Lieutenant-Colonel Robertson with a pursuing column . . . along the Jaloun Road . . . The operations of the pursuing column, which again called into action Lieutenant-Colonel Robertson's energy and intelligence, will be detailed in my Report of the operations against Gwalior.

❊ ❊ ❊

Forrest, IV, pp. 81–103

181
Order of Commander-in-Chief

[Holograph copy]

Allahabad
22 June 1858

The Com^{dr} in Chief congratulates Major Genl Sir Hugh Rose very heartily on the successful result of his rapid advance on Gwalior.

The restoration of the MahaRajah Scindia to his capital by the Force under the Command of the Major General is a happy termination of the brilliant campaign through which the Central India Field Force has passed under his able direction.

That Campaign has been illustrated by many engagements in the open field, by the relief of Saugor, the capture of Ratgurh, Shahgarh and Chandeeree, by the memorable siege of Jhansie, by the fall of Calpee and lastly by the re-occupation of Gwalior.

Again does His Excellency offer his hearty thanks and congratulations to Major Gen[l] Sir Hugh Rose and the gallant troops under his Command.

It must not be forgotten that the advance of the Central India Field Force formed part of a large combination and was rendered possible by the movements of Major General Roberts of the Bombay Army into Rajpootana on the one side & of Major General Whitlock, belonging to Madras, on the other, & by the support they respectively gave to Major General Sir Hugh Rose as he moved onwards in obedience to his instructions.

The two Major Generals have well sustained the honor of their Presidencies.

The siege of Kotah and the action of Banda take rank among the best achievements of the War . . .

OIOC MSS Eur D174, p. 1185

182
Brigadier Smith to COS [Chief of Staff] Rajpootana Field Force

Gwalior

[Printed copy]   25 June 1858

. . . on the morning of the 17th Instant, I marched by Major-General Sir H. Rose's order from Antree through the pass to Kotah-ki-Serai, which lies between three and four miles South-east of Gwalior.

I had reconnoitred the pass the evening before and occupied the difficult points by strong pickets and posts, so that had there been any enemy I should have been prepared.

I met with no opposition whatever and reached Kotah-ki-Serai at 7½ A.M. Upon my arrival I saw the Enemy occupying the heights in front and between me and Gwalior.

I had orders from Sir Hugh Rose to halt at Kotah-ki-Serai and communicate with him, but as the enemy appeared determined to attack me, and being also hampered with a large quantity of baggage and Kotah-ki-Serai not being a secure position, I thought it best to take the initiative. I therefore collected my baggage in and near the fort of Kotah-ki-Serai, placing it under a Troop of Her Majesty's 8th Hussars and a squadron of Lancers, and as strong a guard of Infantry as I could afford. I reconnoitred the ground in front, and found it to be most difficult, intersected with nullahs and impracticable for Cavalry. About 1,500 yards from Kotah-ki-Serai their guns were in position and their line ran all under the hills across the road to Gwalior.

This I ascertained by advancing with my reconnoitring party to within about 400 or 500 yards, when they opened so heavy a fire upon us that we were obliged to retire, not, however, before I had made myself acquainted with the nature of the ground, and thus enabled myself to avoid being entangled in the nullahs above mentioned.

I advanced the Horse Artillery and soon silenced their guns; after three or four rounds they began to retire and I sent my Infantry across the broken ground giving the command to Lieutenant-Colonel Raines, Commanding Her Majesty's 95th (the senior Infantry Officer present),[86] with orders to follow up the enemy as far as he thought advisable . . .

In consequence of threatening movements of the Enemy, as well as the unprotected position of the baggage, I was obliged to send back (to reinforce the Troops already left at Kotah-ki-Serai) one Troop of Her Majesty's 8th Hussars, one Division Horse Artillery and two Companies 10th Native Infantry.

From the nature of the ground already described, I was unable for some time to bring my Cavalry into action, and merely retained them as support and escort to the Troop Horse Artillery under Lieutenant-Colonel Blake,[87] but having advanced to the head of the pass, partially occupied the heights above the plain near the Phool Bagh and placed Infantry to guard the entrance to the defile, and protect a retreat, I thought I might venture to advance with a Squadron of the 8th Hussars and the two Divisions of Horse Artillery remaining at my disposal, and one Troops of the 1st Lancers, sending back for the remaining Troop of the 1st Lancers as a support.

I then ordered the Squadron of Hussars to charge to the front, which they did most gallantly, passing right through the Enemy's Camp, carrying everything before them.

Upon the return of the Squadron both Officers and Men were so completely exhausted and prostrated from heat, fatigue and great exertion they could scarcely sit on their saddles and were for a moment incapable of further exertion. This was a critical moment, as the Enemy were collecting both on the front and flanks, but the 95th had arrived near the Guns, and the 8th Hussars, in spite of their fatigue, formed to their front in line, and to show a greater front I formed them in single ranks. In the mean-time the remaining Troop of the 1st Lancers had arrived to support, as second line. I then retired the Cavalry by alternative Troops, protected by the Artillery, during which movement, both Arms showed the greatest steadiness and entered the ravines under the protection of the Infantry posted there. I then took up a position for the night on the heights, sending for my baggage and placing it in tolerable security, in a sort of amphitheatre formed by a portion of the hills we occupied. I guarded both ends of the defile with strong pickets of Infantry, in strong positions formed by the ground, and also threw out strong pickets, both Cavalry and Infantry, towards the height on our right; the left of our position was defended against any sudden assault by a steep bank and a canal.

❊ ❊ ❊

Forrest, IV, pp. 156–8

183
Bonus to his parents

Morar

[Typewritten copy]   25 June 1858

I forget whether in my last I told you of the battle of Gwalior. On this side we had not much to do, but the troops with Sir Hugh had a very hard and hot day on the 19th; evening however saw them in possession of the old and new towns of Gwalior. The rebels made the best fight we have experienced, and our loss was considerable.[88] Very early the next morning General Napier started in pursuit with Horse Artillery and Cavalry, he is not back yet. I was left behind. When the orders came I was summoned to the General's tent to take his instructions; while he was giving them, I, being dreadfully tired, swayed a bit and leaned against the pole of the tent. He looked at me sharply and said 'you are not fit to go, I must leave you behind.' He was quite kind about it, and I felt he was quite right, I was done. I like him very much indeed. Have I told you that when he joined he said to me, 'I expect you to be ready to turn out at any moment, day or night, but dare say you have not many horses; a horse ready saddled will be at your disposal always in my stable'. Was not that kind and thoughtful? He said, too, that a place would always be laid for me at his table. I have never before met such kindness.

I cannot make out the truth about the death of the Ranee, some say that she was killed in the fight with Brigadier Smith's force, others that she was killed in the battle of Gwalior.[89] She was, it is said, dressed as a man and, of course, rode astride. She was a brave and capable woman, but she was responsible for the massacre of our men and women in Jhansi. I am glad she was killed in fight, the difficulty of disposing of her being thus avoided.

The day after Gwalior, I was riding over the battle ground when to my great astonishment I met an English lady on horseback, a man was with her. I have not been able to find out who she was; I think she was a little out of place, for the plain was strewn with the dead.[90] My object was to find my telescope which I had somehow lost the previous day, I did not find it . . .

But I must return to Gwalior. I think I told you that the fort is an extremely strong one, it is built on a high and huge mass of rock precipitous on all sides, it is over a mile in length but very narrow, if held by a resolute garrison well supplied it might defy an army for months. The rebels evacuated it, but a few desperate men either remained in it, or returned to it after the battle, and the next morning fired on some of our people below. Two officers of the 25th N.I. took a few men, made their way up the steep road to the entrance and actually took the fort. I have not yet been able to learn the exact particulars, but I know that one officer was killed, as were all the men in the place. It was a most plucky business.

OIOC IOR neg. 4395

184
Rose to Elphinstone

Gwalior

[Holograph]   28 June 1858

❊ ❊ ❊

After Konch water became so scarce that we could only march by brigades, till I concentrated them all on the Jumna where the Poonah Pontoons that I had so much trouble lugging along were of great use.

❊ ❊ ❊

I was obliged to go to Golowli in order to communicate with the Force sent by Sir Colin to co-operate with me from the other side, and by making this flank movement, I marched round all the defences which the Enemy had been constructing to oppose my advance to Calpee by the direct road from Jahnsee. The Sepoys always are determined that you shall attack them by the legitimate, straight road, which they fortify accordingly. I always consequently go by the illegitimate, round about road, and turn them, when they bolt. At Konch, I went with my two brigades three miles across country, Siege Artillery and all.

The Sepoy Skirmishers who covered the retreat fought very well at Konch, facing about, kneeling and firing with great coolness; they place groups & knots of men in their line of Skirmishers who act as *bastions*. When their line was broken into they fought desperately, throwing away their muskets and fighting with their swords with fury. I saw one man slash at eight, or more

Dragoons, and he was cut to pieces but fighting to the last. The 52nd Bengal Mutineers were the Skirmishers, and were nearly all destroyed.

At Golowli, they made a desperate attack on my Right. The Sepoys had sworn, by the Jumna, to destroy us, and they had determined, if they failed, to abandon Calpee. Having filled themselves with *bang* they really made a very gallant and vigorous attack, which I came up with just in time to drive back with the Camel Corps, Rifles and 80th; as we mounted the crest of the hill, the Sepoys were marching out of all the ravines towards our two guns, and the Brigadier[91] so hard pressed that he was ordering the Artillerymen to draw their swords and defend their guns. The Sepoys were in great numbers and running forward & at the same time keeping up a very hot fire. Three of my Staff, Wetherall, Cockburn[92] & another had their horses killed or wounded at the same time. I ordered the Rifles to charge the Sepoys with the bayonet which they did most gallantly, driving them back into the Ravines, and bayonetting numbers of them. I ordered the whole line to advance & the rout became general. This defeat decided the fate of Calpee; numbers of the Sepoys had their kit with them, and never went back to Calpee. Therefore when we advanced early next morning to Calpee, they merely covered their retreat with a cannonade from a redoubt, and then ran, throwing away their arms, when pursued, and shewing none of the nerve, as at Konch.

I had warned the Brigadier that his right was to be attacked at Golowli; but he was so self confident that he sent away a regiment, the 25th which I had posted there.

The capture of Calpee was a great blow to the rebels. You never saw such an Arsenal as they had there. Bombay is nothing to it, every imaginable thing, and 60,000 lbs of English powder, not 10,000 as I thought at first. The Sepoys are the most extraordinary compound of intelligence, and luckily for us, of want of commonsense, that can be imagined . . . they had . . . most ingeniously constructed cannon foundries, brass shells etc. which do great credit to their intelligence; and then on the other hand they leave all this quantity of powder with no other protection than a common wooden trap door; one shell would have blown up the whole affair.

OIOC MSS Eur F87, Box 6A, Packet 4

185
Rose to Mansfield

Morar

[Holograph copy]   28 June 1858

I have the honor to acknowledge receipt of your letter of the 7th Instant; and in reply, beg leave to make an explanation, which I trust will convince the Commander in Chief that I have not been guilty of so great a fault as an error in military discipline, an unprecedented proceeding, a departure from the rules of the service, and departure from duty.

Before saying anything on these points, I beg to observe that I received no communication, respecting my retaining the command, of so formal a nature as that conveyed in the second paragraph of your letter, in proof of which I beg to make a short statement.

Before leaving Calpee Sir Robert Hamilton sent me a copy of a letter from the Commander in Chief to the Governor General, which stated that the Central India Field Force was to be broken up after the reduction of Calpee; consequently after the fall of Calpee, my force being dissolved, I requested the Governor General, from whom I was directed to take orders by His Excellency, to allow myself and my staff to return to my Division at Poona immediately, so that we might be saved as much as possible travelling so many hundred miles in the monsoon.

I beg leave therefore to observe that I never formally laid down my Command of the Central India Field Force; but, that by His Excellency's orders, that Force and myself were dissolved; that then Lord Canning offered me in the Telegram, a copy of which I have enclosed, a new Command.

The impression produced on my mind by Lord Canning's kind and flattering Telegram was exactly this, that neither the Governor General nor His Excellency thought it fair to press on me, or hamper me by a formal offer of a mere Brigadier's command at Gwalior, converted into a Divisional one for me, after I had commanded to the entire satisfaction of my Superiors, four Brigades (that is, three Brigades and the Hyderabad Contingent Field Force) of which there were in the field, in no less important a scene than Central India.

I beg also to enclose a copy of my reply to Lord Canning's Telegram, which is written in the same spirit as that of His Lordship.

I beg also to state a fact, not mentioned in your Despatch, that Gwalior was perfectly tranquil, and in its normal state, when I stated my inability to go there on account of ill-health.

With respect to the error in discipline on my part in re-assuming the Command without authority, I beg leave to enclose an Extract from your Despatch of the 1st June, which I received the day on which I re-assumed the Command, and which mainly determined me to do so.

When His Excellency was pleased to express so flattering an opinion of my humble services, the capture by the Rebels of Gwalior, its treasury, strong fortress, formidable artillery, and the defection of Scindia's troops were unknown to His Excellency. It was clear that if the Commander in Chief regretted the loss of my services before the disaster of Gwalior, he would do so still more after that event.

Impressed with this conviction, which was confirmed by the opinion of an officer of excellent judgement and long experience, I acted, as I thought, in the truest and purest spirit of discipline. I put myself out of the question, and thinking only of the wishes of my Superiors, of the good of the Service and of my country, in a state of affairs, which caused perhaps more alarm throughout India and embarrassed Government more than any event since the first outbreak of the mutiny, I gave to His Excellency the humble assistance of my services, the loss of which he was pleased to regret so much; and marched in command of the troops which His

Excellency did me the honor to say, had proved so successful under my orders.

I beg leave to add that, judging from the time that it took for communication to come from His Excellency's Head Quarters to Calpee, where I was, it was impossible for me to have waited for His Excellency's confirmation of this step, and at the same time to have overtaken the troops marching against Gwalior.

With respect to the departure from duty on my part, which His Excellency lays to my charge, in having forwarded to the Governor General the copy of my Telegram to His Excellency, in which I resumed the command, I beg leave to say that I have, since His Excellency directed me to take the orders of the Governor General during his absence in Rohilkund, sent a copy of all Telegrams on matters of importance to His Lordship, and that I do not remember having received any directions from His Excellency annulling these orders, and that as the Governor General had, with His Excellency's consent, offered me the command of the Force marching against Gwalior, I should have failed in courtesy and in duty, if I had withheld from His Lordship information on a point, which in His Excellency's opinion was one of the greatest importance.

With respect to His Excellency's orders to me, not to hold any direct correspondence with the Government of India, I have the honor to request you to acquaint me what course it is His Excellency's wishes that I should pursue when the Government of India address a communication to me, to which they require an answer – I am in possession of two, asking for my opinion respecting the re-organisation of the Armies of India.

<u>Canning to Rose (extract)</u>

[? Allahabad]

[Manuscript telegram]   27 May 1858

I congratulate you heartily on this last and crowning success. You have good reason to be proud of your Campaign. Pray let me know from you as to the time at which the Force, which is to go to Gwalior, can begin to move in that direction. Will your health allow of your remaining in Command of it, as a Divisional Command? The Commander in Chief wishes this, and it will be most satisfactory to me if you can do so . . .

Rose to Canning (extract)

Kalpi

[Manuscript telegram]   30 May 1858

I received your Telegraphic message of the 27th Instant. I am entirely obliged to you for the kind manner in which you express yourself regarding me. Part of the Force for Gwalior is on the road to that place in pursuit of rebels, the remainder can march to Gwalior when ordered. I regret extremely that my present state of health is so under-mined from long exposure to the sun, and over-fatigue, that the Medical Officer strongly urges on me the immediate necessity of leaving this part of India, and returning to the Deccan, where the climate is good, and where my Division is, as soon as practicable, the sun having repeatedly affected me inducing partial Coup de Soleil, from which I was only recovered by strong restoratives, and from the effects of which I still suffer. A sense of duty made me continue in the Field till the close of the operations, contrary to the repeated wishes of the Medical Officer. When the cold weather sets in, I shall be very happy to place my services at the disposal of Your Lordship.

Mansfield to Rose (extract)

(? Allahabad)

[Manuscript copy]   1 June 1858

He [Campbell] regrets much that the state of your health prevents you from retaining Command of the Force which has proved so successful under your Command, and that he is consequently deprived of your assistance in a country which is still the scene of insurrection, although your well-conducted march has broken the principal seats of rebellion.

OIOC MSS Eur D174, pp. 561–4

186
Rose to Duke of Cambridge

Gwalior

[Holograph copy]   28 June 1858

Perhaps no event since the outbreak of the mutiny caused more alarm throughout India than the occupation of Gwalior by the rebels and the treacherous [conduct] of Scindia's troops.

Gwalior itself was a prize of no ordinary value, comprising the city and the Lushkar, with a population of 170,000 souls, the Fort which is the largest, and one of the strongest, in India, Scindia's Treasury, his jewels and those of his family of fabulous value, the Arsenal filled with warlike stores of every description, and upwards of sixty pieces of Seige and Field Artillery.

But other circumstances combined to render the loss of Gwalior the most serious check which Government had yet experienced.

Scindia, the Maharajah or Prince of Gwalior, is our trusted ally, and with one exception, he is the most powerful of the independent Princes of India. The central and geographical position of the Gwalior states gives their rule great political and military power over the whole of India.

Scindia's troops, who went over to the rebels,[93] were the best organised and drilled of all the native levies.

To render this state of affairs still more embarrassing, Gwalior fell into rebel hands at the most unfavourable time of the year for military operations, on the eve of the great rains.

No one, therefore, could foresee the extent of the evil which stared Gov[t] in the face if Gwalior were not promptly wrested from the rebels, if Tantia Topee, with the immense acquisition of political influence and military strength, which the possession of Gwalior gave the rebel cause, had time to organise and march southwards with a fresh army and raise the Deccan and Southern Mahrattas, in favour of the Peishwa's government. The general attachment of these populations to their ancient form of government is too well known to admit of a doubt of their not rallying with enthusiasm round the Pretender's standard.

Malwa and Indore, its capital, would not have hesitated to fraternise with Gwalior, Holkar might have remained faithful to us, but if he had he would have had to abdicate in favour of his brother, who is universally believed to be anti-English.

Sir Colin Campbell having decided that the Central India Field Force was to be broken up, after the fall of Calpe, and to be distributed at Gwalior and Jhansi, I asked Lord Canning, from whom the Commander in Chief directed me to take orders whilst he was in Rohilcund, to give my staff and myself leave to return to my division at Poona before the rains set in.

Lord Canning offered me the Command of the Troops going to Gwalior, which was at that time perfectly quiet. But my health had suffered so much from sun and over fatigue, that I followed the staff surgeon's repeated advice to recruit my health at Poona, and declined the command at Gwalior, where the heat is exceptional even in the rains. I told Lord Canning at the same time that when the operations recommenced in the cool weather I should be most happy to take the field again, as I felt confident that the good air of Poona would bring me round.

When the crisis occurred in the beginning of this month at Gwalior, I had just received a letter from Sir Colin Campbell dated before he knew the crisis, saying how much His Excellency regretted the loss of my services, and as I knew that Lord Canning wished that I should command the Force against Gwalior, I laid aside all considerations as to health and resumed the command.

It was of vital importance to reach Gwalior and take it, as soon as possible, before the rains set in, for a long seige of Gwalior, protracted by the difficulties of carrying on operations in the Monsoon, would have had the worst possible effect on our military prestige and our political affairs.

Lord Canning expressed his constant desire that the Force should not lose an hour in arriving at Gwalior. I therefore made forced marches from Calpe to Gwalior, taking care to avoid exposure to the sun.

The Cantonments of the Gwalior Troops are at Morar, on the river of that name, about five miles from it. I had had a long march and was going to encamp at a village about three miles from Morar; but the enemy having shewn in force, in front of it, I reconnoitred it closely and found that several houses in the Cantonments had not been burned by the rebels; and as I knew that they would burn all that night, I left my projected camping ground, attacked the enemy, and under a short cannonade from them, which my Artillery answered effectually, took the whole cantonments from the rebels and drove them into Gwalior. The 71st had an opportunity of distinguishing themselves very much this day. Some of the most disaffected of Scindiah's troops[94] were in ambuscade in a very difficult position in a nullah. The 71st killed every one of them in the most gallant way, with some casualties on their own side, amongst them their brave leader Lieut Neave.

When the crisis occurred at the beginning of the month at Gwalior, Major Orr's Field Force was on its return to the Deccan; Brigadier Smith's Brigade of the Rajpootana Field Force was on its march from Chanderee to Sepree, part of my force was garrisoning Calpee, part had marched against Gwalior, and part had been left as a garrison at Jhansie.

Both Brigadier Smith's and Major Orr's Force were placed under my orders for the operations against Gwalior.

Gwalior with the old city to the north of the new city or Lushkar to the south, and the Fort in the centre, is a place of great extent and difficult to invest. All the information I could collect concurred in shewing that the South East side of Gwalior was the most favourable for attack. With the view therefore to invest Gwalior as much as possible and attack it at its weakest part, I made the following distribution of my Force.

I left a force under Brigadier General Napier in Morar Cantonments for its protection, and for pursuit, and for the investment of the North of Gwalior. I gave orders to Brigadier Smith to go to Kotah ka Serai to invest the east; to Major Orr to march with the small force he had with him from Jhansi to Punniar to watch the southern issues of Gwalior; finally I directed Colonel Riddell to the Residency, seven miles to the North West of Gwalior to invest its North West and West.

I myself marched on the 18th of June from the Morar Cantonments to Kotah ka Serai to attack Gwalior from that point [with] Brig[r] Smith's Brigade and the two Brigades of the Central India Field Force, with the exception of the troops left in Morar Cantonments, Jhansi, and Cap[t] Ommaney's Battery left in Calpe.[95] All the troops therefore for the attack of Gwalior were concentrated round it by the 19th of June, as I had reported in the beginning of the month that they would be.

My base was Agra, a far better one than either Jhansi or Calpee. Agra was nearer to Gwalior than either of those two places. The roads between Jhansi and Gwalior, and Calpee and Gwalior, become impassable in the monsoon, and the communications between those places are interrupted by the rising of the Rivers Pahooj and Scinde. But a good road connects Gwalior and Agra and the Chumbal is passable even in the rains.

The rebels were so well aware of the weakness of Gwalior to the South East that they had concentrated a large force against Brig Smith when he advanced to Kotah ka Serai. Brig Smith found it necessary to attack them on the 17th, drove them from some heights in front of Kotah ka Serai, and took up a position in front of it, occupying a road which led thro' the hills from Kotah ka Serai to Gwalior, and the heights on the right of it; but the heights on the left, the other side of the road, were held by the enemy; they, the left heights, were separated from the road by an old and very deep cut canal, now dry, impassable for Cavalry and Artillery, and very difficult for Infantry.

In clearing the entry of this road, which is a bad pass from the Gwalior side, a Squadron of the 8th Hussars led by Captain Heneage made a most gallant charge thro' the Enemy's cavalry and Camp into a battery of six light field pieces under the fire of the Fort of Gwalior, routing the Enemy and spiking four guns and bringing away the remainder. The Ranee of Jhansi, the Indian Joan of Arc, was killed in this charge dressed in a red jacket, red trousers and white puggary; she wore the celebrated pearl necklace of Scindia, which she had taken from his Treasury, and heavy gold anklets; as she lay mortally wounded in her Tent she ordered these ornaments to be distributed amongst her Troops; it is said that Tantia Topee intercepted the necklace.

The whole rebel Army mourned for her; her body was burned with great ceremony under a tamarind tree under the Rock of Gwalior, where I saw her bones and ashes.

The Ranee was remarkable for her beauty, cleverness and perseverance, her generosity to her subordinates was unbounded. These qualities, combined with her rank rendered her the most dangerous of all the rebel leaders.

After reconnoitring very closely the Enemy's position on the morning of the 19th of June, I observed that it was a false one; the Enemy had occupied the range of hills in front of Gwalior, three or four miles distant from it and entirely unsupported by the main body in Gwalior. I determined to cut off this advanced force, feeling certain that the success would carry me without all the trouble and risks of a Monsoon siege, into Gwalior.

In order to turn the enemy's rear, I immediately ordered the Sappers and Miners to make, and have ready by nightfall, a bridge across the Canal, close to the rear of our Camp. In the mean time I cannonaded the enemy's batteries on the opposite hills, which annoyed us with a well directed fire, with the 8 inch Howitzer and the two 18[pdrs] which I had brought up during the night to the crest of the hills on the right of the road.

Towards mid-day, the Enemy, under cover of the ravines and broken ground which intervened between his position and ours, advanced in some force, and pressed our outposts which guarded our left and the Canal. Guns and reinforcements were soon moving up to their positions from Gwalior. I did not object to this as I felt certain that the more guns they had on the hill the more we should take next morning, which I had fixed for the General Attack of the Enemy's positions.

Our fire had not been so effective, so L[t] Colonel Hicks reported, as that of the enemy, and he proposed to withdraw the seige guns. As this would have had a bad effect, I told him to cease gradually his fire, which would probably cause the enemy to do the same. So it turned out. We had been firing at a disadvantage, the 8 inch Howitzer on account of the carriage having been shaken by incessant travelling was fired with one pound less than its proper charge; the 18 ᵖᵈʳˢ of the Bombay Arsenals are not sighted, a defect which tells even in Seige but still more in field firing.

Our position was not a good one. We had, it is true, the road thro' the pass, the hills on the right and the steep canal on the left of it. But the Enemy had the hills commanding the advanced part of the road and the Canal. The Enemy occupied also in force the slopes of a hill, threatening from the other side of the Canal my rear and Camp.

Under these circumstances, although I intended to make a general attack on the Enemy at daybreak, it would have been hazardous to allow him to hold his advanced positions and press still more my cramped and irregular position, occupied by Brigadier Smith as a necessity.

Under these circumstances, I determined to drive the Enemy from his position. I did so, with much regret, because my men, already suffering from sun and over work, were wearied by the long march of the day before and a bad bivouack, moreover I wished to keep them fresh for the attack of the next day.

I directed HM 86ᵗʰ and 95ᵗʰ Regᵗˢ to cross the canal, and attack and turn the Enemy's flank. The two gallant Regiments ably led by Lieut Colonels Louth and Raines did this so effectually that driving the enemy across the broken ground and ravines, already mentioned, they took the opposite heights and three English 9ᵖᵈʳˢ in entrenchments in them.

From the top of these heights I saw Gwalior at my feet, the country corresponded exactly with the description which I had elicited from natives and which I have given above.

The heights descended towards Gwalior in a succession of ranges, one lower than the other, the lowest and last commanding the Grand Parade and a great part [of the] Lushkar, all of which I saw I could take from the lowest range undisturbed by the fire of the Fort.

I sent for the Artillery and Cavalry and support from the Camp. The Enemy had concentrated their Artillery in position covering the right of the old city, the palace, the Pool Bagh and the Grand Parade of the Lushkar. They cannonaded from these batteries with great vivacity the heights occupied by the 86ᵗʰ & 95ᵗʰ, the two

18^{pdrs} making very good practice at a corresponding position on our left occupied by the 86th. The 95th advanced the guns taken on the heights and fired with some effect on the batteries below.

I ordered a forward movement, properly supported, against the town. The 86th and 95th drove the rebels from range to range till the 95th and 25th N.I., which I brought up, occupied the lowest one, commanding the Grand Parade of the Lushkar.

The rebels having been driven back from the highest range, the guns and the cavalry were enabled to advance by the road through the pass towards Gwalior, ready to cooperate with the advanced line in the final attack of that place. After debouching from the pass, a spot was found where it was just possibly practicable for guns to cross the canal, but a gun having upset there and blocked up the passage, only one 9^{pdr} reached the heights which I ordered down to the lowest range to cover the attack of the Grand Parade. I directed the 1st Bombay Lancers under Lth Colonel Owen,[96] who much to their credit had succeeded to reach the highest range, to put itself in a road wending thro' the hills so as to be able to join in the attack of the Grand Parade.

The Enemy, driven from the ranges of hills, displayed a large force of foot and horse on the Grand Parade, and on the whole line extending from the center of the Lushkar to the northernmost extremity of the old city, under the Fort; a large body defended the Palace of the Pool Bagh, their object evidently was to support their line of Artillery. The Enfield Rifles annoyed them a good deal.

When the 9^{pdr} had opened its fire with one of the best shrapnel that was ever fired, which cleared the space about the two 9^{pdrs} in position on the Grand Parade; and when the Bombay Troop of Horse Artillery, covered by a squadron of the 14th Lt Dgns and supported by a battery of 9^{pdrs} and cavalry and the 1st Bombay Lt Cavalry, were ready for the attack, a general advance took place. The 95th under Col Raines charged the two guns and the enemy in position on the Grand Parade. Lt Col Owen with the 1st Bombay Cavalry charged across the Grand Parade into the town of the Lushkar, the troop of Horse Artillery and Cavalry under Brigadier Smith attacked the enemy in position at the Pool Bagh and in front of the old city.

The 95th took the two 9^{pdrs} and one or two small pieces of artillery on the Grand Parade, and entering the street leading from it to the Palace, and met the 1st Bombay Cavalry coming back, having had one officer killed, in the streets, and one or two casualties. However we continued our march without opposition to the Palace which is in the centre of the new Town, the Lushkar, and occupied it, the enemy's cavalry flying before us down the streets.

Brigadier Smith met with a good deal of opposition from the Enemy's guns, of which six were horsed, but he captured some of them and the Enemy, retreating, abandoned the rest. Brigadier Smith continued his pursuit till his men and horses, exhausted before the combat began, could go no further.

I ordered the 25th N.I. into the town, the whole of which now fell into our hands, as well as numerous guns abandoned by the Enemy in every direction, altogether 27 in number, exclusive of the guns in the Fort.

Scindia's Agent had reported to me that the Fort was evacuated but on a detachment of the 25th going to occupy it, they were fired on by a small party of fanatics. I ordered it to be closely invested and the next morning it was gallantly captured by Lieut Rose, a Scotch cousin of mine, of the 25th. Every one of the Enemy was killed but Lieut Rose was mortally wounded, and there were several casualties amongst his men.

I had left Brig Gen Napier with a Troop of Horse Artillery, Cavalry and Infantry in the Morar Cantonments, for the purpose of preventing the escape of the enemy in that direction and being fresh for the pursuit.

The Enemy, invested on every side, except the Residency, the North West, which was to have been occupied as I have stated by Col Riddell's Column from Dholpoor, escaped in that direction.

Brig Gen Napier conducted the pursuit with the greatest intelligence and zeal. He came up with the enemy and found them in position at Jowra Alipoor, between Gwalior and Dholpoor. The Chiefs had concentrated here as many troops as they could after their disorderly flight from Gwalior, and were passing them, drawn up in line, in muster. General Napier's Force was concealed from them by a rising ground and the rebels could see nothing of it but the tops of the men's caps, and a few vedettes of the Hyderabad Cavalry pushed on to reconnoitre. Two rebels mounted on running camels left their ranks and came towards the vedettes. One of them, who had been implicated in the meeting and who was always distinguishing himself, with a view to redeem his character, went forward and met the enemy camel men. He asked to whose force they belonged. After some hesitation, they answered, 'To Nana Sahib's Army. To whom do you belong?' 'I,' replied the vedette, 'belong to Rose Sahib's Army'. The Camel Men made off rapidly to their force which got into motion as if to retreat.[97] The rebels when they first perceived the caps of Napier's troops had fired shell at them. Gen Napier moved his troop of Horse Artillery, supported by Hyderabad Cavalry, at a gallop, so as to enfilade the enemy's left flank; their guns on the left fired one or two rounds at the troops and then followed the rest of the main body in full retreat, abandoning their guns before the cavalry could come up with them. General Napier pursued the enemy till his men and horses were no longer able to move; he killed a good many of them and took altogether 25 guns in the pursuit, which with the 27 which my Force took, made 52 pieces of Artillery taken from the Rebels in the field besides 70 Elephants, immense quantities of ammunition and warlike stores, and the Arsenal of Gwalior.

The day after the capture of Gwalior, I conducted Scindia and Sir Robert Hamilton, who arrived from Morar Cantonments, to the Palace in Gwalior, escorted by a Squadron of the 8th Hussars and another of the 14th Lt Dragoons.

The rapid fall of Gwalior has had the happiest of political and military results. The Rebels are no longer an Army of combatants, they are disheartened fugitives, humiliated in their own opinion, and in that of their countrymen, by signal and repeated defeats, without Artillery, warlike stores or reserves. In a political point of view, it is better that Gwalior should have fallen into rebel hands and be retaken as it was. Before, English influence was extinct, and the rebel influence was paramount in Gwalior. Now it is exactly the contrary. The political situation of Gwalior has been completely purified. Before it was Nana Sahib and the Peishwari Government. Now it is English power and grateful Scindia.

My troops deployed in the operations against Gwalior showed the same admirable spirit and discipline which have characterised their conduct since the commencement of the campaign. A hundred men of the H.M. 86th were so weak from the effects of the sun and over fatigue that they were obliged to fall out of the ranks and be carried in doolies on the last march on the 18th of June. The next day the moment they heard the Enemy were to be attacked they turned out, and their noble spirit made them fight as if they were perfectly well. The same spirit of devotion pervades the whole force.

I should feel most grateful if Your Royal Highness were pleased to confer some mark of favour on Her Majesty's 14th Light Dragoons and 86th Regiment. They have shared in every action of the campaign, borne all its hardships with the utmost patience and cheerfulness, and always observed good discipline.

BL Add MSS 42812, ff. 98–112

187
Captain Robert Poore to M.A. Saurin

Gwalior

[Holograph]   30 June 1858

I sent my last letter to my Mother on the 22nd, after we had got the order to march, which was just after the letter was sent, countermanded, as Stiggs had sent to say we were not fit to move (as usual), which as it turned out was lucky as General Napier had come up with the rebels, and they had cut, leaving, I hear, 25 guns in his hands, he reported that he had killed 300 of them, but I daresay half that would be nearer the truth.

This affair at Gwalior has been a mismanaged thing after all, as, with the exception of their guns, the rebels have suffered a very trifling loss, having got off with all their force & treasure. This has to be put down to the utter want of any plan of attack, & of Sir Hugh Rose's not having supported our Force in the proper place on the 17th. He has been a very lucky man, but I should say nothing of a general, however he goes ahead more than most of them, which is the great thing with these fellows. Heneage gets a Victoria Cross & a Brevet Majority for the charge, he is a lucky fellow. In fact as far as I can judge, the whole affair might have been settled & the force of the rebels here completely broken on the 17th if it had been properly managed, and with a very trifling loss to ourselves though no doubt it is easy enough to see what might have been done when one knows the ground and knows what has happened after the affair is over . . . On Thursday we turned out about 5 a.m. in light marching order & Sir H. Rose came round to thank the dif. regts . . .

(Sat. 26th June) I went up to see the Fort, did not see much of it as I went to sleep, & as it began to rain when I awoke I made the best of my way back to camp, found it had been raining pretty smartly on the plain, in fact, a sort of water course that serves as a road as well, & that was perfectly hard & dry when I crossed in the morning, was so deep & rapid when I crossed coming back that my horse was taken off his feet for a stride or two, it rained a good bit more during the day, its quite astonishing in what a short space of time a tremendous river is formed, they disappear about as quickly.

(Sun. 27th June) There was some rain again today. A division of the Horse Artillery Troop with us that had been with Napier's Column returned this morning.

(Mon. 28th June) Morning spent in trying to make the men recommend one of their number for the Vic. Cross, of which you have no conception of the difficulty, as they are so jealous of one another.[98] Started at 11 a.m. with 2 others and went all over the Fort, they had 5 guns up there, 2 six pounder, iron guns (one of which had burst), an old iron gun supposed to be a 20 pounder, a 4 pounder (out of which they had got an astonishing range and accuracy of firing, particularly considering their bullets are hammered into shape and consequently not round) & a 24 pounder brass gun. There were also some very old temples belonging to a religion that existed before Hindooism, and now nearly extinct (Gins I think they call them.)[99] The hill on which the wall of the Fort runs round is about 1½ miles in length & varying from 100 to 300 yards in breadth, scarped by steep rock on all sides: lots of tanks of water all over it & some of these with good water, a beautiful view from all sides. You must know that when the Fort was attacked there were only 8 men left in it (they were fanatics & had sworn to die or else) and an Officer of the attacking Force (i.e a Company of the 25th N.I.), they were all killed except one man who has either bolted or else still lies hid there, most probably the former.

(Tues. 29th June) We had another Vic. Cross worry, as there were to be the names of one officer, one Sergeant and one man in each troop sent in for recommendation nothing particular beside. It was not certain yesterday the exact number to be recommended . . .

NAM 9504–22–1

188
Mansfield to Rose

Allahabad

[Holograph copy]   7 July 1858

No. 100 Confidential

Your Despatch of the 28th June 1858, in answer to one from me, No. 88, dated 7th June 1858, has been laid before the Commander in Chief.

I have the honor, by desire of His Excellency, to say that he should have wished to have allowed the matter, which formed the subject of these letters to drop, were it not for one or two assumptions which it is necessary to answer.

In the first place, it was never the intention of the Commander-in-Chief to reduce you to a Brigade Command with the title of a Divisional Commander.

On the contrary, he expressed his desire to the Governor General that you should command, not only in Gwalior, but throughout the wide districts in which your very successful operations have been carried on, after you left Saugor. The reason given by His Excellency to His Lordship as the advantage that would be gained to the State by the presence of an Officer in that country, still unhappily in insurrection, in which he had gained so wide a reputation, as a successful Military Commander.

2. With regard to your re-assumption of the Command of the Central India Field Force, without, as the Commander-in-Chief considers, due authority, His Excellency is compelled to re-iterate that you were at that time in Telegraphic communication with him. The orders for the march of the Force from Kalpee, the movement of the Seepree Brigade to your aid, and of the Budpore Brigade from Agra, were actually given before you were aware of the Gwalior outbreak. Thus it is evident that there was ample time for the interchange of communications between His Excellency and you.

It would have been consonant with the rules of the Service for you to have asked permission to revoke your former decision of resigning the command. But it was against all rule and precedent that you should do so without having in the first instance demanded permission. If you consider the favourable inclination of His Excellency towards you, that it was at his instance you were first appointed to the command of the trans-Jumna country, you can hardly doubt what would have been the reply of His Excellency to your request.

3. His Excellency well knew from your own reports, as well as from those of Sir R. Hamilton, the dangerous state of the Districts through which your Columns have lately passed. He well knew, although the insurrection might be partially quelled, that it was by no means utterly put down. If the outbreak of Gwalior had not actually taken place, there was ample reason for great anxiety on the part of His Excellency that an Officer of tried ability in War should be appointed to hold the great command he destined for you, and which has now been conferred on your successor. It was with extreme regret that he hears of your ill-health on public, as well as on private grounds.

4. I am commanded to say that however much the Commander in Chief may have felt what drew forth my letter of the 7th June, he would not have taken notice of it in the manner he did, had His Excellency not had previous occasion to find one of his orders, given in the most positive manner with regard to the disposition of troops, set aside by you but a very short time before. The result being that his combinations were interfered with; and a wide

Province was exposed, for a time, to pillage and incendiarism. The means he had disposed to meet such evils – which he anticipated with the utmost certainty – having been estranged in direct contravention of his Orders.[100]

5. On that occasion, His Excellency abstained from putting on Official Record his opinion of this step. But when he perceived that his authority was again set aside, so shortly after his previous friendly remonstrance, he felt that it was due to himself, and to his office, to speak in such a manner that there might be no mistake in future. He is sure that on reflection you will admit that you would not suffer any subordinate of your own to take such a like liberty with yourself.

6. With regard to your question about corresponding with Government, His Excellency is surprised that it should have been put. On consideration you will comprehend that the injunction conveyed in my letter of June the 7th, regarding direct correspondence with the Government affected you only in your position as a General Officer Commanding a Division in the Presidency of Bengal, about which there could be no doubt.

On the other hand, there can equally be no doubt that you are at liberty, as any other officer of inferior rank would be, to answer questions put to you direct from the Supreme Government.

OIOC MSS Eur D174, pp. 564–6

189
Rose to Cambridge

Poona

[Holograph copy]   10 August 1858

❊ ❊ ❊

As long as I was under the sun of Central India, I was so weak from its effects that I could only perform the duties which were necessary for the success of the operations. But I was not able to write reports of them, except the Telegrams, until long after they were due.

I had no plans of any of the scenes of operations except one of the 'enceinte' of the Fort of Calpee; my whole available time was spent in collecting information respecting them; the information I thus obtained was one of the main causes of my success.

At the attack of Koonch I was three times dismounted by the sun, but recovered by strong restoratives of which a skin full of water poured over me is the best. Before Calpee I had more attacks of sun. These attacks prostrate the strength for a length of time. The fact is that myself and the very great majority of my Force would, in ordinary circumstances, have been in the sick list but this would never have done, for then we could not have succeeded. I have only spoken about myself in order to account for the very tardy arrival of my report of the operations, and for which I venture to ask Your Royal Highness's kind consideration. I am now engaged in sending in to the Commander in Chief my final report respecting the operations against Calpee and Gwalior.

I found that my health would not stand a Gwalior sun which in the rains is as bad as in summer. I am already getting quite round, thanks to the good air of Poona, and am quite ready for an autumn or winter campaign.

BL Add MSS 42812, ff. 113–14

190
Rose to Mansfield

Poona
[Holograph copy]   11 October 1858
Private

I am very sorry to have to write to you on a painful subject.

Consideration for the service alone prevented me from enlarging in my despatches on the conduct of Brigadier Steuart C.B. Commanding 2nd Brigade (of the 14th Light Dragoons) at Koonch and subsequently, which retarded and acted very unfavourably on my operations, and the health of his Brigade.[101]

Putting the most charitable construction I can on that conduct, truth and duty compel me to say that it would not be right that

Brigadier Steuart should ever again command troops on service, the reward to which under other circumstances he would probably have been entitled for the Special Mention and Mentions of his conduct at Rathghur and Jhansi. All this is the more regretted because I hear that he behaved gallantly at Ramnuggur[102] as a young man. But like others he has been the victim of twenty years in India, too much smoking etc.

❊ ❊ ❊

BL Add MSS 42812 ff. 130–1

191
Captain Maclachlan[103] to Rose

[Holograph]

[Indecipherable]
17 December 1858

Having been requested by you to state what I recollect concerning certain Drum Head Courts Martial assembled at Sehore in January last; and more especially that held on Jumal Khan and others, referred to in the 22nd para. of the Judge Advocate General's Report on these trials, dated 10th November 1858, I beg to bring to your notice what you may possibly recollect that in every case which I had the honor of laying before you for confirmation you required and obtained from me a verbal summary of the evidence, both for and against the Prisoners, previous to your decision being given.

2. This I was at the time well able to afford, from pencil notes made by me of the leading points of the evidence adduced, but as these were not kept I cannot at this distant period point out the particular overt acts, for which each individual was tried, or the nature of the evidence against him.

3. You are well aware of the reasons which rendered it entirely impracticable to record the evidence on these Courts and I may notice here that they had only three days to dispose of the Charges against the Mutineers of the Bhopal Contingent.

4. You arrived at Sehore on the 10th January. No Court Martial was held on that day, as it was, I believe, employed by you in

enquiring into their conduct and another day was spent in bringing in the disarmed Regiments from a village, distant some six or eight miles, from our Camp. Eventually, so urgent was the necessity of the Force moving on the 15th that several prisoners had to be left behind untried.

5. Although in one day three important trials were concluded yet I would beg to state that the evidence in these cases was much the same against all the Prisoners tried under the various charges, the Courts usually commenced their Proceedings early, and in more than one instance, did not terminate them until dark, sitting without interruption all the time. By the evidence not being recorded much time was saved, while every care and attention that these important trials demanded was bestowed on them by the Court.

6. In the case particularly brought to my notice, that of Jumal Khan, and those tried for mutiny at Bursiah[104] the evidence I perfectly remember was that though insufficient to convict them of the whole charge, it was clear from it that, through fear, they had deserted their post which it was their duty to have defended to the last thereby and by withholding their assistance when required, being the cause of the life of the Deputy Collector at that station being sacrificed and a large amount of treasure lost, this the Court considered an act of mutiny, caused by fear or defection, although not proved to have been through disaffection. The Prisoners stated in their defence that reports had been made to Sehore and Bhopal as to the state of the country and that they had called for assistance, but their defence for which the Court made every allowance depended on their own statements.

7. The Court gave this case their most careful and anxious consideration, and having well weighed and sifted the evidence, found them 'Guilty' of not having rendered assistance, from fear of the number of Prisoners and others who were present at Bursiah, when the Political Assistant was murdered and of having left their posts on the same account, they were sentenced to (7) seven years imprisonment with hard labour.

8. On my taking the proceedings to you for Confirmation you remarked upon it, after hearing all the facts of the case, in words to the following effect 'that fear in a soldier was the same as

cowardice, one of the greatest of military crimes and that under the influence of it these men had yielded up a sacred trust – that such should not have been recorded by the Court as a palliation of their offence, and that you considered it their duty to mark by a more severe sentence their sense of the magnitude of the crime of which these men were found guilty'. These remarks were, I believe, also personally communicated to the President, who laid them before the Court.

9. Agreeing with you, on reconsideration, the Court saw fit to alter their sentence to Transportation for life, adding to it however for assigned reasons a Recommendation to Mercy.

10. What I have above stated is as nearly as I can recollect a brief outline of the trial in question, affording as much information as I can give, without Notes and documents to which to refer, and I trust I may be in conclusion allowed to add that although the cases tried by the Court Martial, and which I assisted as officiating Judge Advocate, were numerous and the time allowed short, yet no Prisoner situated as these men were, could have received more patient, impartial and anxious hearing, both with regard to the Prosecution and Defence, than those men of the Bhopal Contingent did, from the tribunal of British officers before whom they were arraigned.

BL Add MSS 42807 ff. 47–9

192
Rose to Canning

<table>
<tr><td>[Holograph]
Private</td><td>Burhanpur[105]
23 December 1858</td></tr>
</table>

I only write a few lines to say how *very much pained* I am that you should have thought that the delay in sending in the Report on the operations before Calpe & Gwalior argued any degree of want of respect for yourself or Lord Clyde.

But I was utterly unable besides the discharge of such duties, to compose a despatch on long, intricate, and very difficult operations, more especially as the subject of these despatches [Kalpi and Gwalior] was a very delicate one. In the first place, Lord Clyde had disapproved strongly my reinforcing myself with part of Lieutenant Colonel Maxwell's Column. Of course in my report of the operations, it was necessary that I should show the necessity for my having done so. But to do so was very delicate because I had to take care not to let it appear that my opinion was opposed to Lord Clyde's. I was therefore obliged to show the necessity of obeying my first and most important instructions, which were to take Calpe, and if I showed that the state of health of my force was such that I could not take Calpe without reinforcements, then in that case I became absolved from blame, having done what was necessary for the fulfillment of my primary instructions, and for the good of the country.

There again nothing could be worse than the unfortunate Brigadier Steuart of the 14th Light Dragoons. It was necessary for the sake of the truth, and in justice to the troops to show in my report that they were not to blame for the delay and very unfavourable results of Brigadier Steuart's misconduct. But it was also necessary for the credit of the Army not to proclaim to the world that Brigadier Stewart has lost his name and his head.[106] However, I thought it right to let the Duke of Cambridge know that the unfortunate Brigadier ought never again to be placed at the head of Troops, and an answer which I received from Sir C. Yorke a few days ago tells me that that opinion is shared at the Horse Guards. The most singular part of the whole affair is that he was considered the best cavalry officer in India.

I am all in the right about the Sehore Courts Martial, and your former opinion as to my conduct in that matter will be quite justified by my answer to General Birch's letter and the Judge Advocate General's Report. Nothing can be stronger than the documents and facts which prove the necessity of my immediate advance to Saugor, and consequently the evil of delaying that advance by not availing myself of the latitude allowed Drum Head Courts Martial *not* to record evidence.

The Judge Advocate General is mistaken in thinking that the Bhopal Sepoys accused of mutiny at Bursah were not found guilty of mutiny. The Court found them guilty of mutiny but with the palliating circumstance of having so erred that is aided, or abetted the mutiny, thro' 'fear' and not feloniously, as will be seen by the statement of the officiating Assistant Judge Advocate, who fortunately is here with his Troop of Horse Artillery. I could not approve the finding because fear, or cowardice (they are the same) which makes a soldier misbehave or give up his post to the Enemy, is punished by the common British Articles of War, by death.

Sleeping on a post is punishable with death by the Articles of War, it involves no turpitude or moral offence, but its punishment is severe because it places in danger the safety of an Army or of a cause.

Abandoning a post through *fear* places in peril the same important interests, and it is worse than sleeping on a post, because it is base to abandon thro' fear a Post or Government Officer or any trust confided to Soldiers.

❋ ❋ ❋

BL Add MSS 42812 ff. 139–40

193
Rose to Robertson

[Holograph copy]

Mahabaleshwar
20 April 1859

❋ ❋ ❋

I am extremely mortified that the C.I.F.F. are not to get a clasp for Calpee or anything else.[107] I suppose it is all Lord Clyde. He said from the beginning that Gen. Roberts and Gen. Whitlock's Force had done equally as much as the C.I.F.F. It is true that this unjust deduction created general indignation in the Military world, but that only makes Lord Clyde more angry. Wetherall wrote to me from Allahabad that everybody there understands the cause of Lord Clyde's and Sir William Mansfield's annoyance with the C.I.F.F. and that we had been much too successful. Did you ever hear such patriotism? Angry that their own brothers in arms conquered in a more difficult struggle.

BL Add MSS 42812 f. 139

194
Birch to Secretary, Military Department, Bombay

Calcutta

[Holograph copy]   9 May 1859

With reference to your letter N° 59 dated the 27th January 1859 and its enclosures, I am directed to acquaint you for the information of the Governor of Bombay that His Excellency the Governor General in Council is of opinion that the explanation of that Officer is entirely satisfactory as regards the necessity of using all possible expedition in the trial of the mutineers at Sehore.

Whether, as it was, the length of Sir H. Rose's stay at Sehore would not have allowed of the men being tried in batches smaller than the extraordinarily large number of 149, and therefore with a better hearing of each case, appears doubtful, but under the very difficult circumstances of the moment His Excellency in Council does not think it is necessary to say more on this point.

The punishment awarded to Jumal Khan and others, the severest punishment short of Death, is heavier, I am to observe, than that which has been awarded in many cases of mutiny of the like inactive kind but it was necessary to make a stern example in this case and the Governor General in Council does not find fault with the sentence. The men in question will be considered amongst those whose cases will, at a fitting time, come under review by the Government of India.

I am to request that a communication to this effect may be made to Major General Sir H. Rose and that he may be assured that nothing was further from the intention of the Governor General in Council than to imply any unduly harsh disposition on his part towards the mutineers who came within his reach for punishment, but the scantiness of the information conveyed in former papers on this subject made it indispensable that the Governor General in Council should have further particulars brought before him.

BL Add MSS 42807 f. 58

195
Rose to Cambridge

Mahabaleshwar

[Holograph copy]   22 May 1859

❊   ❊   ❊

[regarding Colonel Riddell] He commanded a moveable column but from the extreme difficulty of moving it it was called the Immoveable Column.

❊   ❊   ❊

I gave Colonel Riddell a positive order to cross the River Chumbaul and occupy with his column the Residency about seven miles N.E. of Gwalior, which would have completed the investment of Gwalior, and prevented the escape of Tantia Topee and the Rebel Army.

However, Colonel Riddell did not obey the order, did not cross the Chumbaul, and did not occupy the Residency, by which point of course the Rebels escaped.

Instead of the Residency being held, I received no end of excuses from Colonel Riddell for his disregard of my order, that is the ford across the Chumbaul was very bad; the rocks large and slippery; all of which excuses were proved to be valueless by a

Battery of Artillery passing over the same Ford directly afterwards.

❖ ❖ ❖

BL Add MSS 42813, ff. 148–9

196
Sir Robert Hamilton to Sir John Kaye

Stratford on Avon

[Typed copy]   27 August 1860

❖ ❖ ❖

The Ranee lived in the Palace, a very fine house in the Town, when the shells began to thicken she went up to the Fort and lived in the Palace there. I have no plan but I can give you an idea of the end of the Fort which Sir Hugh attempted to breach, he bombarded it and threw shells into the Palace, but the rock was the firmest and finest of defences – and inside was a reservoir or tank and of this I was aware and *told* Sir Hugh Rose and when I saw the Battery making told the Capt. and also our Engineer Boileau M.E. who reported it to Sir Hugh but he would not desist and we wasted no end of ammunition. The breach was made near the Gate (not the one the poor folks came out to be slaughtered) and the escalade attempted on the wall, the cantonments were some distance from the City, the Fort had a wall all round it and it enclosed the town, the palace was within matchlock range of the Fort and it was very difficult to get out the first day after the Town was captured, for immediately the Palace Gate moved a shot came slap upon it – the Doctor was wounded and I think killed just whilst looking after wounded in Dhoolies.[108]

❖ ❖ ❖

The Ranee escaped (à la Bazaine) by a tortuous secret path along the face of the bluff rock, guided by a faithful Thakoe.[109] I went to see it and it is a wonder she did not slip and break her neck. She was killed at Gwalior at the corner of the Parade in the [missing], whereon a cluster of [missing] were seen. I had always desired that the Enfield Rifle might fire at them. In this way a group came on the Parade, at a Tukeeah (B)[110] whilst the battle was raging but quite out of shot, however some rifles (A) let drive at them and they dispersed; two shots had taken effect, one on the Ranee the other on her attendant. The Ranee died almost before she was put in a Palkee and hurried off to a Mundil[111] (C) on the other side of the town . . . I went to the spot with Dr Christison[112] and collected bits of bone from the ashes – which he preserved, the attendant was a Masalmanee, and I had her exhumed, both were shot in the breast and fatal wounds.

OIOC MSS Eur D706/2, ff. 26–7

197
Sir R. Hamilton to Sir John Kaye

[Typed copy]

Stratford on Avon
20 March 1860

. . . When I reached Calcutta Lord C. asked me to give a memo. of what I thought necessary to tranquillise Central India – my charge extended from Goozerat to the Jumna including Rewah and *down* to Ajunta. I drew out a sketch of operations and it was sent to Sir Colin to whom the memo. had been transferred and with the C. and Mansfield and maps I pointed out and went over the whole *line* from Indore to the Jumna. 'When will you reach Calpee' was the C.C. question and I replied 'If no unforeseen obstacles occur by the 1st May – but you must give us some Europeans'. In his broadest Scotch the C. 'I canna' gie you a man'. Lord C. said he would arrange for one regiment and I could tell you more of this. It was no time to dawdle – Sir C. said and who will you have for your General? I went to Bombay, Lord Elphinstone outdid himself and Sir H. Rose and I were started together and reached Indore on 14th Decr. The plan of operations to the very marches was carried out and we reached Calpee and took it on the 23 May. I kept no copy of the plan and memo. I gave Lord C. because it was secret and I did not wish to risk losing it, but I asked him when all was over for a copy and you will see his notice of my request.[113]

I got on without any reference or dispute with Sir H. Rose to the marvel of every one, I carried all I wanted and it was no time for correspondence or reference. He put *all* the responsibility upon me and I cared not for it we got supplies, money and every thing, thanks to Holkar, Tehree Bhopal and Sindia and we should have reached Calpee but for the run of the Kotah rebels in our rear compelling us to halt at Jhansi.

❊ ❊ ❊

OIOC MSS Eur D706/2, f. 34

198
Hamilton memorandum

[Holograph]   [Undated but post-1866]

❊ ❊ ❊

The Amil of Mahedpore was sent for by Durand for some cause, and he fell under Sir Hugh's wrath, was tried by a Ct. Martial and blown away – and the unfortunate massacre of the Bhopal Contingent, tried, sentenced, and executed, some 90 men, in ten hours was a disgrace to our Name and narrowly escaped Parliamentary notice. I would not give particulars and Gen. Travers[114] was indignant yet kept silence. All my trials were held before a Jury of Vakeels who had to say Guilty or Not Guilty and tho I sentenced and executed many I have never felt one life was sacrificed in revenge. The Drum Head Ct Ml, with Captain Ashburn as Judge Advocate General[115] and 3 or 5 young officers were simple farces ending fatally – as Sir Hugh was for hanging every 'black fellow'. Luckily there was no party like the Jamaican one in Parliament or Sir H.R. might have been a General Eyre.[116]

OIOC MSS Eur D706/2, f. 22

Notes

Introduction

1 The best single volume history is S.N. Sen, *Eighteen Fifty-Seven* (New Delhi, 1958), commissioned by the Indian Government to commemorate the centenary of the Mutiny. For the general reader Christopher Hibbert, *The Great Mutiny: India 1857* is the best modern account, with an excellent bibliography. J.W. Kaye, *History of the Sepoy War in India* (London, 1859–60) and its continuation by G.B. Malleson, *A History of the Indian Mutiny* (London, 1878–80), six volumes in all, remain essential reading. P.J.O. Taylor, *A Companion to the 'Indian Mutiny' of 1857* (New Delhi, 1996) is a valuable source of factual information, as is his *What Really Happened During the Mutiny* (New Delhi, 1997).

2 The only significant exception was Bakht Khan, a subadar in the Bengal Artillery, who commanded the rebel forces at Delhi in the early stages of the siege, but he quickly disappeared into obscurity.

3 The first historians to interpret the insurrection in these terms were Marx and Engels in their book *The First War of Independence*, published in 1860.

4 Small groups of sepoys and some minor nobles may well have discussed the possibility of an uprising, but if so this can only have been on a local scale.

5 Sen and Kaye provided valuable analysis, as does Hibbert. Beyond that, the literature is voluminous and some of it is usefully brought together in Ainslie T. Embree, *1857 in India: Mutiny or War of Independence* (Lexington, Mass., 1963). Not to be overlooked is F.W. Buckler, 'The Political Theory of the Indian Mutiny' (*Transactions of the Royal Historical Society*, Series 4, Vol. V, 1922) in which he argued that technically it was the East India Company which was in rebellion against the Emperor; it was answered, not wholly convincingly, by Dewar and Garrett 'A reply to Mr F.W. Buckler's Political Theory of the Indian Mutiny' *Transactions*, Series 4, Vol. VII, 1924.

6 Sen, p. 412.

7 The operation of the doctrine of lapse is examined in some detail in Kaye, Vol. I, pp. 69–111. For a list of states annexed between 1849 and 1856, see *Parliamentary Papers* (House of Commons) 1856, Vol. XLV, p. 102. It is by no means clear that Dalhousie appreciated the deeper effects of his 'doctrine' or saw it as anything but a useful piece of financial and political aggrandisement.

8 See John Pemble, *The Raj, the Mutiny and the Kingdom of Oudh* (Hassocks, 1977).

9 See Kaye, Vol. I, pp. 175–9 and Malleson, Vol. III, pp. 21–2. In Oudh it was calculated that the *taluqdars* lost about 40% of the villages over which they claimed rights – Pemble, p. 155. In the Bombay Presidency which included the Maratha heartland more than 20,000 estates were confiscated.

10 For a contemporary criticism of this Commission see Robert Knight, *The Imam Commission Unmasked* (London, 1859).

11 The affair of the greased cartridges is very ably analysed in J.A.B. Palmer, *The Mutiny Outbreak at Meerut in 1857* (Cambridge, 1966).

12 *Report of the Commissioners appointed to inquire into the organisation of the Indian Army* (HMSO, 1859), Appendix 61, p. 77 – evidence of Major-General R.J.H. Birch, Military Secretary to the Government of India.

13 The Bengal regiments which mutinied in Central India were the 1st Bengal Light Cavalry, the 14th Bengal Irregular Cavalry, the 12th, 15th, 23rd, 30th, 31st (part), 42nd, 50th, 52nd and 72nd Bengal Native Infantry, 4 Troop, 1st Bengal Horse Artillery, 2 Company, 7th Bengal (Foot) Artillery and 6 Field Battery, Bengal Artillery. The 20th and 27th Bombay Native Infantry, the 1st Bombay Lancers, the 1st Cavalry Hyderabad Contingent and the Malwa, Kotah, Bhopal and Gwalior Contingents also mutinied either in whole or part.

14 Whitlock fought a minor action at Jhigan on 11 April and a somewhat more serious one outside Banda on 18 April. After halting at Banda for some weeks he moved on to Kirwi, 40 miles east of Banda, which he captured on 6 June together with a huge amount of booty.

15 The Banda and Kirwi booty was valued at some £700,000. Rose and his men claimed a share of the prize money on the argument that they had materially assisted Whitlock by their own campaign. Judgement was given for Whitlock and his men in 1866. Rose was reputed personally to have lost prize money worth £30,000. Ironically, the real winner was Campbell who, as Commander-in-Chief, received £60,000. The arguments are set out in *Prize Money or the Right of Major General Whitlock and his Troops to the Banda and Kirwee Booty* (London, 1862). See also Brian Robson, 'The Banda and Kirwi prize money' in *Soldiers of the Queen* (Victorian Military Society), 97, pp. 11–13.

16 The Bundelas had ruled Central India in the 16th century. For a detailed discussion of the precise meaning of the term 'Rajput' see Dirk Kolff, *Naukar, Rajput and Sepoy: the ethnohistory of the military labour market in Hindustan 1450–1850* (Cambridge, 1990).

17 Eric Stokes pioneered this new approach in *The Peasant Armed: The Indian Revolt of 1857* (Oxford, 1986); it has been developed with rich results in Dr Tapti Roy's *The Politics of a Popular Uprising: Bundelkhand in 1857* (Delhi, 1994).

18 Roy, p. 159.

19 Mehemet Ali, an Albanian adventurer, made himself master of Egypt in 1805, occupied Palestine and Syria in 1831 and threatened to march on Constantinople and dethrone the Sultan in 1839. France and Britain then stepped in to assist the Sultan.

20 See C. Rathbone Low, *Soldiers of the Victorian Age* (London, 1880), Vol. II, p. 173.

21 'certainly his pale, thin and delicate appearance did not suggest the endurance, energy and ability to command, which he afterwards displayed in so eminent a degree.' – Sylvester (Annand, p. 91, see note 26 below); 'He was laughed at and called a griff by a good many' – Lowe, p. 154.

22 i.e. since the 1st Bengal Irregular Cavalry, and the 42nd and part of the 31st Bengal Native Infantry had mutinied in June 1857. In fact, Saugor was in no immediate danger, although isolated.

23 An observer had noted during the Malwa campaign that 'These drunken fellows, off-duty men of the 86th and Artillery, with some native troops, killed everyone they met, irrespective of age or sex. Their behaviour on this occasion placed them on the same level as the worst of their adversaries' – Sylvester, diary for 25 October 1857. 'At Jhansi, any man over the age of 16 was automatically executed if caught escaping from the city' – G.C. Stent, *Scraps from my Sabretasche* (1882), p. 205.

24 See Peter Stanley, *White Mutiny: British military culture in India 1825–1875* (London, 1998); see also A.H. Shibley 'Reorganisation of the Indian Armies, 1858–1879' (unpublished PhD thesis, London University).

25 For a wickedly amusing portrait of him in retirement, see Allan Fea, *Recollections of Sixty Years* (London, 1927). Fea, a journalist, was his private secretary for a short period in the 1880s.

26 Sylvester left three accounts; the first was published in 1860 as *Recollections of the Campaign in Malwa and Central India*, the second, written in retirement, was published as *Cavalry Surgeon* in 1971, excellently edited by A. Mackenzie Annand, while the third, Sylvester's diary, lies unpublished in the India Office Library, although I have used extracts here.

I Bombay to Jhansi, June 1857 to March 1858 – Introduction

1 Woodburn's force comprised five troops 14th Light Dragoons, 25th Bombay Native Infantry (BoNI), one battery Bombay Artillery (European), one Coy. Madras Sappers and Miners. It was joined at Mhow by four coys. HM 86th Foot, a battery of Bengal European Artillery, and an all-arms force of the Hyderabad Contingent.

2 Durand's abandonment of Indore remains controversial – see J.W. Kaye, *History of the Sepoy War in India* (1859–60), Vol. III, pp. 342–50, and S.N. Sen, *Eighteen Fifty-Seven* (1958), pp. 313–14; for a defence of Durand see Lieutenant-General James Travers, *The Evacuation of Indore 1857*

(privately printed, n.d.) and H.M. Durand, *Central India in 1857*, both very much *parti pris*.

3 For a vivid account see Sylvester.

4 **1st Brigade (C.S. Stuart)**: wing 14th Light Dragoons, troop 3rd Bombay Light Cavalry, detachment Hyderabad Contingent Cavalry, 86th Foot, 25th BoNI, 21 Company RE, 4 Company 2 Battalion, Bombay (European) Artillery, detachment 5 Company 14 Brigade RA (with siege train).

   2nd Brigade (C. Steuart): HQ and wing 14th Light Dragoons, HQ and five troops 3rd Bombay Light Cavalry, 3/4 Cavalry Hyderabad Contingent, 3rd Bombay European Regiment, 24th BoNI, B Company, Madras Sappers and Miners, 2nd and 5th Companies, Bombay Sappers and Miners, 1st Troop (European) Bombay Horse Artillery, 2 Company Reserve Battalion, Bombay Artillery, detach. 4 Company 2 Battalion Bombay Artillery (with siege guns), Hyderabad Contingent Cavalry, Artillery and Infantry.

   The Begum of Bhopal sent 700 levies with three 9-pounder guns.

5 See C. Rathbone Low, *Soldiers of the Victorian Age*, Vol. II, p. 173.

6 Fazl Mahomed had simply seized the opportunity to become independent of Bhopal.

7 The employment of Afghan, Baluch and even Arab mercenaries, known generically as *vilayatis* (foreigners), had a long tradition in Central India.

8 Mardan Singh was primarily actuated by the desire to recover Chanderi, ceded to Sinhia. He rebelled after failing to get support from the British. He was ultimately pardoned.

9 For example, Captain J.G. Lightfoot, of the Bombay Horse Artillery, thought Rahatgarh 'a very badly managed affair' (Lightfoot MSS, in private hands).

10 Indra Singh, the Raja of Shahgur, remained in rebellion until August 1858 but was pardoned also.

11 Whitlock's force – the Saugor and Nerbudda Field Force – consisted initially of one brigade, comprising Wing 12th Lancers, 2nd Cavalry, Hyderabad Contingent, 3rd Madras European Regiment, 1st and 50th Madras Native Infantry (MNI), A and E Troops, Madras Horse Artillery, 6 Company 14 Battalion RA, A and B Companies, 4 Battalion, Madras Artillery, Company Madras Sappers and Miners. At Banda he was joined by a second brigade which included HM 43rd Foot and the 19th MNI.

12 Some 950 men of the 31st Bengal Infantry had remained loyal at Saugor – some assisted Rose at Rahatgarh – see *Services of the late 31st now the 2nd Native Light Infantry in the Mutiny* (Indian Mutiny Pamphlets, No. 4 – NAM '1857' 54).

I Bombay to Jhansi, June 1857 to March 1858

1 Edward Lowry, 25th Bombay Native Infantry (BoNI).

2 See also Sylvester's account – Annand, A.M. (ed.) *Cavalry Surgeon: the Recollections of Deputy Surgeon-General John Henry Sylvester, FGS, Bombay Army* (1971), pp. 62, 65.

3 Mir Fidr Ali, who had fired at Captain Abbott, 1st Cavalry, Hyderabad Contingent.

4 Major Francis William Henry Follett, 25th BoNI.

5 i.e. C.S. Stuart, commanding Malwa Field Force.

6 Richard Herbert Gall.

7 John Alexander Matthew Macdonald, 3rd Bombay European Regiment.

8 Sutherland George Gordon Orr, Madras Infantry seconded to Hyderabad Contingent.

9 John Dobree Woolcombe, Bombay Artillery.

10 Townshend James William Hungerford, Bengal Artillery.

11 C.S. Stuart.

12 Henry Otway Mayne, 1st Cavalry, Hyderabad Contingent, acting as the Force's intelligence officer. Raised Mayne's Horse, later part of the Central India Horse.

13 Hyderabad Contingent.

14 Either the town attached to the fort or the town wall itself.

15 See Sylvester's account also – Annand, pp. 78–9.

16 A tattoo is a pony.

17 Mutineers from the United Malwa Contingent.

18 Alexander Peter Le Mesurier, commanding fortress of Asirgarh, 80 miles SE of Mhow, on a main E–W route; Peter Melvill Melvill, Secretary of Military Department, Bombay.

19 George Hare, 20th Madras Native Infantry (MNI), seconded to Hyderabad Contingent.

20 Samuel Landon and John Louis, 3rd Bombay European Regiment.

21 John Liddell, commanding 3rd Bombay Europeans.

22 John William Fleming Sandwith.

23 David Davidson, Commissary General, Bombay Army.

24 John Baptiste Ramsay, Assistant Commissary General, Bombay Army.

25 George Cator Turner Stockley.

26 The local corruption of Ahmadnagar, 130 miles E of Bombay.

27 Sir James Outram, commanding the garrison of the Alambagh outside Lucknow, under constant attack from the rebel army in Lucknow.

28 Sent by the Maharajah of Indore, to whom Hamilton had been guardian.

29 Armed civilian guards.

30 Khandwa, 80 miles S of Indore, now an important railway junction.

31 Hoshangabad, on the Nerbudda, on the route from Nagpur to Bhopal.

32 George Henry Robertson.

33 George Meyrick Dew, 14th Light Dragoons.

34 Henry Dyett Abbott and William Murray, both Madras Infantry seconded to Hyderabad Contingent.

35 Henry Clerk, ditto.

36 Sorghum or millet (*Holcus sorghum*).

37 C.M. Martin, late 1st Bengal Light Cavalry, attached to 14th Light Dragoons.

38 Giles Keane, HM 86th.

39 3rd Bombay Europeans. East India Company height standards were sometimes lower than those of the British Army.

40 Maximum ranges and weight of projectiles were:

18 pounder gun	2,300 yards	18 pounds
10 inch howitzer	2,000	85
8 inch howitzer	1,700	41
10 inch mortar	2,500	93
8 inch mortar	1,700	46
5½ inch mortar	1,000	16

Mortars were fired at a fixed elevation of 45° and range was varied by adjusting the charge; they normally fired explosive shells. Guns and howitzers varied the range by adjusting elevation; guns normally fired solid balls or spherical case (a form of shrapnel), howitzers shells or case.

41 The Malwa Field Force arrived Nimach 27 November and departed 6 December 1857.

42 The Deccan Field Force became Rose's 2nd Brigade.

43 1st (Eagle) Troop, Bombay Horse Artillery.

44 This return omits 21 Company RE and the Hyderabad Contingent Field Force (1,200). Adding these and the remaining wing of the 86th, but omitting the 71st, produces a total of some 5,700. No daily parade states have been located.

45 Presumably the 71st Highlanders from Malta, which joined on 3 May 1858.

46 See also Document 165.

47 Nasik, 100 miles NE of Bombay, on the road to Indore.

48 Heavy guns and mortars could be mounted on a wheeled or a static (fortress) carriage.

49 i.e. the Commander-in-Chief Bombay (Sir Henry Somerset).

50 Frederick Alexander Kane, 15th BoNI.

51 Government cash.

52 The reference to Saugor makes it clear that this is addressed to Steuart.

53 Malegaon, 150 miles SW of Mhow, on the main road from Bombay to Mhow.

54 A covered litter.

55 Steuart.

56 Indian artillerymen (from *gola*, meaning a ball).

57 George Timins, Bengal Native Infantry, commanding United Malwa Contingent.

58 William Ross Shakespear, 3rd Madras Light Cavalry, 1st Political Assistant to Hamilton and his son-in-law.

59 See Document 76; Beauvais was presumably a local Uncovenanted Civil Servant since he does not appear in the East India Register.

60 Amjeera, 20 miles W of Dhar.

61 The garrison at Cawnpore under Major-General Charles Windham was defeated by Tantia Topi at the end of November.

62 From the 31st Bengal Native Infantry at Saugor, most of whom had remained loyal.

63 Sydney Turnbull, Bombay Artillery, killed at Jhansi 3 April 1858.

64 Probably John Forbes, Major, 3rd Bombay Light Cavalry.

65 Henry Hastings Affleck Wood, Bombay Army; George Elliott Ashburner, 8th BoNI; Henry Charles Jones, 2nd BoNI; all members of Rose's staff.

66 Francis Cobbe, Madras Artillery, on political duties.

67 William Gordon Cumming, 17th BoNI, on political duties.

68 Agar, 75 miles N of Indore; Shahjahanpur, 75 miles NE of Indore; Biaora, 115 miles NE of Indore.

69 i.e. the ruler's Council.

70 The revenue collector for the district of Mehidpur, 60 miles N of Indore, where the United Malwa Contingent had mutinied earlier.

71 Superintendent of Dak (post) on the Indore–Agra road.

72 Raghugarh, Barsad and Bajrungarh are villages on the Indore–Agra road.

73 A *coss* was roughly 2 miles but varied with locality.

74 Kolaras, 15 miles S of Sipri; Mummia not located but possibly a transcription error for Miana, just N of Guna.

75 An agent employed to collect and transmit local news.

76 Titles adopted by the Nana Sahib.

77 Campbell had retrieved Windham's defeat (see Note 61) on 6 December 1857.

78 Deputy Postmaster at Mandisore.

79 A Muslim holy war.

80 *Tehsildar* and *Kotwal* – revenue officer and chief of police; *Soubah* is short for Subadar, meaning here the head of a small district.

81 Elphinstone's telegram has not been located.

82 Rose reached Saugor on 3 February; Whitlock on the 28th.

83 Walter Coningsby Erskine, Commissioner for the Saugor and Nerbudda Territory, accompanying Whitlock as Political Officer. Succeeded as 12th Earl of Kellie 1866.

84 i.e. Chanderi.

85 Naraioli, 10 miles NW of Saugor.

86 Benaika, 20 miles N, and Narsimhapur, 70 miles S, of Saugor.

87 Literally 'wet hens' i.e. wimps or soft-centred.

88 i.e. by moving directly on Jhansi via Guna.

89 Alexander Ross Elliott Hutchinson, Bengal Infantry, Political Assistant on Hamilton's staff, and yet another son-in-law.

90 Samuel Charters Macpherson, 8th Madras NI, Political Agent at Gwalior.

91 The opium trade with China was the only trading activity left to the Company.

92 Sage, commanding at Saugor. Relieved in March 1858.

93 Richard Western, Madras NI, on political duties.

94 i.e. Sir Colin Campbell.

95 Mardan Singh, Raja of Banpur.

96 James Hope Grant.

97 Herbert Bruce, 2nd Bombay Europeans, intelligence officer to Campbell, later Chief of Police, Lucknow.

98 The fertile area between the Jumna and Ganges (*do ab* – two waters).

99 Joseph Bonus, Bombay Engineers, Assistant Field Engineer with Rose's force.

100 Dinkar Rao Rajwade, Chief Minister (Dewan) of Gwalior.

101 The Gwalior Contingent, the major element in Tantia Topi's attack on Windham.

102 The sepoys enjoyed certain privileges, e.g. in civil courts.

103 Mutineers of the Bhopal Contingent – see also Documents 40, 47, 94.

104 A misprint for the 25th BoNI.

105 The peasants.

106 Balampur, 13 miles E of Bhopal; Bhilsa, 34 miles beyond Balampur.

107 Thomas Wood, 14th Light Dragoons.

108 The Gonds and Bhils, who had seized the opportunity to indulge in banditry.

109 i.e. the 14th had served the longest in India, since 1841.

110 3rd Dragoon Guards and 8th Hussars.

111 Alas for the sepoys, quite untrue, as is the other 'news'.

112 The officers mentioned here were John Liddell, commanding 3rd Bombay Europeans, Henry Archibald Mallock, Bengal Artillery, John Granville Lightfoot, Bombay Horse Artillery, and Arthur Scudamore, 14th Light Dragoons.

113 One wing had joined Stuart at Mhow in August 1857, the remainder joined at Chanderi in March 1858.

114 Biaora, 55 miles S of Guna.

115 A *Faujdar* (or *Phousdar*) was a Mughal police official.

116 i.e. the Shahzada Firuz Shah (see Section Introduction, p. 00); he was not there.

117 *Abeen* is coloured liquid traditionally thrown at Holi; *Kafir* is literally an unbeliever.

118 The Nana Sahib's nephew.

119 The Gwalior Contingent, cantoned at Morar, outside Gwalior.

120 *pan* is a paste of betel, areca nut, lime etc. for chewing; *goolal* the coloured powder thrown during Holi.

121 At Barodia.

122 Not understood – possibly a transcription error from original.

123 Pay in British service was 7 rupees a month.

124 George Frederick Edmonstone, Foreign Secretary to Government of India, with Canning at Allahabad.

125 Khuria, 35 miles NW of Saugor.

126 From Jubbalpore.

127 Rahatgarh – see also Section Introduction.

128 Archibald John Maddy Boileau, Madras Engineers, Commanding Engineer.

129 Probably Karim Khan, captured in 1817.

130 See note 116.

131 Khemlassa, 40 miles NW of Saugor.

132 Of Afghan descent, mainly located E of Delhi, in Rohilkhand.

133 Harry North Dalrymple Prendergast – see Biographical Notes.

134 Glastonbury Neville, RE.

135 Charles Augustus Goodfellow and William George Douglas Dick, Bombay Engineers.

136 Possibly a reference to the Sehore executions – see Documents 40 and 94.

137 18 miles E of Saugor.

138 The first Order using the title 'Central India'.

139 The reward for the Nana.

140 Not understood.

141 The Brinjaras were hereditary carriers whose oxen were famous.

142 John Henry Carne, Bengal Civil Service, Assistant Magistrate at Chirkari.

143 40 miles N of Saugor on the Jhansi road.

144 Actually, the Narut Pass, some miles W of the Madanpur Pass.

145 He survived.

146 76 miles from Jhansi.

147 HM 34th Foot was with Windham at Cawnpore and the medal was presumably taken from a dead body there.

148 i.e. the Indian *scale* of baggage, notoriously lavish.

149 Malthoni, just S of the Marut Pass.

150 Midway between Saugor and Jhansi.

151 Panna, 50 miles SW, and Rewa, 90 miles SE, of Banda.

152 Colonel Edward Robert Wetherall joined as Chief of Staff on 16 April.

153 *Jemadar* is used here in the alternative sense of 'head man'.

154 i.e. the loyal elements.

155 Alfred Butler Little, 25th BoNI.

156 A tunnel through the hills surrounding the fort of Chanderi.

157 Ralph Fitzgibbon Lewis; Harry James Grant Gordon, Madras Engineers; John Miles.

158 Two marches S of Jhansi.

159 Richard Hart Keatinge, Bombay Artillery.

160 Steuart.

161 Barwa Sagar, S of the Betwa river, 10 miles SE of Jhansi.

162 50 miles SW of Jhansi.

163 Thomas Fenwick, RE.

164 Lawrence St Patrick Gowan.

165 John Foster Forbes; William Butler Gossett, RE. There is no Germe in any Army list so it is presumably an error.

II Jhansi to Kalpi, March to May 1858 – Introduction

1 It was known generally as the Mound Bastion but Rose, in a throw-back to his Crimean days, on occasion referred to it as the Mamelon.

2 The story of the Rani is well known in outline but important elements are still obscure. A Maratha from a prominent family, she was the widow of the last ruler of Jhansi, Ganghadar Rao. Under the doctrine of lapse, the British had refused to allow his adopted son, Damodar Rao, to succeed and to allow the Rani to act as Regent. Deeply attached to Jhansi, she lived there quietly until the regular troops mutinied in June 1857, massacring 66 European men, women and children in peculiarly horrifying circumstances. There is no convincing evidence of the Rani's responsibility but she was acclaimed ruler and, receiving no help from the British against attacks from the enemies of Jhansi such as Orcha and Dhatia, threw in her lot with the rebels.

3 '. . . though we occasionally took prisoners at the outposts, but as they were not required in camp, we summarily disposed of them.' A.M. Annand (ed.), *Cavalry Surgeon* (1971), p. 109. 'No quarter was given; those attempting to escape from the city were cut off . . . There was not a night passed but a large number of prisoners were taken by our cavalry picquets and many of these were summarily disposed of.' G.C. Stent, *Scraps from my Sabretasche* (1882), pp. 197–205. 'The orders were to spare nobody over sixteen years – except women, of course.' Charles Combe, *Letters from Persia and India 1856–59*, 7 April 1858.

4 The main battering gun was the 18 pounder; trials in 1861 showed that the error was 120 yards at a range of 1,760 yards – see B.P. Hughes *British Smooth-Bore Artillery* (1969). The problems of ammunition supply in an extended siege need no underlining.

5 There is no evidence of any co-ordination between Tantia and the Jhansi garrison.

6 British casualties in Major R.G. Burton *The Revolt in Central India* (1908), pp. 259–60.

7 Tantia Topi may have visited Gwalior before returning to Kalpi, the implication being that he was already plotting a possible move on Gwalior – see Section III.

8 The troops of the loyal Maharaja of Kotah (Kota) had mutinied in October 1857, murdering the Political Agent, Major Burton, and his two sons. Kotah was captured on 29 March 1858 by the Rajputana Field Force under Major-General H.G. Roberts (see Biographical Notes), based on Nasirabad. Charles Napier had considered Roberts 'the best officer in the Bombay Army, and perhaps in India, of his rank . . . capable of commanding any Army in the field'; his operations in 1858 scarcely bear that out.

II Jhansi to Kalpi, March to May 1858

1 Clearly an error – the 2nd Brigade cavalry (14th LD, 3rd BoLC, Hyderabad Contingent) did not exceed 900.

2 *Tamarindus indica* – its slightly acid fruit gave a refreshing drink believed to relieve fevers.

3 It seems improbable after eight months and may have been simply another camp rumour.

4 The lake was on the E side of the city – Liddell and his Bombay Europeans were presumably covering the Right Attack.

5 i.e. with mortars and guns.

6 Dhanoni, 7 miles east of the Madanpur.

7 Rajwas, 15 miles S of the Narut and centrally placed for all three passes.

8 Salt was a major source of revenue and a special police force was employed to prevent smuggling. It is a vivid illustration of Rose's shortage of men. Bartle is not in the *East India Register* so he was probably a member of the local Uncovenanted Civil Service.

9 Turnbull – see Document 83.

10 John Sinclair, Madras Native Infantry, killed at Jhansi.

11 Jaitpur, between Jhansi and Banda, and SW of Chirkari.

12 Despat, a *thakur* in rebellion until killed in 1862; Adil Mahomed Khan not identified; Nurwar 25 miles N of Sipri.

13 It is not clear if this information about Tantia's intentions and strength reached Rose.

14 Mau, between Jaitpur and Jhansi.

15 It contained a high velocity gun, which the Indians called 'Ghana Garjana' (Roaring Cloud).

16 Arthur Need, 14th Light Dragoons.

17 They were not related.

18 A *tope* is a grove of trees.

19 An auxiliary corps of Gonds and Bhils had been raised to assist.

20 Orai, 20 miles SW of Kalpi; Jalaun 25 miles W of Kalpi; Hamirpur, on the Jumna, 25 miles SE of Kalpi.

21 i.e. the Nana Sahib. *Sircar* means 'head of affairs'.

22 Bhander, 25 miles NE of Jhansi, on the route to Kunch.

23 This account has been translated from Marathi into Hindi, and from Hindi into English.

24 A sacred form of basil (*ocimum sanctum*).

25 A Hindu devotion involving sacrificial fire.

26 Cupboards or wardrobes.

27 Store rooms.

28 Literally, the Drum Room.

29 Religious buildings; sometimes rest-houses.

30 i.e. Campbell's capture of Lucknow on 14–21 March 1858.

31 Nevertheless, Rose continued to use Orr and the Hyderabad Contingent Cavalry on detached missions until the end of the campaign. No evidence has been found of misbehaviour at Garakhota or Barodia and the reluctance of Clerk's troop to charge overwhelming odds at the Betwa scarcely merits such sweeping condemnation.

32 But there was some evidence of agitation in the 3rd.

33 Francis Wingrave Pinkney, Madras Infantry, Commissioner of Jhansi; William Muir, Secretary to Government of North West Provinces.

34 The Unao Gate on the north side of the city – see Documents 119, 130.

35 Thomas Stack, surgeon to 86th Foot.

36 Francis Robert Fox, 14th Madras Native Infantry, attached to Madras Sappers and Miners.

37 Atherton Allen Park.

38 Howard Codrington Dowker, later a lieutenant-general.

39 Major R.G. Burton, *The Revolt in Central India 1857–1859* (Simla, 1908), Appendix 12, gives total casualties as 59 killed and 274 wounded.

40 Rose's despatch and other testimony make it clear that he heard on 30 March and moved on the evening of the 31st.

41 Tantia led the rebel army; the Rao Sahib does not appear to have been present.

42 *Revolt in Central India*, op. cit., Appendix 12, gives 17 killed and 63 wounded.

43 See Document 119.

44 Lieutenant Hugh Robert Meiklejohn and 2nd Lieutenant William George Douglas Dick.

45 *Revolt in Central India*, op. cit., Appendix 12, gives 42 killed and 211 wounded.

46 Tantia himself put his army at 20,000 men with 25 guns. Rose, not surprisingly, put it higher.

47 i.e. drawn by elephants.

48 Captain James Leith, 14th Light Dragoons; for Need, see Note 16.

49 An obvious misprint for 'Bombay'.

50 A leather or skin bag.

51 William Henry Slingsby Beamish, 14th Light Dragoons.

52 i.e. an April Fool.

53 Actually her late husband's adopted son, Damodar Rao.

54 Kotra, 55 miles NE of Jhansi; Mau.

55 A hill station 40 miles S of Poona, then the hot-weather seat of the Bombay Government.

56 Allan Octavian Hume, Commissioner at Etawa, 65 miles NW of Kalpi, on the Jumna. Later, a founder of the Indian National Congress.

57 Akbarpur, in the Doab, mid-way between Cawnpore and Kalpi. The force there under Colonel Maxwell had already been ordered to co-operate with Rose.

58 Not located.

59 A landing or crossing place.

60 30 miles beyond Jhansi, on the Kalpi road.

61 Artillerymen.

62 A *fakir* is a Muslim religious mendicant. It is possible that Rose confused this with *ghazi*, a fanatic.

63 i.e. from wheels to a static mounting to ensure greater accuracy and less wear by limiting recoil.

64 See Document 119.

65 During the siege Rose had set up a semaphore station on a hill S of Jhansi.

66 Gurserai, 50 miles ENE of Jhansi.

67 Punch, 45 miles NE of Jhansi; Lohari, off the main road, about 60 miles NE of Jhansi.

68 See Document 138.

69 *garhi* – see Glossary.

70 Mutinied at Jhansi June 1857.

71 Chamra (Chamer), 3 miles W, and Umri, 3 miles SW, of Kunch.

72 'There was something awe-inspiring to us – comparatively so many pigmies – in the majesty with which it rolled onward and with a terrific roar overhung as a moving mountain range, and then overwhelmed us.' A.M. Annand (ed.) *Cavalry Surgeon* (1971), p. 136.

73 8 miles W of Kalpi.

74 A misprint for *thakur*.

75 Probably Lieutenant-General David Barr, retired.

76 Pearson Scott Thompson, 14th Light Dragoons.

77 Sylvester (Annand, pp. 127–8) has a slightly different account.

78 Itaura, 10 miles from Kalpi.

79 8 miles SE of Kunch.

80 Not located.

81 John Campbell Partridge.

82 Charles Douglas, Bengal Artillery; Richard Kirwan MacQuoid, Madras Infantry, attached Hyderabad Contingent.

83 Bhagalpur, between Kalpi and Cawnpore.

84 Auriya, NW of Kalpi, on the Jumna.

85 i.e. the Rani – *baee* (or *bhai*) meant senior wife or dowager.

86 Steuart, who was invalided home.

87 Lord Harris, Governor of Madras.

88 Francis Shortt Arnott, Surgeon.

89 Starting with some 1,200 European infantry, Rose had lost 261 killed and wounded and an unknown number from disease; he had been reinforced by the 71st (500).

90 Sylvester gives the composition as 170 3rd Bombay LC, troop 14th LD, 200 Hyderabad Cavalry, company 3rd Bombay Europeans, 116 24th BoNI, No. 2

Company Bombay Sappers and Miners, 2 guns – about 800 total – commanded by Major Forbes, 3rd BoLC, Annand, op. cit., p. 141.

91 Deopura, 5½ miles S of Kalpi.

92 See Section I, note 11.

Kalpi to Gwalior, May to June 1858 – Introduction

1 88th Foot, No. 17 Field Battery and 3 Coy. 1 Battalion Bengal Artillery, Camel Corps (Rifle Brigade and 88th Foot), Sikh cavalry and infantry, total about 2,000 men.

2 The Nawab was defeated by Whitlock outside Banda on 18 April and retreated with his troops to Kalpi.

3 Sylvester claimed that the sepoys were inflamed with opium, hemp (cannabis) and captured brandy – A.M. Annand (ed.), *Cavalry Surgeon*, p. 147. This was probably camp rumour.

4 At the critical moment Stuart was reputed to have shouted to his staff 'We must all die like Scotsmen'.

5 See Biographical Notes.

6 The Gwalior Contingent mutinied in June 1857, murdering some of its officers and eventually joining Tantia Topi. The Maharaja (Sindia) had maintained his position there; it was accepted that if he had defected Central India could not have been held or regained.

7 For which he was subsequently severely rebuked by Campbell [166].

8 Riddell's movements were so slow that Rose referred to it as the 'Immoveable Column' [195].

9 Michael William Smith, 3rd Dragoon Guards – see Biographical Notes. In its wanderings the brigade marched 2,028 miles between February 1858 and January 1859 when it was disbanded. It was accompanied throughout by the famous Mrs Fanny Duberly who recorded the journey in *Campaigning Experiences in Rajputana and Central India* (1859).

10 The fortress is 1¾ miles long, with a circumference of about 5 miles, with walls 30 feet high, resting on a flat topped hill, with precipitous sides rising some 300 feet from the surrounding plain.

11 *Lashkar* means camp and commemorates the spot where Daulat Rao Scindia pitched his camp when taking possession of the city in 1794.

12 The Rani was killed during this fighting but the exact circumstances of her death remain unclear [183, 186, 196]. See also S.N. Sen, *Eighteen Fifty-Seven* (New Delhi, 1958), pp. 294–5.

13 See H.G. Rawlinson, 'The capture of Fort Gwalior 20 June 1858', *Journal of the Society for Army Historical Research*, Vol. 8 (1930), pp. 198–200.

14 His deposition (G.B. Malleson, *A History of the Indian Mutiny 1857–1858* (1878–80), Vol. III, Appendix I, pp. 514–24) is the source of almost all that we know about him.

III Kalpi to Gwalior, May to June 1858

1 Richard Thomas Hare.

2 Alexander Davidson Turnbull, Bengal Engineers.

3 Charles Harris Blunt, Bengal Artillery.

4 A body of irregular cavalry raised in the Punjab for the emergency.

5 Running S from Kalpi.

6 Jagamanpur, 40 miles NW of Kalpi, close to the Jumna.

7 In fact, Rose refused the command with some hauteur.

8 William Malcolm Leckie, Bombay Infantry.

9 There is no name on the manuscript but internal evidence identifies it as Shakespear's.

10 See also Document 145.

11 Kadaura, 20 miles S of Kalpi.

12 Presumably he means that they were armed with rifles but part of the Corps came from the Rifle Brigade.

13 The preliminaries to the monsoon.

14 Government had decided to garrison Gwalior with regular troops to dominate Central India.

15 No other evidence of discontent in the Contingent has been noticed.

16 A misprint for 'Goonah'.

17 Cuthbert Davidson, Resident at Hyderabad; the Contingent was under political control because it was paid for by the Nizam.

18 Francis Wheler, succeeded Sage at Saugor in February 1858.

19 John MacDuff, HM 74th Foot.

20 i.e. civilian insurgents, not professional troops.

21 The battle was on the 22nd and Rose occupied Kalpi on the 23rd.

22 Not surprisingly in view of Rose's reputation.

23 38 miles W of Kalpi, on the road to Gwalior.

24 In Rohilcund, about 150 miles N of Kalpi. If these rebels were crossing the Jumna it was a serious development.

25 Colonel R.H. Birch.

26 Whitlock's victory at Banda, by forcing the Nawab to flee to Kalpi with his troops, made Rose's task harder.

27 This is specious nonsense; neither Campbell nor Mansfield had any knowledge of Central India.

28 Barjur Singh, of Bilayan.

29 100 miles W of Nagpur, garrisoned by the Hyderabad Contingent until 1903.

30 M.W. Smith.

31 An artful attempt to forestall the rebuke which he subsequently received – see Document 166.

32 17 miles W of Kalpi.

33 Morar.

34 On the Chambal river, 30 miles N of Gwalior.

35 St George Daniel Showers, commanding at Agra 1858–61.

36 William Riddell, commanding 3rd Bengal European Regiment.

37 A contingent contributed by the state of Patiala, in the Punjab.

38 Raised by Captain John Richard Meade in March, a constituent part of the later Central India Horse. Meade captured Tantia Topi in April 1859.

39 John Fowler Bradford, commanding Meerut Division.

40 Alfred Light, Bengal Artillery.

41 William George Le Mesurier, RA.

42 An error for 'June 1858'.

43 The Pahuj river, 48 miles W of Kalpi.

44 Rose was expecting to attack Gwalior from the N.

45 The Antri pass, 20 miles S of Gwalior.

46 Possibly an error for Magroni, between two branches of the Scinde, 35 miles S of Gwalior.

47 29 miles W of Kalpi.

48 55 miles WNW of Kalpi, four marches from Morar.

49 Amain, 11 miles beyond Indurki.

50 i.e. Gwalior.

51 Lt-Col. Thomas William Hicks, commanding the artillery of the CIFF.

52 Not traced and possibly a mistake.

53 17 miles W of Jhansi.

54 See Document 165.

55 Moth, roughly halfway between Kunch and Jhansi.

56 Dinkar Rao.

57 Between Gwalior and Sipri, the scene of a battle on 29 December 1844 during the Gwalior War.

58 A misprint for *fakir* – see Document 172.

59 Sindia's mother, the wife of the famous Dhaulat Rao Scindia and equally powerful in her own right.

60 Cf. Sylvester 'It is most difficult to write anything which could convey a description of our impedimenta; long strings of laden camels, ponderous elephants, thousands of bullocks, laden with round shot and shell; bags of grain, spare stores of every description; led horses; trains of mules; huge pieces of cannon; unwieldy mortars; pontoon bridges; scaling ladders; sick in dhoolies; sick in wheeled ambulances; sick on camels; sick on foot; and worse than all, an immense number of wheeled vehicles of the worst possible description, many broken down and all drawn by galled and exhausted cattle tended and driven by timid natives or unwilling agriculturalists pressed for service.' A.M. Annand (ed.), *Cavalry Surgeon* (1971), p. 141.

61 Dagaon, 20 miles from Morar.

62 Supaioli, one march from Morar.

63 John North Crealock – see Biographical Notes.

64 Crealock was hearing the sound of Rose's action at Morar.

65 The Morar river, flowing S past Gwalior.

66 A canal flowed S through the pass through the hills S of Gwalior.

67 Henry Foster and Surgeon John Ewing, 95th Foot; the officer of the 1st Bombay Light Cavalry (Lancers) not identified.

68 Captain Clement Walker Heneage, 8th Hussars, who led this charge, received the VC - he had charged with the Light Brigade at Balaclava. See also Document 177.

69 Lieutenant Wyndham Neave.

70 Cornet William Mills, 1st Bombay Light Cavalry (Lancers).

71 See also Document 179.

72 i.e. by driving a nail or spike into the touch hole so that the gun could not be fired until the spike had been drilled out.

73 Napier defeated the fleeing rebels under Tantia Topi at Jaora Alipur on 23 June.

74 Robert Poore, 8th Hussars, with Smith's brigade.

75 Horace Montague.

76 Amputations in India were almost invariably fatal through shock or gangrene.

77 Edward Seager, commanding 8th Hussars. He was a 'ranker' but died a lieutenant-general in 1883.

78 John Reilly, another Crimean veteran.

79 An error for the 19th.

80 The Phul Bagh (Garden of Flowers), the summer palace and gardens a mile E of the Lashkar.

81 Lieutenant Wellington Rose (a distant cousin of Sir Hugh) who, with Lieutenant William Francis Frederick Waller, both of 25th BoNI, led the sortie – see also Document 178. Waller received the VC but it was not at this time awarded posthumously.

82 When the Gwalior Contingent mutinied in June 1857 they spared the European women and children, some of whom escaped to Agra but others, it would appear, remained in hiding. It is not known who precisely were the people see by Poore.

83 i.e. on 17 June. She was accompanied by a female attendant, not sisters – see Document 196.

84 The early Enfields suffered a good deal from ammunition problems.

85 Strictly speaking, learned men.

86 Julius Augustus Robert Raines, retired as major-general 1871.

87 Edward Samuel Blake, Bombay Artillery.

88 Rose's despatch (Forrest, IV, p. 129) gives 29 killed and 65 wounded.

89 See also Document 196.

90 It was, of course, Mrs Duberly.

91 Stuart.

92 Thomas Hugh Cockburn, HM 43rd Light Infantry.

93 i.e. the Gwalior Contingent.

94 These were State troops, not the Contingent.

95 Montague Willes Ommaney, Bengal Artillery.

96 Conrad John Owen.

97 This curious encounter is corroborated by Combe, *Letters from Persia and India 1856–1859*, diary entry for 23 June 1858.

98 The VC carried an annuity with it which may explain some of the rivalry.

99 The Jain religion pre-dates Hinduism, with which it shares some beliefs.

100 A somewhat ponderous reference to the transfer of some of Maxwell's force at Kalpi.

101 Steuart's offences are not entirely clear but Rose appeared to believe that he had been dilatory at Kunch and slow and fumbling in the approach to Kalpi.

102 22 November 1848, during the Second Sikh War.

103 Thomas James MacLachlan, Bombay Artillery.

104 25 miles N of Bhopal.

105 100 miles S of Indore.

106 'Losing one's name' is a traditional Army expression for having committed a (usually minor) offence.

107 The CIFF eventually got the clasp 'Central India' to the Indian Mutiny medal, along with Whitlock's and Roberts' men and many others.

108 Surgeon Stack, 86th Foot, killed near the Palace during the assault.

109 Achille François Bazaine, Marshal of France; the reference is not understood. The place where the Rani is alleged to have jumped her horse over the Fort wall, as pointed out today, seems from personal inspection to be impossible. 'Thakoe' presumably should read 'Thakur'.

110 The dwelling of a holy man; unfortunately the plan evidently attached has disappeared.

111 A temple near the Phul Bagh.

112 Assistant Surgeon Alexander Christison, Bengal Medical Establishment, attached to Gwalior Contingent.

113 No copy has been traced, alas!

114 James Travers, commanding Bhopal Contingent.

115 But see Document 191.

116 Edward Eyre, Governor of Jamaica, put down a rebellion with great harshness in 1865, and was recalled and tried for murder.

Biographical Notes

Broun-Ramsey, James Andrew, 10th Earl of Dalhousie (1812–60). MP for Mid-Lothian 1837–8. Succeeded to Earldom 1838. Vice-President and President of Board of Trade 1843–6. Governor-General 1848–56.

Burne, Owen Tudor (1837–1909). Commissioned 20th Foot 1855. Service in Crimea 1855–6, Mutiny 1857–8. Private Secretary to Viceroy 1868–72 and 1876–8, Secretary of Political Department at India Office 1874–87. Council of India 1887–97. KCSI 1879.

Canning, Charles John, 1st Earl (1812–62), third son of George Canning, the statesman. MP for Warwick 1836–7. Succeeded as Viscount 1837. Under Secretary, Foreign Affairs 1841–6, Postmaster-General 1853–5. Governor-General of India 1855–62. Earl 1859, Knight of Garter 1862.

Campbell (MacLiver), Colin, 1st Baron Clyde of Clydesdale (1792–1863). Commissioned 9th Foot 1808. Service in Peninsula 1808–13, China 1842–6, Second Sikh War 1848–9, Crimea 1854–6, Mutiny 1857–9. Lieutenant-Colonel 1832, Major-General 1854, Field Marshal 1862. KCB 1849, Baron 1859. C-in-C India 1857–60.

Campbell, Robert Dennistoun (1817–59). Commissioned 4th Light Dragoons 1833. Service in First Afghan War 1838–9, Crimea (with 71st Highlanders) 1856, Mutiny 1858–9. CB 1859.

Crealock, John North (1836–95). Commissioned 95th Foot 1854. Service in Mutiny 1857–9, Zulu War 1879–80, Egyptian Campaign 1882. Commanded 95th 1880–5, Regimental District 1885–7, Division, Madras Army 1892–5. CB 1879, Major-General 1892.

Duberly, Frances Isabella (1829–1903). Married Henry Duberly, Paymaster 8th Hussars, 1849. Accompanied him to Crimea 1854–6, to Mutiny 1857–9. Published reminiscences of both campaigns.

Durand, Henry Marion (1812–71). Commissioned Bengal Engineers 1828. Service in First Afghan War 1838–40, Gwalior campaign 1843, Second Sikh War 1848–9, Mutiny 1857–9. Colonel 1858, Major-General 1867. CB 1858, KCSI 1867. Council of India 1859–61, Foreign Secretary, India 1861–5, Military Member of Governor-General's Council 1865–70, Lieutenant-Governor of Punjab 1870–1 (killed when his elephant howdah struck a gateway at Tank, in Waziristan).

Elphinstone, John, 13th Baron (1807–60). Succeeded 1813. Commissioned Royal Horse Guards 1826, retired 1835. Governor of Madras 1837–42, of Bombay 1853–60. GCB 1858, raised to UK peerage 1859.

Hamilton, Robert North Collie, 6th Baronet (1802–87). Joined Bengal Civil Service 1819. Collector, Delhi 1836, Commissioner, Agra 1840–3, Resident, Indore 1844–54, Agent to Governor-General in Central India 1854–9, Provisional Member of Governor-General's Council 1859. KCB 1859. Retired 1859.

Holkar, Tukaji Rao, Maharaja of Indore (1832–86). Ascended throne 1843, given full powers 1852.

Jhansi, Lakhshmibai, Rani of (?1828–58). A Maratha, possibly the daughter of Moropant Tambe, adviser to Chumaji Appa, brother of the last Peishwa of Poona, Baji Rao II. Married Gangadhar Rao, Raja of Jhansi 1842. Killed at Gwalior June 1858.

Mansfield, William Rose, 1st Baron Sandhurst of Sandhurst (1819–76). Commissioned 53rd Foot 1835. Service in First Sikh War 1845–6, Second Sikh War 1848–9, Mutiny 1857–9. Military Adviser to Ambassador at Constantinople 1855–6, Consul-General, Warsaw 1856–7. Chief of Staff to C-in-C India 1857–60, C-in-C Bombay 1860–5, C-in-C India 1865–70. C-in-C Ireland 1870–5. Major-General 1858, General 1872. KCB 1857, Baron 1871.

Maxwell, George Vaughan (1818–92). Commissioned 88th Foot 1838. Service in Crimea 1854–6, Mutiny 1857–9. Lieutenant-Colonel 1854, Major-General 1864. Commanded Brigade 1864, Aldershot Brigade 1870–4.

Napier, Robert Cornelis, 1st Baron Napier of Magdala (1810–90). Commissioned Bengal Engineers 1826. Service in First Sikh War 1845–6, Second Sikh War 1848–9, Mutiny 1857–9, China 1860, Abyssinia 1867–8. C-in-C Bombay 1865–8, C-in-C India 1870–6, Governor of Gibraltar 1876–73. KCB 1859, Major-General 1861, General 1874, Field Marshal 1883, Baron 1868.

Orr, William Adam (1810–69). Commissioned Madras Artillery 1826. Seconded to Hyderabad Contingent 1842. Brevet Major 1854.

Pant, Dhundu, the Nana Sahib (1825–?59). Adopted son and heir of the last Peishwa of Poona, Baji Rao II. In nominal command during siege and massacre of Cawnpore 1857. Thereafter played little direct part in Mutiny. Fled to Nepal in 1859 but date of death unknown.

Prendergast, Harry North Dalrymple (1834–1913). Commissioned Madras Engineers 1854. Service in Persian War 1857, Mutiny (VC) 1857–8, Abyssinian Expedition 1867–8, Third Burma War 1885–6. Major-General 1882, Lieutenant-General 1886, General 1887. KCB 1885, GCB 1902. Commanded Burma Division 1882–4, GOC Burma 1885–6. Resident, Travancore, Mysore 1887, Baroda 1889, Agent to Governor-General Baluchistan 1889, Resident, Mysore 1891–2.

Roberts, Henry Gee (1800–60). Commissioned Bombay Cavalry 1818. Service in Sind 1843–4, Mutiny 1857–8. Lieutenant-Colonel 1843, Major-General 1859. KCB 1859. Commanded Northern Division, Bombay Army and Rajputana Field Force 1857–8.

Rose, Hugh Henry, 1st Baron Strathnairn of Strathnairn and Jhansi (1801–85). Commissioned 93rd Foot 1820. Service in Syria 1840, Crimea 1854–6, Mutiny

1857–8. Consul-General, Syria 1841–8, Secretary to Embassy, Constantinople 1851–4, Poona Division 1857–60, C-in-C Bombay 1860, C-in-C India 1860–5, C-in-C Ireland 1865–70. Major-General 1854, General 1867, Field Marshal 1877. KCB 1855, GCB 1858, KCSI 1861, GCSI 1866, Baron 1866.

Sindhia, Jiaji Rao, Maharaja of Gwalior (1835–66). Ascended throne of Gwalior 1843.

Smith, Michael William. Commissioned 3rd Dragoon Guards 1830. Service in Crimea (with Turkish cavalry) 1854–6, Mutiny 1858–60. Colonel 1854, Major-General 1864, Lieutenant-General 1873, General 1877. Poona Division 1862–7, Colonel 20th Hussars 1870.

Somerset, Sir Henry (1794–1862). Commissioned 25th Foot 1811. Service in Peninsula 1813–14, Waterloo 1815, South Africa. Major-General 1851, Lieutenant-General 1857. C-in-C Bombay Army 1855–60.

Steuart, Charles (1807–73). Commissioned 14th Light Dragoons 1825. Service in Second Sikh War 1848–9, Persia 1857, Mutiny 1857–8. Lieutenant-Colonel 1850, Colonel 1854, Major-General 1864. CB 1857, Colonel of 11th Hussars 1873.

Stuart, Charles Shepherd (1804–79). Commissioned Bombay Infantry 1819. Service in Indian Mutiny. Lieutenant-Colonel 1851, Colonel 1854, General 1877. CB 1858, KCB 1859, GCB 1875.

Sylvester, John Henry (1830–1903). Commissioned into Medical Service of East India Company 1853. Service in Persia 1857, Mutiny 1857–9, Ambeyla Expedition 1863. Retired 1873. Surgeon-Major 1865, Deputy Surgeon-General 1880.

Topi, Tantia (or Tatya), real name Ramchandra Panduranga (c. 1814–59). A Maratha Brahmin born near Ahmadnagar. Companion and adviser to Dhundu Pant, the Nana Sahib (q.v.). Executed at Sipri 18 April 1859.

Whitlock, George Cornish (1798–1868). Commissioned Madras Infantry 1818. Service in Third Maratha War 1819, First Burma War 1826, Coorg campaign 1834, Mutiny 1857–60. Lieutenant-Colonel 1845, Lieutenant-General 1864. Commanded Northern Division, Madras Army 1860–3, Colonel 108th Foot (formerly 3rd Madras European Regiment) 1862. KCB 1859.

Bibliography

(All books published in London unless noted otherwise)

1 Manuscript sources

British Library

    Add MSS 42796–838 papers of Hugh Henry Rose, 1st Baron Strathnairn

British Library, Oriental and India Office Collections

    MSS Eur   C 241   papers of J.H. Sylvester, Bombay Medical Service

               D 174   papers of Sir William Mansfield (Lord Sandhurst)

               D 951   papers of Sir Owen Tudor Burne

               D 538   papers of Sir George Clerk

               D 706   papers of G.B. Malleson (3 bundles)

               D 1007 Central India Field Force Order Book January–June 1858

               F 83   papers of Lord Elgin

               F 87   papers of 13th Lord Elphinstone, Boxes 6, 9

    LMIL/17/2/306 (Parts 1 and 2) General Orders 1858

    Foreign Department, Political Proceedings, 1858–9

    Foreign Department, Political Consultations, 1858–9

    Foreign Department, Secret Proceedings, 1858–9

    Foreign Department, Secret Consultations, 1858–9

    IOR neg. 4395 Letters of Lieutenant Joseph Bonus, Bombay Engineers

    Home Miscellany Series 724–727a Mutiny papers of Sir J. Kaye

National Army Museum

    6307–60 Thomas Wood papers

    6807–264 Letters of George Lynedoch Carmichael, 95th Foot

    6802–5 Journal of the Route of the Column under the Command of Major-General George Cornish Whitlock

National Library of Scotland

    MSS 3797–9 papers of Hugh Henry Rose, 1st Baron Strathnairn

Scottish United Services Museum

    M1994.100.2 Diary and notebook of Hugh Henry Rose, 1st Baron Strathnairn

Sherwood Foresters Museum, Nottingham

    Mutiny diary of John North Crealock, 95th Foot.

2 Official publications and works of reference

Army Lists, 1821–85.

Bombay Army List, 1858.

Buckland, C.E., *Dictionary of Indian Biography* (1906).

Burton, Major R.G., *The Revolt in Central India 1857–59*. Compiled in the Intelligence Branch, Army Headquarters (Simla, 1908).

Forrest, G.W., *Selections from the Letters, Despatches and other State Papers preserved in the Military Department of the Government of India* (4 vols., Calcutta, 1893–1912).

Farrington, Anthony, *Guide to the records of the India Office Military Department* (1982).

Hodgson Index, National Army Museum.

Indian Army List, 1858–66.

Ladendorf, Janice M., *The Revolt in India 1857–58* (Zug, 1966).

Madras Army List, 1858.

Rizvi, S.A.A. and Bhargava, M.L. (eds.), *Freedom Struggle in Uttar Pradesh* (6 vols., Lucknow, 1959).

Seton, R., *The Indian 'Mutiny' 1857–58: Guide to source material in the India Office Library and Records* (1986).

Taylor, P.J.O., *A Companion to the 'Indian Mutiny'* (Delhi, 1996).

What Really Happened During the Mutiny (Delhi, 1997).

Whitworth, R.C., *An Anglo-India Dictionary* (1885).

3 Biographies, memoirs and secondary works

Annand, A.M. (ed.), *Cavalry Surgeon: the recollections of Deputy Surgeon-General John Henry Sylvester, FGS, Bombay Army* (1971).

[Anon.] *A Sortie from Fort St George, being a narrative of the services of the Madras troops under Major General Whitlock K.C.B. during the war in Central India in the years 1858–59 by one who served in the campaigns* (Madras, 1860).

[Anon.] *Prize Money: or the right of Major-General Whitlock K.C.B. and his troops to the Banda and Kirwee booty* (1862).

Burne, Sir O.T., *Rulers of India: Clyde and Strathnairn* (Oxford, 1891).

Burton, Major R.G., *A History of the Hyderabad Contingent* (Calcutta, 1912).

C.C. [Charles Combe], *Letters from Persia and India 1856–59* (privately printed, n.d.).

Chaudhuri, S.B., *Civil Rebellion in the Indian Mutinies, 1857–1859* (Calcutta, 1957). *Theories of the Indian Mutiny 1857–59* (Calcutta, 1959).

Duberly, Mrs Henry, *Campaigning Experiences in Rajpootana and Central India during the Suppression of the Mutiny* (1859).

Embree, Ainslie T., *1857 in India: Mutiny or War of Independence?* (Lexington, Mass., 1963).

Forrest, G.W., *A History of the Indian Mutiny, Reviewed and Illustrated from Original Documents*, 3 vols. (1904–12).

Gall, R.H., *Letters of the late Maj. Genl. R.H. Gall* (Hitchin, 1881).

Gimlette, Lt. Col. G.H.D., *A Postscript to the records of the Indian Mutiny: an attempt to trace the subsequent careers and fate of the rebel Bengal regiments, 1857–1858* (1927).

Hibbert, Christopher, *The Great Mutiny India 1857* (1978).

Hughes, Major-General B.P., *British Smooth-Bore Artillery: the muzzle loading artillery of the 18th and 19th centuries* (1969).

Jacob, John, *A few remarks on the Bengal Army and Furlough Regulations* (1851).

Jocelyn, Colonel J.R.J., *The History of the Royal and Indian Artillery in the Mutiny of 1857* (1915).

Kaye, J.W., *History of the Sepoy War in India* (1859–60).

Knight, Robert, *The Imam Commission Unmasked* (1859).

Kolff, Dirk, *Naukar, Rajput and Sepoy: the ethnohistory of the military labour market in Hindustan 1450–1850* (Cambridge, 1990).

Lang, John, *Wanderings in India and other sketches of life in Hindostan* (1859).

Low, Charles Rathbone, *Soldiers of the Victorian Age* (2 vols., 1880).

Lowe, Thomas, *Central India during the Rebellion of 1857 and 1858: A Narrative of Operations from the suppression of the Mutiny in Aurungabad to the Capture of Gwalior* (1860).

Macpherson, William (ed.), *Memorials of Service in India from the correspondence of the late Major Samuel Charters Macpherson CB* (1865).

Majumdar, R.C., *The Sepoy Mutiny and the Revolt of 1857* (2nd edition, Calcutta, 1963).

Malleson, Colonel G.B., *A History of the Indian Mutiny 1857–1858, Commencing from the close of the second volume of . . . Sir John Kaye's History of the Sepoy War* (3 vols., 1878–80).

Pemble, John, *The Raj, the Indian Mutiny and the Kingdom of Oudh 1801–1859* (Sussex, 1977).

Press List of 'Mutiny Papers': being a collection of the correspondence of the mutineers at Delhi, reports of spies to English officials and other papers (Calcutta, 1921).

Prichard, Iltudus Thomas, *The Mutinies in Rajpootana, being a personal narrative of the mutiny at Nusseerabad* (1860).

Roy, Tapti, *The Politics of a Popular Uprising: Bundelkhand in 1857* (Delhi, 1994).

Sen, S.N., *Eighteen Fifty-Seven* (New Delhi, 1958).

Smyth, Sir John, *The Rebellious Rani* (1966).

Srivastava, K.L., *The Revolt of 1857 in Central India* (Delhi, 1966).

Stanley, Peter, *White Mutiny: British Military Culture in India 1825–1875* (1998).

Stent, G.C., *Scraps from my Sabretasche, being personal adventures while in the 14th (King's Light) Dragoons* (1882).

Stokes, Eric, *The Peasant Armed: the Indian Revolt of 1857* (Oxford, 1986).

Sylvester, Assistant Surgeon J.H., *Recollections of the Campaign in Malwa and Central India* (Bombay, 1860).

Tahmankar, D.V., *The Ranee of Jhansi* (1958).

Walker, Andrew, *Our Bones are Scattered: The Cawnpore massacre and the Indian Mutiny of 1857* (New York, 1996).

4 Articles

Indian Historical Records Proceedings

Bhargava, K.D., 'A note on Tantia Topi' (XXIV, 1948).

Taimuri, M.H.R., 'Some unpublished documents on the death of the Rani of Jhansi' (XXIX, 1953).

Journal of the Society for Army Historical Research

Laws, Colonel M.E.S., 'A contemporary account of the battle of Banda' (XXXII, 160–4).

Rawlinson, H.G., 'The capture of Fort Gwalior 20th June 1858' (VIII, 200).

Transactions of the Royal Historical Society

Buckler, F.W., 'The Political Theory of the Indian Mutiny' (Fourth Series, V, 1922).

Dewar, Douglas, and Garrett, H.L.O., 'A reply to Mr F.W. Buckler's "Political Theory of the Indian Mutiny"' (Fourth Series, VII, 1924).

Index

Abbott, Maj. H. D., 14, 114, 128, 154, 228, 238, 294 n. 33
Agar, 26, 294 n. 68
Akbarpur, 160, 162, 301 n. 57
Amain, 226–7, 236, 305 n. 49
Amjira (Amjeera), 24, 295 n. 60
Antri, pass, 225, 228, 239, 255, 305 n. 45
Army, Bengal, xiii, xv
Army, Bombay, xiii
Army, Madras, xiii
Arnott, Surgeon, 189, 251, 302 n. 88
Ashburner, Capt. G., 25, 289, 296 n. 65
Asirgarh, 9, 10, 12
Attack, Left (Jhansi), 116, 117
Attack, Right (Jhansi), 116, 117, 120, 123
Auriya, 186

Baise Baee, 235, 242, 243
Bajrungarh, 28
Banda, xvi, 74
    Nawab of, 186, 188, 192, 202, 250, 255, 303 n. 2
    prize money, xvi, 291 n. 15
    Whitlock reaches, 291 n. 14
Banpur, Raja of (Mardan Singh), 3, 4, 33, 34, 55, 107, 126, 130, 157, 171, 297 n. 95

Barodia, 3, 65, 71, 81, 84, 85, 86, 87, 126
Bartle, Mr, 127, 144
Barwa Sagar, 145
Beamish, Lt W. H. S., 154, 301 n. 51
Beauvais, Mr, 23, 295 n. 59
Betwa, river, 109, 117, 129, 211
    battle of, 117, 133, 142–3, 145–6, 148–50, 152
Bhandore, 138
Bhils (Bheels), tribe, xvi, 12, 25, 153, 300 n. 19
Bhilsa, 20, 49, 51
Bhopal
    Begum of, xvi
    Contingent, 22–3, 24, 44–5, 47, 48, 108, 226, 280, 282, 284
Birch, Col. R. H., 101, 217, 220, 225, 285
Blake, Lt-Col. E. S., 256, 306 n. 87
Blunt, Maj. C. H., 197, 198, 304 n. 3
Boileau, Maj. A. J. M., 66, 75, 76, 81, 109, 130, 132, 298 n. 128
Bonus, Lt J., 44, 47, 75, 93, 121, 132, 146, 148, 173, 177, 178, 179, 190, 199, 203, 231, 240, 257, 297 n. 99
Bradford, Maj. Gen. J. F., 223, 305 n. 39

315

Brinjaras (Banjaras), 86
Bullock train, 20
Bundelas, xvi, 213, 229, 291 n. 16
Bundelkhand, xvi, 213, 239, 291
    n. 16

Campell, Sir Colin (Lord Clyde),
    4, 37, 42, 92, 157, 195, 214,
    220, 254, 283, 284–5, 288, 308
    and Jhansi, 74
Campbell, Lt-Col. R. D., xix, 308
Canning, Lord, xix, 4, 22, 26, 34,
    62, 73, 108, 171, 219, 261–4,
    266, 282, 289, 308
Carne, J. H., 90, 298 n. 142
Cawnpore (Kanpur), 24, 204
Chambal, river, xvi
Chanderi, 37, 70, 81, 93, 104, 212
    captured by Stuart, xviii, 4,
        105–6, 111–14
    re-occupied by rebels, xviii, 191,
        210
    recaptured by Smith, 209, 212
Chirkari, 4, 59, 60, 61, 74, 90–1,
    101, 110, 116
Christison, Asst Surgeon A., 307
    n. 112
Clerk, Lt H., 294 n. 35
Cobbe, Capt. F., 25, 296 n. 66
Cockburn, Capt. T. H., 306 n. 92
Crealock, Capt. J. N., 239, 308
Cumming, Capt. W. Gordon, 25,
    295 n. 67

Dalhousie, Marquis of, xiv, 290,
    308
Davidson, Col. C., 10, 304 n. 17
Davidson, Col. D., 210, 294 n. 23
Delhi prize money, 82–3
Deopura, 199

Despat, *thakur*, 130, 300 n. 12
Dew, Lt G. M., 13, 294 n. 33
Dhanoni, 125
Dhar, 1, 7, 8
Dholpore, 221, 222–3, 229, 242,
    244
Dick, Lt W., 80, 146, 298 n. 135,
    301 n. 44
Doab, the, 43, 215–16, 297 n. 98
Douglas, Capt. C., 183, 184, 302
    n. 82
Dowker, Lt H. C., 147, 156, 171,
    183, 184, 301 n. 38
Duberly, Mrs Frances (Fanny),
    258, 303 n. 9, 306 n. 90, 308
Durand, Col. H. M., 1, 7, 11, 22,
    25, 210, 292 n. 2, 308

Edmonstone, G. F., 62, 90, 109,
    185, 201, 297 n. 124
Enfield (rifle), use of, 104–5, 199
    defective ammunition for, 249
Ellichpur, 219
Elphinstone, Lord, 1, 24, 26, 34,
    37, 40, 41, 308
Erskine, Maj. W. C., 33, 41, 296
    n. 83
Etawa, 134, 162, 186
Ewing, Surgeon J., 240, 306 n. 67
Executions, 6–7, 9, 23, 24, 44, 47,
    50, 108, 195, 289
Eyre, Governor Edward, 308

Fenwick, Capt. T., 111, 112, 298
    n. 163
'Flying camps', 116
Follett, Maj. F. W. H., 7, 294 n. 4
Forbes, Maj. J., 25, 54, 66, 296
    n. 64
Forbes, Maj. J. F., 299 n. 165

Force
  Central India Field, xvii, 193,
    202, 220, 284
  Nerbudda, xvii, 55, 73
  Rajputana, 218
  Saugor Field, 293 n. 11
Foster, Lt H., 240, 306 n. 67
Fox, Lt F. R., 146, 301 n. 36

Gall, Maj. R. H., 7, 14, 107, 111,
  132, 136, 152, 160, 170, 174,
  179, 254, 294 n. 6
Garakhota, 3, 33, 70, 74–5, 78–9,
  81
Gati, Kati, 105, 112, 113
Golaoli, 119, 188, 200, 204, 250,
  252, 259
Gonds, tribe, xvi, 136, 153, 300
  n. 19
Goodfellow, Lt C. A., 78, 80, 120,
  298 n. 135
Goraria, 1
Gordon, Lt H. J. G., 113, 114, 298
  n. 157
Gossett, Lt W. B., 113, 299 n. 165
Gowan, Lt L. St. P., 113, 154, 298
  n. 164
Guna (Goonah), 2, 29, 43, 47, 56,
  105, 162
Guns and mortars, ranges and
  weights, 295 n. 40
Gurserai, 172, 302 n. 66
Gwalior
  Contingent, 1, 61, 133, 182, 185
  description, 195, 258, 265–7
  events at, 194, 216, 230, 231,
    234, 273
  Maharaja of (Sindhia), xvi, 27,
    38–9, 194, 212, 216, 217, 230,
    235, 241, 242, 310

  recaptured by Rose, xviii, 195,
    242, 257–74

Hamilton, Sir R. C. N., xvi, 4, 12,
  24, 25, 27, 28, 29, 43, 44, 57,
  62, 89, 104, 206, 217, 219,
  228, 242–3, 254, 287, 309
  plans campaign, xvi, 288–9
  relations with Rose, 2, 32, 35,
    36–7, 38–40, 41–2, 43, 44, 224
  annexes Shahgarh, 100
  disobeys instructions to relieve
    Chirkari, 4, 109–10
Hamirpur, xvi, 160, 300 n. 12
Hare, Capt. G., 9, 64, 68, 80, 107,
  123, 183, 206, 228, 294 n. 19
Hare, Capt. R. T., 198, 304 n. 1
Heneage, Capt. C. W., 245, 268,
  275, 306 n. 68
Hicks, Lt-Col. T. W., 226, 228,
  232, 269, 305 n. 51
Holkar *see* Indore
Honner, Brig. Sir R. W., 209, 222
Hoshangabad, 12, 24, 294 n. 31
Hume, A. O., 159, 160, 162, 294
  n. 56
Hungerford, Capt. T. J. W., 7, 16,
  294 n. 10
Hutchinson, Capt. A. R. E., 38,
  40, 296 n. 89

Imam Commission, xv, 291 n. 10
India, Central
  definition of, xvi
  political structure, xvi
Indore, 20, 34–5, 57
  attack on Residency, 1, 27
  executions at, 23, 24, 27, 29, 44
  Maharaja of (Holkar), xvi, 22,
    27, 42, 309

Indurki, 230, 232, 235, 236
Intelligence, xx

Jabalpur (Jubbalpore), xv, xvi, 3
Jacob, Brig.-Gen. John, xvi
Jagamanpur, 201, 304 n. 6
Jaitpur, 129
Jalaun, xvi, 138, 201, 234, 300 n. 20
Jaora Alipur, action at, 195, 272–3,
    306 n. 73
Jhansi, xiv, xv, 4, 42, 73, 81, 156,
    161, 164
  description of, 115, 165–6
  siege of, 109, 115–17, 153,
    164–8, 287
  capture of, 118, 134–7, 139–41,
    142, 143–4, 146–8, 151–2,
    153–5, 169–71
  Rani of, 33, 34, 79, 105, 107,
    110, 118, 142, 186, 192, 201,
    214, 250, 299 n. 1, 309
  escape of, from, 156, 170–1, 287,
    307 n. 109
  Rani, death of, 241, 242, 247,
    258, 268–9, 288
Jones, Capt. H. C., 25, 295 n. 65
Jumna (Yamuna), river, xvi, 119,
    159, 162, 185, 192, 199, 202,
    204, 215, 250, 259

Kalpi, xvi, xviii, 48, 49, 52, 58, 73,
    91, 118, 138, 158, 159, 160–1,
    186, 188, 192, 200, 203, 211,
    213, 249
  capture of, 193, 200, 201–2, 207,
    213, 230, 250–3, 260
Kane, Maj. 20, 295 n. 50
Keane, Maj. G., 7, 16, 56, 295 n. 38
Keatinge, Capt. R. H., 107, 111,
    112, 113, 289 n. 159

Khan, Adil Mahomed, 130
Khan, Bakht, 290 n. 2
Khan, Fazl Mahomed, 3, 57, 60,
    64, 69, 293 n. 6
Khandwa, 12, 294 n. 30
Khuria, 63, 65, 71
Kirwi, prize money, xvi, 291 n. 15
Kota (Kotah), rebels, 40, 157, 158,
    159, 161, 255, 299 n. 8
Kotah-ki-Serai, 194, 239, 255–6
Kotra, 160, 173, 301 n. 54
Kunch, xviii, 175
  battle of, 118, 176–8, 181–2,
    183–5, 230, 259

Landon. Capt. S., 10, 11, 294 n. 20
Lapse, doctrine of, xiv–xv, 290 n. 7
Lashkar (Lushkar) (New Town),
    the, 195, 265, 270–1
Leckie, Capt. W. M., 203, 304 n. 8
Leith, Capt. J., 301 n. 48
Le Mesurier, Col. A. P., 9, 10, 12,
    294 n. 18
Le Mesurier, Maj. P., 223
Lewis, Lt R. F., 114, 147, 298 n.
    157
Liddell, Lt-Col. J., 10, 11, 54, 56,
    66, 68, 118, 123, 134, 169,
    229, 294 n. 21, 297 n. 112
Light, Capt. A., 223, 305 n. 40
Lightfoot, Capt. J. G., 54, 64, 67,
    293 n. 9, 297 n. 112
Little, Capt. A. B., 105, 113, 114,
    298 n. 155
Lohari, 118, 173–4, 179, 302 n. 67
Louis, Lt J., 10, 294 n. 20
Lowry, Capt. E., 6, 7, 293 n. 1
Lowth, Lt-Col. R. H., 134, 144,
    270
Lucknow (Lakhnao), 142

Macdonald, Maj. J. A. M., 7, 294 n. 7

Macduff, Brig. J., 211, 304 n. 19

MacLachlan, Capt. T. J., 191, 307 n. 103

Macpherson, Maj. S. C., 39, 46, 71, 208, 212, 216, 296 n. 90

MacQuoid, Lt R. K., 183, 302 n. 82

Madanpur, pass, seizure of, 4, 92, 93, 94–9, 100, 125, 126, 129

Mallock, Lt H. A., 54, 66, 297 n. 112

Malthoni, 88, 94, 126

Malwa, xvi
  campaign in, xxvi, 1

Mandisore (Mandisaur), action at, 12–17, 26, 28, 31

Mansfield, Maj.-Gen. W. R., 74, 103, 162, 209, 214, 215, 217, 222, 223, 247, 261, 264, 276, 279, 285, 309

Martin, Lt C. M., 15, 22, 294 n. 37

Mau (near Jhansi), 157, 175, 300 n. 14

Maxwell, Col. G. V., 160, 162, 185, 192–3, 197, 200, 205, 206, 215, 250, 309

Mayne, Capt. H. O., 8, 22, 45, 159, 162, 191, 222, 294 n. 12

Mehidpur, Amil of, 27, 36, 289, 296 n. 70

Meiklejohn, Lt H. R., 146, 301 n. 44

Melvill, Col. P. M., 9, 10, 12

Miles, Lt J., 114, 298 n. 157

Mills, Cornet W., 243, 306 n. 70

Montague, Lt H., 245, 306 n. 75

Morar
  Rose seizes cantonments, 194, 237, 240–1, 266–7
  river, 237

Moth, 160, 171, 232

Mound, bastion, 117, 124, 131, 135, 136, 166, 167

Muir, William, 145, 301 n. 33

Murray, Capt. W., 14, 183, 184, 294 n. 33

Mutiny
  in Bengal Army, xiii
  in Bombay Army, xiii
  causes of, xiv–xvii, 46, 71–2
  nature of, xiii

Napier, Brig.-Gen. Robert, xviii, xix, 193, 241, 242, 244, 247, 258, 272–3, 309

Naraioli, 295 n. 85

Narsimhapur, 33, 86, 99

Narut, pass, 4, 125, 129

Neave, Lt W., 306 n. 69

Need, Capt. A., 300 n. 16

Nerbudda (Narbada), river, xvi, xix, 202

Neville, Capt. G., 78, 298 n. 134

Nimach (Neemuch), xv, 1, 13

Ommaney, Capt. M. W., 268, 307 n. 95

Orai, 138, 157, 185, 186, 250, 300 n. 20

Orcha gate, 117, 135, 166

Orr, Capt. S. G. G., 7, 15, 55, 294 n. 8

Orr, Maj. W. A., 12–14, 26, 65, 88, 107, 118, 126, 129, 131, 160, 173, 175, 176, 182, 183, 205, 208, 219, 221, 225, 226, 228, 309

Oudh (Awadh), annexation of, xv
  taluqdars of, xv

unemployment after annexation, xv

Owen, Lt-Col. 271, 307 n. 96

Pahuj, river, 235, 305 n. 43
Panna, 101, 109, 110, 298 n. 151
Pant, Dhundu *see* Sahib, Nana
Park, Lt A. A., 147, 301 n. 37
Partridge, Lt J. C., 184, 302 n. 81
Peishwa *see* Rao, Baji, II
Phul Bagh, 243, 246, 256, 306 n. 80
Pinkney, Capt. F. W., 145, 177, 301 n. 33
Piplia, 14
Pontoons, 99, 192, 251, 259
Poore, Capt. R., 244, 274, 306 n. 80
Prendergast, Lt H. N. D., 76, 122, 150, 298 n. 33, 309
Prettijohn, 25
Prize money, xvi, 82–3

Rahatgarh (Rathgarh), seizure of, xviii, 3, 34, 49, 53–4, 56, 57–8, 59–60, 64, 65–70, 75–8
Raines, Lt-Col. J. A. R., 270–1, 306 n. 86
Rajwas, 126
Ramsay, Capt. J. B., 10, 293 n. 24
Rao, Baji, II, Peishwa, xiv
Rao, Damodar, 301 n. 53
Rao, Dinkar, 234, 235
Reilly, Lt J., 245, 247, 306 n. 78
Rewa, 101, 110, 298 n. 151
Riddell, Col. W., 186, 194, 195, 222, 254, 286, 305 n. 36
Roberts, Maj.-Gen. H. G., 157, 158, 161, 164, 218, 255, 299 n. 8, 309

Robertson, Lt-Col. G. H., 13, 16, 35, 193, 208, 216, 220, 226, 227, 232, 239, 254, 284
Rose, Sir H. H., xi, 77, 218–19, 309
early career, xvii
appointed to command CIFF, xvi
at Indore, 2, 20, 22, 24, 26–7, 32, 35, 38, 40
and executions at Sehore, 2, 47, 48, 108, 176, 195, 226, 280–2, 283–4
at Jhansi, 120–4
at Betwa river, 109, 133, 142, 145, 148, 152
at Kunch, 118, 176, 181, 183
at Kalpi, 193, 206, 207
at Gwalior, 194–5, 232, 237–9, 241, 242, 257–8, 265–74
rebuked by Campbell, 223–4, 261–3, 276–8
character, xx, 80, 93, 203, 292 n. 25
generalship, xi, 3
physical stamina, xviii, 278–9, 292 n. 21
relations with Hamilton, 2, 17, 32, 35, 36, 38–9, 41–2, 43, 44, 84
relations with other commanders, xiv
later career, xix
Rose, Lt Wellington, 243, 244, 272, 306 n. 81
Roy, Babu Ramcomal, 31

Sage, Brig. W., 41, 48, 49, 296 n. 92
Sahib, Bala, 104, 150

Sahib, Nana, xiv, xxi, 30, 43, 60, 84, 103, 158, 309

Sahib, Rao, xiv, xxi, 58, 134, 139, 171–2, 186, 192, 202, 250

Sandwith, Capt. J. F. W., 10, 294 n. 22

Sattara, xiv, 27

Saugor (Sagar), xv, 21, 23, 40, 41, 43, 78, 212
  garrison relieved, xviii, 3, 62, 65
  and Nerbudda Territory, xvi, 212

Scudamore, Maj. A., 54, 67, 87, 88, 98, 184, 297 n. 112

Seager, Maj. E., 245, 246, 306 n. 77

Sehore, xvi, xvii, 2, 22, 108, 176, 195, 280, 283, 285
  executions at, 2, 47, 48, 108, 176, 226, 280–2, 283–4

Shah, Firuz (Shahzada), 1, 57, 70

Shahghar, Raja of (Indra Singh), 3, 4, 34, 96, 100, 130, 171

Shahjahanpur, 26, 55, 296 n. 68

Shakespear, Lt W. R., 23, 59, 88–9, 107, 120, 176, 204, 242, 295 n. 58

Showers, Brig. St G. D., 222–3, 230, 305 n. 35

Sinclair, Capt. J., 147, 300 n. 10

Sindhia see Gwalior

Sipri (Shivpuri), 43

Smith, Brig. M. W., 191, 194, 209, 220, 221, 225, 226, 228, 235, 239, 255, 310

Somerset, Lt-Gen. Sir H., 26, 158, 174, 310

Stack, Surgeon T., 301 n. 35

Steuart, Brig. C., xviii, xix, 10, 12, 21, 33, 41, 67–8, 203, 241, 310

Rose criticises, 279–80, 283, 307 n. 101

Stuart, Brig. C. S., xvii, 12, 22, 56, 83, 102, 107, 109, 169, 193, 206, 220, 228, 252–3, 310
  succeeds Woodburn, 1
  campaign in Malwa, 1, 7, 12–17
  captures Chanderi, xviii, 4, 105–6, 111–14

Stockley, Capt. G. C. T., 10, 23, 25, 294 n. 25

Sylvester, Surgeon J. H., 7, 9, 292 n. 26, 310

Tehri, 92, 101

Telegraph system, xx, 28

thakurs, xvii, 172

Thompson, Capt. P. S., 180, 302 n. 76

Timins, Maj. G., 23, 295 n. 57

Topi, Tantia (Tatya), xiv, xxi, 48, 52, 59, 60, 110, 116–17, 129, 139, 158, 171–2, 201
  background, 310
  at Betwa river, 133, 145
  at Kalpi, 186, 192
  at Gwalior, 194–5, 232
  defeated at Jaora Alipur, 195
  later career and execution, 195
  Rose's assessment of, 155, 172

Turnbull, Capt. A. D., 198, 304 n. 2

Turnbull, Lt-Col. S., 24, 25, 26, 54, 67–8, 92, 97, 130, 146, 296 n. 63

Unao, gate, 146, 170, 300 n. 34

Units, British
  8th Hussars, 243, 256–7, 268

14th Light Dragoons, 6, 7, 8, 14, 17, 24, 44, 51, 56, 57, 67, 80, 98, 111, 137, 143, 144, 148, 171, 213, 246, 274

21 Coy RE, 111

5th Foot (Fusiliers), 220, 221, 234

71st Highlanders, 81, 118, 160, 164, 178, 209, 213, 234, 238, 241, 243, 246, 248

86th Foot, 2, 8, 15, 48, 56, 111, 114, 137, 146, 213, 243, 244, 270–1, 274

88th Foot, 162, 197, 198, 199, 200

95th Foot, 239, 243, 245, 256–7, 270–2

Camel Corps (88th and Rifle Brigade), 193, 197, 198, 200, 205, 251, 253

Units, Indian

1st Bengal Light Cavalry, 1, 291

3rd Bengal Irregular Cavalry, 212

1st Bombay Lancers, 245, 256–7, 271–2, 291 n. 13

3rd Light Cavalry, 8, 66, 84, 88, 144, 160, 171, 197, 209, 220

1st Cavalry, Hyderabad Contingent, 1, 7, 8, 291 n. 13

3rd Cavalry, Hyderabad Contingent, 13, 14, 15, 111, 136, 144

4th Cavalry, Hyderabad Contingent, 14

Mayne's Horse, 294

Meade's Horse, 22, 242, 305 n. 38

Towana (Tiwana), Horse, 197

1st Troop, Bombay Horse Artillery, 67, 293 n. 4

A, E Troops, Madras Horse Artillery, 293 n. 11

4 Coy 2 Batt., Bombay Artillery, 293 n. 4

No. 4 Light Field Battery, 111, 293 n. 4

No. 18 Light Field Battery, 197, 293 n. 4

2 Coy, Bombay Reserve Artillery, 293 n. 4

Nos 1, 2, 4 Coys Artillery, Hyderabad Contingent, 293 n. 4

Bombay Sappers and Miners, 67, 111, 113

Madras Sappers and Miners, 293 n. 11

3rd Bengal European Regiment, 222

3rd Bombay European Regiment, 2, 17, 44, 51, 55, 69, 81, 87, 111, 132, 136, 137, 146, 169, 220, 244

3rd Madras European Regiment, 293 n. 11

12th Bengal Native Infantry (BNI), 182, 291 n. 13

15th BNI, 291 n. 13

19th BNI, 291 n. 13

30th BNI, 291 n. 13

31st BNI, 4, 65, 80, 98, 105, 210, 212, 291 n. 13

32nd BNI, 291 n. 13

34th BNI, 291 n. 13

42nd BNI, 4, 65, 80, 98, 105, 210, 212, 291 n. 13

50th BNI, 291 n. 13

52nd BNI, 33–4, 70, 80, 98, 101, 182, 291 n. 13

57th BNI, 182

70th BNI, 80

72nd BNI, 1, 291 n. 13

20th Bombay Native Infantry
(BoNI), 291 n. 13

24th BoNI, 2, 44, 51, 55, 67, 88,
137, 220

25th BoNI, 2, 6, 8, 15, 36, 48,
106, 111, 114, 137, 195, 197,
208, 213, 239, 244, 271

27th BoNI, 291 n. 13

1st Madras Native Infantry
(MNI), 293 n. 11

50th MNI, 293 n. 11

3rd Infantry Hyderabad
Contingent, 183

5th Infantry Hyderabad
Contingent, 183, 184

Contingents
Bhopal, 1, 22–3, 44–5, 48, 176,
225–6, 280, 289, 291 n. 13

Gwalior, 1, 61, 182, 185, 213,
240, 250, 291 n. 13, 306 n. 6

Hyderabad, 36, 193, 208,
209–10, 235

Kotah, 291 n. 13

United Malwa, 23, 291 n. 13

vilayatis, xvii, 28, 29, 154, 161,
170, 244, 293 n. 7

Waller, Lt W. F. F., 306 n. 81

Western, Capt. R., 297 n. 93

Wetherall, Col. E. R., 189, 219,
285, 298 n. 152

Wheler, Brig. F., 211, 304 n. 18

'Whistling Dick' bastion, 131, 135

Whitlock, Maj.-Gen. G. C., xvi, 3,
33, 37, 70, 99, 101, 144, 188,
211, 255, 303 n. 2, 310

Windham, Maj.-Gen. C. A., 155,
296 n. 61

Wood, Capt. H. A. A., 25, 296 n.
55

Wood, Pte T., 50, 230, 297 n. 107

Woodburn, Maj.-Gen. A., 1, 292
n. 1

Woolcombe, Capt. J. D., 7, 15, 294
n. 9